STUDY GUIDE

for use with

FINANCIAL ACCOUNTING
FOURTH EDITION

Kermit D. Larson

The University of Texas at Austin

1989
IRWIN
Homewood, IL 60430
Boston, MA 02116

© Richard D. Irwin, Inc., 1979, 1983, 1986, and 1989

Printed in the United States of America.

ISBN 0–256–07262–0

2 3 4 5 6 7 8 9 0 P 5 4 3 2 1 0 9

To The Student

This booklet is designed to help you review the material covered in *Financial Accounting,* 4th edition. You should understand that the booklet is not intended to substitute for your review of *Financial Accounting.* Instead, the objectives of this booklet are as follows:

1. To remind you of important information that is explained in the text. For example, the topical outline of each chapter reminds you of important topics in the chapter. In reading the outline, you should ask yourself whether or not you understand sufficiently the listed topics. If not, you should return to the appropriate chapter in *Financial Accounting* and read carefully the portions that explain the topics about which you are unclear.

2. To provide you with a quick means of testing your knowledge of the chapter. If you are unable to correctly answer the "Problems" that follow the chapter outline, you should again return to the appropriate chapter in *Financial Accounting* and review the sections about which you are unclear.

Your best approach to the use of this booklet is as follows:

First, read the learning objectives and ask whether your understanding of the chapter seems adequate for you to accomplish the objectives.

Second, review the topical outline, taking time to think through (describing to yourself) the explanations that would be required to expand the outline. Return to *Financial Accounting* to cover areas of weakness.

Third, answer the requirements of the problems that follow the topical outline. Then check your answers against the solutions that are provided after the problems.

Fourth, return to *Financial Accounting* for further study of the portions of the chapter about which you made errors.

Contents

1 | Accounting, an Introduction to Its Concepts

Your objectives in studying this chapter should include learning how to:

1. Describe the function of accounting and the nature and purpose of the information it provides.

2. List the main fields of accounting employment and the kinds of work carried on in each field.

3. Briefly explain the accounting concepts and principles introduced in the chapter and describe the process by which generally accepted accounting principles are established.

4. Recognize and be able to indicate the effects of transactions on the elements of an accounting equation.

5. Describe the information contained in the financial statements of a business and be able to prepare simple financial statements.

6. Briefly explain the differences between a single proprietorship, a partnership, and a corporation, comparing the differing responsibilities of their owners for the debts of the business.

7. Define or explain the words and phrases listed in the chapter Glossary.

Topical Outline

I. Accounting as a profession

  A. Accounting is a service activity. Its function is to provide quantitative information about economic entities.

  B. All states license CPAs (certified public accountants).

II. The work of an accountant typically includes:

  A. Public accounting; the services of certified public accountants involve:

  1. Auditing—critical examination of an entity's accounting records and statements that is made for the purpose of determining whether the statements fairly reflect the entity's financial position and operating results, in accordance with generally accepted accounting principles.

  2. Management advisory services—the design, installation, and improvement of a client's accounting system, plus advice on financial planning, budgeting, forecasting, and inventory control.

  3. Tax services—the preparation of tax returns, with advice as to how transactions may be completed in such a way as to incur the smallest tax liability.

  B. Private accounting; the work of accountants employed by a single enterprise involves:

  1. General accounting—the recording of transactions, processing of the recorded data, and preparation of financial statements.

  2. Cost accounting—the determination and control of costs, and assessing the performance of managers who are responsible for costs.

  3. Budgeting—the process of developing formal plans for future business activities, which then serve as bases for evaluating actual accomplishments.

  4. Internal auditing—checking records and operating procedures for the purpose of making sure that established accounting procedures and management directives are being followed. Also includes evaluation of operating efficiency.

  C. Governmental accounting; a variety of accounting positions in governmental agencies.

III. Important accounting statements include:

  A. The income statement, which indicates whether a business earned a net income (a profit) by showing the:

  1. Revenues earned—an inflow of assets received in exchange for goods or services provided to customers as part of the major or central operations of the business.

  2. Expenses incurred—outflows or the using up of assets as a result of the major or central operations of a business.

  3. Net income (excess of revenues over expenses) or net loss (excess of expenses over revenues).

  B. The balance sheet—shows the financial position of a business on a specific date by listing the:

  1. Assets—probable future economic benefits obtained or controlled by a particular entity as a result of past transactions or events.

  2. Liabilities—probable future sacrifices of economic benefits arising from present obligations of a particular entity to transfer assets or to provide services to other entities in the future as a result of past transactions or events.

  3. Equity—the residual interest in the assets of an entity that remains after deducting its liabilities. Also called net assets.

C. Statement of changes in owner's equity—discloses all changes in owner's equity during the period, including investments by the owner, withdrawals by the owner, and net income or net loss.

D. Statement of cash flows—discloses the inflows and outflows of cash during the period, classified in terms of cash flows from operations, cash flows from investing activities, and cash flows from financing activities.

IV. Generally accepted accounting principles—broad rules adopted by the accounting profession as guides in measuring, recording, and reporting the financial affairs and activities of a business.

    A. Sources of accounting principles

        1. American Institute of Certified Public Accountants (AICPA).

        2. Accounting Principles Board (APB)—established by the AICPA in 1959.

        3. Financial Accounting Standards Board (FASB)—replaced the APB in 1973.

        4. Securities and Exchange Commission (SEC)—the dominant authority in establishing accounting principles; relies heavily on the FASB.

    B. Important accounting principles and concepts

        1. Business entity concept—a business is a separate entity that is distinct from its owner or owners and from every other business.

        2. Cost principle—assets and services plus any resulting liabilities are to be recorded in the accounting records at cost, which is the cash or cash-equivalent amount of the consideration given in exchange for the purchased assets and services.

        3. Objectivity principle—the amounts used in recording transactions are to be based on verifiable evidence such as business transactions between independent parties.

        4. Continuing-concern concept—the assumption that a business will continue to operate and that the assets held for use in the business will not be sold.

        5. Stable-dollar concept—the idea that the purchasing power of the unit of measure used in accounting, the dollar, does not change.

        6. Realization principle—the inflow of assets associated with a revenue does not have to be in the form of cash; a revenue should be recorded as a revenue at the time, but not before, it is earned; and the amount of a revenue should be measured in terms of the cash plus cash-equivalent amount of other assets received.

V. Business organizations include three general types:

    A. Single proprietorship—a business owned by one individual. There are no legal requirements to be met in starting a single proprietorship business. The most numerous of all business concerns.

    B. Partnership—a business that is owned by two or more people but is not organized as a separate legal entity. A partner is personally responsible for all the debts of the partnership.

    C. Corporation—a business that is established under the laws of a state or the federal government as a separate entity. The owners of a corporation are called stockholders because their ownership of the corporation's equity is divided into units that are called shares of stock.

VI. Recording transactions

    A. Accounting equation (or balance sheet equation)

        Assets = Liabilities + Owner's Equity

    B. Double-entry system—every transaction recorded affects two or more items in the accounting equation, so that the equation remains in balance.

Problem I

The following statements are either true or false. Place a (T) in the parentheses before each true statement and an (F) before each false statement.

1. ( ) The phase of accounting that has to do with determining and controlling costs, and assessing the performance of managers who are responsible for costs is called auditing.

2. ( ) The dollar is used in recording and reporting accounting information because it is a stable unit of measure.

3. ( ) Land appraised at $40,000 and worth that much to its purchaser should be recorded at its worth ($40,000), even though it was purchased through hard bargaining for $35,000.

4. ( ) If a business is to be liquidated and its assets sold, the losses incurred in converting assets into cash must exceed the equity of the owner or owners before the creditors will lose.

5. ( ) Net income + Owner's investments − Owner's withdrawals = The increase in owner's equity during the year.

Problem II

You are given several words, phrases or numbers to choose from in completing each of the following statements or in answering the following questions. In each case select the one that best completes the statement or answers the question and place its letter in the answer space provided.

_____ 1. Financial statement information about Company B is as follows:

December 31, 1989:
   Assets $42,000
   Liabilities 17,000
December 31, 1990:
   Assets 47,000
   Liabilities 14,800
During 1990:
   Net income 18,000
   Owner investments .... ?
   Owner withdrawals 10,800

The amount of owner investments during 1990 is:

a. $ 7,200.
b. $14,400.
c. $25,000.
d. $ –0– .
e. some other amount.

_____ 2. The term "management advisory services" describes:

a. the phase of public accounting dealing with the critical examination of an entity's accounting records and statements.
b. the phase of public accounting dealing with the design, installation, and improvement of a client's accounting system.
c. the phase of accounting dealing with the development of formal plans for future business activities, which serve as bases for evaluating actual accomplishments.
d. the phase of public accounting dealing with the preparation of tax returns and advice as to how transactions may be completed in such a way as to incur the smallest tax liability.
e. the phase of accounting dealing primarily with recording transactions and preparing financial statements.

Problem II *(continued)*

_____ 3. The cost principle:

    a. states that the inflow of assets associated with a revenue does not have to be in the form of cash; a revenue should be recorded as a revenue at the time, but not before, it is earned; and the amount of a revenue should be measured in terms of the cash plus cash-equivalent amount of other assets received.

    b. requires that wherever possible the amounts used in recording transactions be based on verifiable evidence such as business transactions between independent parties.

    c. states that all expenses incurred in earning a revenue be deducted from the revenue in determining net income.

    d. requires assets and services plus any resulting liabilities to be recorded in the accounting records at cost.

    e. is another name for the recognition principle.

_____ 4. The APB was a(n):

    a. professional association of certified public accountants.

    b. committee of the American Institute of Certified Public Accountants that, prior to the FASB, was responsible for formulating generally accepted accounting principles.

    c. agency of the federal government that was established to administer the provisions of various securities and exchange laws.

    d. organization of persons interested in accounting; generally identified as the professional association of academic accountants in America.

    e. certification of an individual's professional level of competence in the field of internal auditing.

_____ 5. If on January 16, 1990, Mary Kay Company rendered services for a customer in exchange for $175 cash, what would be the effects on the accounting equation?

    a. Assets, $175 increase; Liabilities, no effect; Owner's Equity, $175 increase.

    b. Assets, no effect; Liabilities, $175 decrease; Owner's Equity, $175 increase.

    c. Assets, $175 increase; Liabilities, $175 increase; Owner's Equity, no effect.

    d. Assets, $175 increase; Liabilities, $175 decrease; Owner's Equity, $350 increase.

    e. There is no effect on the accounting equation because Mary Kay Company is a single proprietorship.

Problem III

Many of the important ideas and concepts discussed in Chapter 1 are reflected in the following list of key terms. Test your understanding of these terms by matching the appropriate definitions with the terms. Record the number identifying the most appropriate definition in the blank space next to each term.

_____ AAA

_____ Accounting

_____ Accounting concept

_____ Accounting equation

_____ Accounts payable

_____ Accounts receivable

_____ AICPA

_____ APB

_____ Assets

_____ Audit

_____ Balance sheet

_____ Balance sheet equation

_____ Bookkeeping

_____ Budgeting

_____ Business entity concept

_____ Business transaction

_____ CIA

_____ CMA

_____ Continuing-concern concept

_____ Controller

_____ Corporation

_____ Cost accounting

_____ Cost principle

_____ CPA

_____ Creditor

_____ Debtor

_____ Equity

_____ Expense

_____ FASB

_____ FEI

_____ GAAP

_____ General accounting

_____ Generally accepted accounting principles

_____ Going-concern concept

_____ Income statement

_____ Internal auditing

_____ IRS

_____ Liabilities

_____ Management advisory services

_____ NAA

_____ NASBA

_____ Net assets

_____ Net income

_____ Net loss

_____ Objectivity principle

_____ Partnership

_____ Realization principle

_____ Recognition principle

_____ Revenue

_____ SEC

_____ Shareholder

_____ Single proprietorship

_____ Stable-dollar concept

_____ Statement of cash flows

_____ Statement of changes in owner's equity

_____ Statement of financial position

_____ Stock

_____ Stockholders

_____ Tax services

Problem III *(continued)*

1. A financial report showing the assets, liabilities, and equity of an enterprise on a specific date. Also called a statement of financial position.

2. The accounting rule that wherever possible the amounts used in recording transactions be based on verifiable evidence such as business transactions between independent parties.

3. American Institute of Certified Public Accountants, the professional association of certified public accountants in the United States.

4. A service activity that provides quantitative information about economic entities; the information is primarily financial in nature and is intended to be useful in making economic decisions.

5. The phase of public accounting dealing with the preparation of tax returns and with advice as to how transactions may be completed in such a way as to incur the smallest tax liability.

6. An inflow of assets received in exchange for goods and services provided to customers as part of the major or central operations of the business.

7. A financial statement showing revenues earned by a business, the expenses incurred in earning the revenues, and the resulting net income or net loss.

8. Another name for the balance sheet equation.

9. A business that is established under the laws of a state or the federal government as a separate entity.

10. The accounting rule that requires assets and services plus any resulting liabilities to be recorded in the accounting records at cost, which is the cash or cash-equivalent amount of the consideration given in exchange for the purchased assets and services.

11. The residual interest in the assets of an entity that remains after deducting its liabilities.

12. Financial Accounting Standards Board, the seven-member board that currently has the authority to issue pronouncements of generally accepted accounting principles.

13. A business that is owned by two or more people and that is not organized as a separate legal entity.

14. Another name for the balance sheet.

15. Another name for the realization principle.

16. The use of a business's own accounting employees to check records and operating procedures for the purpose of making sure that established accounting procedures and management directives are being followed.

17. The excess of revenues over expenses.

18. The process of developing formal plans for future business activities, which then serve as bases for evaluating actual accomplishments.

19. The phase of accounting that has to do with determining and controlling costs, and assessing the performance of managers who are responsible for costs.

20. Another name for the continuing-concern concept.

21. The excess of expenses over revenues.

22. A person or organization that is obligated to pay a liability.

23. Outflows or the using up of assets as a result of the major or central operations of a business.

24. The owners of a corporation.

25. The idea that accounting reports should be based on the assumption that the purchasing power of the unit of measure used in accounting (the dollar) does not change.

26. The chief accounting officer of a large business.

27. Amounts owed to a business by its customers for goods or services sold to them on credit.

28. The accounting rule which states that the inflow of assets associated with a revenue does not have to be in the form of cash; a revenue should be recorded as a revenue at the time, but not before, it is earned; and the amount of a revenue should be measured in terms of the cash plus cash-equivalent amount of other assets received.

Problem III *(continued)*

29. A completed exchange of economic consideration; for example, goods, services, money, or the right to collect money, between two or more parties.

30. Equity of a corporation that is divided into units or shares.

31. Broad rules adopted by the accounting profession as guides in measuring, recording, and reporting the financial affairs and activities of a business.

32. A critical examination of an entity's accounting records and statements that is made for the purpose of determining whether the statements fairly reflect the entity's financial position and operating results in accordance with generally accepted accounting principles.

33. A financial statement that discloses all changes in owner's equity during the period, including investments by the owner, withdrawals by the owner and net income or net loss.

34. The phase of public accounting dealing with the design, installation, and improvement of a client's accounting system, plus advice on financial planning, budgeting, forecasting, and inventory control.

35. Securities and Exchange Commission, an agency of the federal government that was established to administer the provisions of various securities and exchange laws.

36. An individual or organization to whom a debt is owed.

37. Probable future sacrifices of economic benefits arising from present obligations of a particular entity to transfer assets or to provide services to other entities in the future as a result of past transactions.

38. The record-making phase of accounting.

39. The American Accounting Association, an organization of persons interested in accounting; generally identified as the professional association of academic accountants in America.

40. The assumption that a business will continue to operate and that the assets held for use in the business will not be sold.

41. Liabilities resulting from the credit purchase of goods or services.

42. Probable future economic benefits obtained or controlled by a particular entity as a result of past transactions or events.

43. The idea that a business is a separate entity that is distinct from its owner or owners and from every other business.

44. An expression in dollar amounts of the equivalency of the assets, liabilities, and equity of an enterprise, usually stated as Assets = Liabilities + Owner's Equity.

45. Financial Executives Institute.

46. A business owned by one individual.

47. Accounting Principles Board, a committee of the AICPA that was responsible for formulating generally accepted accounting principles prior to the FASB.

48. Certified public accountant, an accountant who has met legal requirements as to age, education, experience, residence, and moral character and is licensed to practice public accounting.

49. Another name for a stockholder.

50. That phase of accounting dealing primarily with recording transactions, processing the recorded data, and preparing financial statements.

51. Generally accepted accounting principles.

52. National Association of Accountants.

53. A financial statement that discloses the inflows and outflows of cash during the period, classified in terms of cash flows from operations, cash flows from investing activities, and cash flows from financing activities.

54. An abstract idea that serves as an important assumption underlying generally accepted accounting principles and procedures.

55. Certified Internal Auditor, a certification of an individual's professional level of competence in the field of internal auditing.

56. Internal Revenue Service.

57. Another name for equity, or the residual interest in the assets of an entity that remains after deducting its liabilities.

58. National Association of State Boards of Accountancy.

59. Certificate in Management Accounting, a certification of an individual's professional level of competence in management accounting.

Problem IV

Complete the following by filling in the blanks.

1. The _____ principle of accounting requires that assets and services be recorded at cost. Assets and services are recorded at cost because normally costs are based on verifiable evidence and thus meet the requirements of the _____ principle, the accounting principle which requires that transaction amounts be objectively established. It is important that transaction amounts be objectively established because if accounting information is to be fully useful, it must be based on _____ data and information.

2. The _____ is a form of business organization that requires the organizers to obtain a charter from one of the states or the federal government.

3. Under the _____ concept, for accounting purposes, every business is conceived to be a separate entity, separate and distinct from its _____ or _____ and from every other _____.

4. Does a balance sheet show current market values for the assets listed on it? _____ _____ (Yes or No) If the dollar amounts do not represent current market values, what do they represent? _____ _____.

5. Equity on a balance sheet is the _____ of the owner in the net assets of the business.

6. The statement of changes in owner's equity discloses all changes in owner's equity during the period, including _____ by the owner, _____ _____ by the owner, and _____ _____.

7. The balance sheet equation is _____ equal _____ plus _____. It is also called the _____ equation.

8. Probable future sacrifices of economic benefits arising from present obligations of a business to transfer assets or to provide services to other entities as a result of past transactions are _____.

Problem IV *(continued)*

9. Accounting is a service activity, the function of which is _____
_____
_____.

10. The assets of a business are the _____
_____
owned by the business.

11. Bookkeeping is the _____-making part of accounting, and bookkeeping and accounting _____ (are, are not) the same thing.

12. There are several kinds of accounting work done by employees of business firms. These include

    (a) _____, (b) _____

    _____, (c) _____, and

    (d) _____.

13. An income statement prepared for a business shows whether or not the business earned a
_____ or suffered a _____.

14. Revenues are inflows of _____ or other
_____ received in exchange for goods or services provided to
customers.

15. A balance sheet prepared for a business shows its financial position on a specific
_____. Financial position is shown by listing the
_____ of the business, its _____,
and the _____ of the owner or owners in the business.

16. Expenses are goods and services _____ in
operating a business or other economic unit.

17. The accounting equation for a single proprietorship is _____
_____.

Problem V

The assets, liabilities, and owner's equity of Susan Thompson's law practice are shown on the first line in the equation below; and following the equation are eight transactions completed by Ms. Thompson. Show by additions and subtractions in the spaces provided the effects of each transaction on the items of the equation.   Show new totals after each transaction as in Illustration 1-8 in the text.

			ASSETS			= LIABILITIES	+ OWNER'S EQUITY
	Cash	+ Accounts Receivable +	Prepaid Rent	+ Law Library	+ Office Equipment =	Accounts Payable +	S. Thompson, Capital
	$4,000			$8,000	$7,250		$19,250
1.							
2.							
3.							
4.							
5.							
6.							
7.							
8.							

1. Paid the rent for three months in advance on the law office, $3,000.
2. Purchased a new typewriter for the office, paying cash, $900.
3. Completed legal work for Ray Holland, a client, and immediately collected $2,500 in cash in full payment therefor.
4. Purchased on credit from Legal Book Publishers law books costing $700.
5. Completed on credit $1,500 of legal work for Julie Landon and immediately entered in the accounting records both the right to collect and the revenue earned.
6. Paid Legal Book Publishers for the books purchased in Transaction 4.
7. Received $1,500 from Julie Landon for the legal work of Transaction 5.
8. Paid the weekly salary of the office secretary, $575.

Problem V *(continued)*

Refer to your completed work on the previous page and fill in the blanks.

a. Did each transaction affect two items of the equation? _____. (Yes or No)

b. Did the equation remain in balance after the effect or effects of each transaction were entered?

_____. (Yes or No)

c. If the equation had not remained in balance after the effect or effects of each transaction were entered, this would have indicated that _____

_____.

d. Ms. Thompson earned $2,500 of revenue upon the completion of Transaction 3 and the asset that flowed into her practice as a result of this transaction was in the form of _____

_____.

e. Ms. Thompson earned $1,500 of revenue upon the completion of Transaction 5, and the asset that flowed into the law practice upon the completion of this transaction was _____

_____.

f. The right to collect $1,500 from Julie Landon was converted into _____

_____ in Transaction 7. Nevertheless, although the $1,500 was not received in cash until Transaction 7, the revenue was earned upon the completion of the _____

_____ in Transaction 5.

g. The $1,500 collected in Transaction 7 was recognized as revenue in Transaction 5 because of the requirements of the _____ principle, which (1) defines a revenue as an inflow of assets, not necessarily _____ in exchange for goods or services; (2) requires that the revenue be recognized at the time, but not before, it is

_____, which generally is at the time title to goods sold is

_____ or services are _____; and (3) requires that the amount of revenue recognized be measured by the cash received plus the cash equivalent of any other _____ received.

Solutions for Chapter 1

Problem I	Problem II
1. F	1. D
2. F	2. B
3. F	3. D
4. T	4. B
5. T	5. A

Problem III

AAA	39	General accounting		50
Accounting	4	Generally accepted accounting		
Accounting concept	54	principles		31
Accounting equation	8 or 44	Going-concern concept	20 or	40
Accounts payable	41	Income statement		7
Accounts receivable	27	Internal auditing		16
AICPA	3	IRS		56
APB	47	Liabilities		37
Assets	42	Management advisory services		34
Audit	32	NAA		52
Balance sheet	1	NASBA		58
Balance sheet equation	44	Net assets	57 or	11
Bookkeeping	38	Net income		17
Budgeting	18	Net loss		21
Business entity concept	43	Objectivity principle		2
Business transaction	29	Partnership		13
CIA	55	Realization principle	28 or	15
CMA	59	Recognition principle		15
Continuing-concern concept	40	Revenue		6
Controller	26	SEC		35
Corporation	9	Shareholder		49
Cost accounting	19	Single proprietorship		46
Cost principle	10	Stable-dollar concept		25
CPA	48	Statement of cash flows		53
Creditor	36	Statement of change in		
Debtor	22	owner's equity		33
Equity	11	Statement of financial		
Expense	23	position		14
FASB	12	Stock		30
FEI	45	Stockholders		24
GAAP	51 or 31	Tax services		5

Problem IV

1. cost, objectivity, objective
2. corporation
3. business entity, owner, owners, business
4. No. Costs or costs less accumulated depreciation. (The phrase "accumulated depreciation" will be explained further in Chapter 3.)
5. interest or ownership right
6. investments, withdrawals, net income or net loss
7. Assets, Liabilities, Owner's Equity, accounting
8. liabilities
9. to provide quantitative information, primarily financial in nature, about economic entities
10. property or property rights
11. record, are not
12. (a) general accounting
    (b) cost accounting
    (c) budgeting
    (d) internal auditing
13. net income, net loss
14. cash, assets (properties)
15. date, assets, liabilities, equity
16. used up (consumed)
17. Assets = Liabilities + Owner's Equity
    or
    Assets − Liabilities = Owner's Equity

Problem V

	Cash +	Accounts Receivable +	Prepaid Rent +	Law Library +	Office Equipment =	Accounts Payable +	S. Thompson, Capital
	$4,000			$8,000	$7,250		$19,250
1.	−3,000		+3,000				
	$1,000		$3,000	$8,000	$7,250		$19,250
2.	−900				+900		
	$ 100		$3,000	$8,000	$8,150		$19,250
3.	+2,500						+ 2,500
	$2,600		$3,000	$8,000	$8,150		$21,750
4.				+ 700		+ 700	
	$2,600		$3,000	$8,700	$8,150	$ 700	$21,750
5.		+1,500					+ 1,500
	$2,600	$1,500	$3,000	$8,700	$8,150	$ 700	$23,250
6.	− 700					− 700	
	$1,900	$1,500	$3,000	$8,700	$8,150	$ 0	$23,250
7.	+1,500	−1,500					
	$3,400	$ 0	$3,000	$8,700	$8,150	$ 0	$23,250
8.	− 575						− 575
	$2,825	$ 0	$3,000	$8,700	$8,150	$ 0	$22,675

a. Yes
b. Yes
c. an error had been made
d. cash
e. the right to collect $1,500 from Julie Landon, an account receivable
f. cash, legal work
g. realization (or recognition), cash, earned, transferred, rendered, asset or assets

2 Recording Transactions

Your objectives in studying this chapter should include learning how to:

1. Explain the mechanics of double-entry accounting and tell why transactions are recorded with equal debits and credits.

2. Describe the rules of debit and credit and apply the rules in recording transactions.

3. State the names of several commonly used accounts and the nature of the items recorded in those accounts.

4. Tell the normal balance of any asset, liability, or owner's equity account.

5. Record transactions in a General Journal, post to the ledger accounts, and prepare a trial balance to test the accuracy of the recording and posting.

6. Define or explain the words and phrases listed in the chapter Glossary.

Topical Outline

I. Steps in the accounting process include:

   A. Analyzing the economic events of an entity and recording the effects of those events.

   B. Classifying and summarizing the recorded effects in reports or financial statements that individuals find useful in making economic decisions about the entity.

II. Accounting records include:

   A. Business papers—printed documents (sales slips, invoices, checks) that businesses use in the process of completing business transactions and that provide evidence of the transactions.

   B. Journal—a book of original entry in which transactions are first recorded and from which transaction amounts are posted to the ledger accounts.

   C. Ledger—a group of accounts used by a business in recording its transactions.

III. Accounts are separate locations in an accounting system, one of which is used in recording and summarizing the increases and decreases in each type of revenue, expense, asset, liability, or owner's equity item.

   A. Types of accounts include:

      1. Asset accounts (Cash, Notes Receivable, Accounts Receivable, Prepaid Expenses, Supplies, Equipment, Buildings, Land, etc.)

      2. Liability accounts (Accounts Payable, Notes Payable, Unearned Revenues, Other Short-Term Payables, etc.)

      3. Owner's equity accounts (Capital account, Withdrawals account, Revenue and Expense accounts)

   B. T-account—a simple form of account that illustrates the debits and credits required in recording a transaction.

   C. Balance-column account—an account that has debit and credit columns for entering changes in the account and a column for entering the new account balance after each debit or credit is posted to the account.

IV. The mechanics of double-entry accounting—Assets = Liabilities + Owner's Equity. Every transaction is recorded in two or more accounts with equal debits and credits.

   A. Debit—the left-hand side of a T-account.

   B. Credit—the right-hand side of a T-account.

   C. Asset accounts are debited for increases and credited for decreases.

   D. Liability and owner's equity accounts are debited for decreases and credited for increases.

   E. Owner's equity is increased by owner's investments and by revenues; owner's equity is decreased by expenses and by withdrawals.

      1. Investments by the owner are credited to the owner's capital account.

      2. Withdrawals of assets are debited to the owner's withdrawals account.

      3. Revenues are credited to a revenue account.

      4. Expenses are debited to an expense account.

V. Journalizing—the process of recording transactions in a journal. The transaction date, the names of the accounts involved, the amount of each debit and credit, and an explanation of the transaction are recorded for each transaction.

VI. Posting—the process of copying information from a journal to a ledger.

VII. Trial balance—a list of the accounts that have balances in the ledger, the debit or credit balance of each account, the total of the debit balances, and the total of the credit balances. A trial balance tests the equality of the debit and credit balances to provide evidence of accuracy in the accounts.

VIII. Bookkeeping techniques—locate and correct errors by checking journalizing and posting procedures.

Problem I

The following statements are either true or false. Place a (T) in the parentheses before each true statement and an (F) before each false statement.

1. (   ) Debits are used to record increases in assets, withdrawals, and expenses.
2. (   ) To credit a liability account means to increase it.
3. (   ) The journal record makes it possible to trace the debits and credits into the accounts for the purpose of locating errors.
4. (   ) An unearned revenue is an owner's equity account that will be satisfied by delivering the product or service paid for in advance.
5. (   ) The cost of renting an office during the current period is an expense; however, the cost of renting an office six periods in advance is an asset.

Problem II

You are given several words, phrases or numbers to choose from in completing each of the following statements or in answering the following questions. In each case select the one that best completes the statement or answers the question and place its letter in the answer space provided.

_____ 1. Hal Hammer, the owner of Hal Company, had a capital balance of $12,300 on June 30 and $23,800 on July 31. Net income for the month of July was $14,000. What were the owner's withdrawals during July?

  a. $22,100.
  b. $25,500.
  c. $ 2,500.
  d. $11,500.
  e. $ –0– .

_____ 2. Which of the following transactions does not affect the owner's equity in a proprietorship?

  a. Investments by the owner
  b. Withdrawals of cash or other assets by the owner
  c. Cash receipts for revenues
  d. Cash receipts for unearned revenues
  e. Cash payments for expenses

_____ 3. A ledger is a(n):

  a. book of original entry in which a complete record of transactions are first recorded.
  b. group of accounts used by a business in recording its transactions.
  c. book of original entry in which any type of transaction can be recorded.
  d. book of special journals.
  e. accountant's book of FASB rules and principles.

Problem II *(continued)*

_____ 4. The following transactions occurred during the month of October:

    1) Paid $1,500 cash for store equipment.
    2) Paid $1,000 in partial payment for supplies purchased 30 days previously.
    3) Paid October's utility bill of $600.
    4) Paid $1,200 to owner of the business for his personal use.
    5) Paid $1,400 salary of office employee for October.

What was the total amount of expenses during October?

    a. $3,000.
    b. $4,500.
    c. $2,000.
    d. $3,500.
    e. $5,700.

_____ 5. The journal entry for the completion of legal work for a client on credit and billing the client $1,700 for the services rendered would be:

    a. Accounts Receivable 1,700
          Legal Fees Earned 1,700
    b. Legal Fees Earned 1,700
          Accounts Receivable 1,700
    c. Accounts Payable 1,700
          Legal Fees Earned 1,700
    d. Legal Fees Earned 1,700
          Revenues 1,700
    e. Accounts Receivable 1,700
          Unearned Revenues 1,700

Problem III

Jon Wheeler has just begun a new small repairs business he calls Wheeler's Repair Shop, and the first ten transactions completed by the business follow:

a. Mr. Wheeler sold a personal investment in Southern Cable stock for $1,921.50 and began his business by depositing $1,800 of the proceeds in a bank account opened in the name of the business.
b. Paid three months' rent in advance on the shop space, $675.
c. Purchased repair equipment for cash, $700.
d. Completed repair work for customers and collected cash therefor, $505.50.
e. Purchased additional repair equipment on credit from Comet Company, $415.50.
f. Completed repair work on credit for Fred Baca, $175.
g. Paid Comet Company $290.50 of the amount owed to it.
h. Paid the local radio station $75.00 for an announcement of the shop opening.
i. Fred Baca paid for the work of Transaction (f).
j. Mr. Wheeler withdrew $350 cash from the business to pay personal expenses.

Required:

1. Record the transactions directly in the T-accounts provided on the next page. Use the transaction letters to identify the amounts in the accounts.
2. Prepare a trial balance on the form provided on the next page.

Problem III *(continued)*

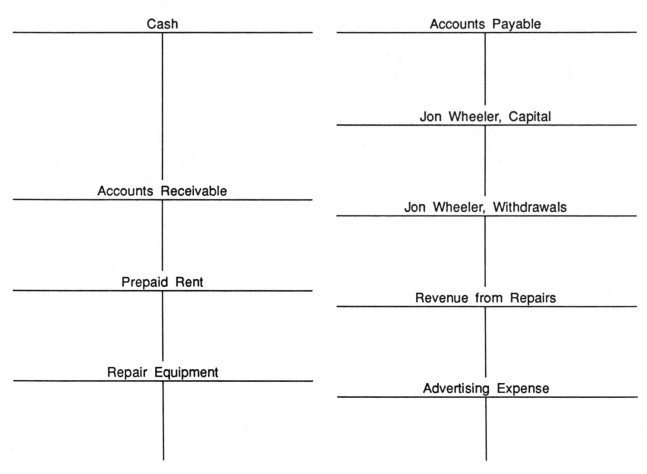

Cash	Accounts Payable
Accounts Receivable	Jon Wheeler, Capital
Prepaid Rent	Jon Wheeler, Withdrawals
Repair Equipment	Revenue from Repairs
	Advertising Expense

WHEELER'S REPAIR SHOP
Trial Balance
_____, 19__

Problem IV

Journalize the following transactions and post to the accounts following.

a. On November 5 of the current year Sherry Dale invested $1,500 in cash and office equipment having a fair value of $950 in a real estate agency.

b. On November 6 she purchased for cash office equipment costing $425.

DATE	ACCOUNT TITLES AND EXPLANATION	P.R.	DEBIT	CREDIT

GENERAL LEDGER

Cash   Account No. 1

DATE	EXPLANATION	P.R.	DEBIT	CREDIT	BALANCE

Office Equipment   Account No. 8

DATE	EXPLANATION	P.R.	DEBIT	CREDIT	BALANCE

Problem IV *(continued)*

	Sherry Dale, Capital				Account No. 15	

DATE		EXPLANATION	P.R.	DEBIT	CREDIT	BALANCE

Problem V

Many of the important ideas and concepts discussed in Chapter 2 are reflected in the following list of key terms. Test your understanding of these terms by matching the appropriate definition with the terms. Record the number identifying the most appropriate definition in the blank space next to each term.

____ Accounts

____ Account balance

____ Account number

____ Balance column account

____ Book of final entry

____ Book of original entry

____ Business papers

____ Capital account

____ Chart of accounts

____ Compound journal entry

____ Credit

____ Debit

____ Double-entry accounting

____ Drawing account

____ Folio column

____ General Journal

____ Internal transactions

____ Journal

____ Journal page number

____ Ledger

____ Personal account

____ Posting

____ Posting Reference column

____ Prepaid expenses

____ Promissory note

____ Source documents

____ T-account

____ Trial balance

____ Unearned revenue

____ Withdrawals account

Problem V *(continued)*

1. Liabilities created by the receipt of cash from customers in payment for products or services that have not yet been delivered to the customers; the liabilities will be satisfied by delivering the product or service.

2. A list of the accounts that have balances in the ledger, the debit or credit balance of each account, the total of the debit balances, and the total of the credit balances.

3. An account that has debit and credit columns for entering changes in the account and a column for entering the new account balance after each debit or credit is posted to the account.

4. Another name for business papers.

5. A book of original entry in which transactions are first recorded and from which transaction amounts are posted to the ledger accounts.

6. A unique number that is assigned to an account as a means of identifying that account.

7. A simple form of account that is widely used in accounting education to illustrate the debits and credits required in recording a transaction.

8. A posting reference number entered in the Posting Reference column of each account to which an amount is posted and which shows the page of the journal from which the amount was posted.

9. Another name for the withdrawals account.

10. An account used to record the owner's investments in the business plus any more or less permanent changes in the owner's equity.

11. The left-hand side of a T-account, or entries that increase assets, or decrease liabilities, or decrease owner's equity.

12. Assets created by payments for economic benefits that do not expire until some later time; then, as the benefits expire or are used up, the assets become expenses.

13. Another name for the withdrawals account.

14. The account used to record the transfers of assets from a business to its owner.

15. Another name for the Posting Reference column.

16. A list of all the accounts used by a company, showing the identifying number assigned to each account.

17. A journal entry that has more than one debit or more than one credit.

18. A book of original entry that is designed so flexibly that it can be used to record any type of transaction.

19. A journal in which transactions are first recorded.

20. A ledger to which amounts are posted.

21. The right-hand side of a T-account, or entries that decrease assets, or increase liabilities, or increase owner's equity.

22. A formal written promise to pay a definite sum of money on demand or at a fixed or determinable future date.

23. A group of accounts used by a business in recording its transactions.

24. Transcribing the debit and credit amounts from a journal to the ledger accounts.

25. A name sometimes given to economic events that have an effect on an entity's accounting equation but that do not involve transactions with outside parties.

26. A system of accounting in which each transaction affects and is recorded in two or more accounts with equal debits and credits.

27. A column in a journal and in each account that is used for cross-referencing amounts that have been posted from a journal to the account.

28. Separate locations in an accounting system, one of which is used in recording and summarizing the increases and decreases in each type of revenue, expense, asset, liability, or owner's equity item.

29. Printed documents that businesses use in the process of completing business transactions and that provide evidence of the transactions.

30. The difference between the increases and decreases recorded in an account.

Problem VI

Complete the following by filling in the blanks.

1. A group of accounts used by a business in recording its transactions is called _____

    _____.

2. Transactions are first recorded in a _____ and are then posted to the ledger accounts.

3. The balance of an account is _____

    _____.

4. A journal entry linking together the debits and credits of a transaction makes it possible to

    _____ into the accounts and to see that they are equal and were properly recorded.

5. A T-account has a left side and a right side; and in entering increases and decreases in a T-account,

    the _____ are placed on one side of the account and the

    _____ are placed on the other side. This placement makes it possible to add the increases, add the decreases, and subtract the sum of the decreases from the sum of the increases to learn the amount of the item recorded in the account that the business has, owns, or owes.

6. The last step in posting an amount is _____

    _____

    _____.

7. Accounts are a device used by a business in recording and summarizing the _____

    _____ and _____ in each asset, liability, and owner's equity item appearing on its balance sheet and each revenue and expense on its income statement.

Problem VI *(continued)*

8. The steps in preparing a trial balance are: _____

    _____

    _____

    _____

    _____

    _____

    _____

    _____

    _____

    _____.

9. Revenues increase owner's equity and are _____ to revenue accounts.

    Expenses decrease owner's equity and are _____ to expense accounts.

10. a. The normal balance of an asset account, such as Cash is _____.

    b. The normal balance of a liability account is _____.

    c. The normal balance of the owner's capital account is _____.

    d. The normal balance of the owner's withdrawals account is _____.

    e. The normal balance of a revenue account is _____.

    f. The normal balance of an expense account is _____.

11. Increases in assets are recorded as _____ (debits, credits) and decreases

    are recorded as _____. Likewise, increases in liability and owner's equity

    items are recorded as _____ and decreases are recorded as

    _____.

12. When an account has an opposite from normal kind of balance, this opposite from normal kind of

    balance is indicated by _____

    _____

    _____.

Problem VI *(continued)*

13. Debits to accounts _____ (are, are not) always increases.

14. A trial balance that fails to balance is proof that _____

_____ either in recording transactions, in posting, or in preparing the trial balance.

15. A trial balance that balances is not absolute proof that there were no errors in recording, posting,

and preparing the trial balance because _____

_____

_____.

Solutions for Chapter 2

Problem I   **Problem II**

1. T	1. C
2. T	2. D
3. T	3. B
4. F	4. C
5. T	5. A

Problem III

Cash

(a)	1,800.00	(b)	675.00
(d)	505.50	(c)	700.00
(i)	175.00	(g)	290.50
		(h)	75.00
		(j)	350.00

Repair Equipment

(c)	700.00
(e)	415.50

Jon Wheeler, Withdrawals

(j)	350.00

Accounts Receivable

(f)	175.00	(i)	175.00

Accounts Payable

(g)	290.50	(e)	415.50

Revenue from Repairs

(d)	505.50
(f)	175.00

Prepaid Rent

(b)	675.00

Jon Wheeler, Capital

(a)	1,800.00

Advertising Expense

(h)	75.00

WHEELER'S REPAIR SHOP
Trial Balance, Current Date

Cash	$ 390.00	
Prepaid rent	675.00	
Repair equipment	1,115.50	
Accounts payable		$ 125.00
Jon Wheeler, capital		1,800.00
Jon Wheeler, withdrawals	350.00	
Revenue from repairs		680.50
Advertising expense	75.00	
Totals	$2,605.50	$2,605.50

Problem IV

GENERAL JOURNAL

PAGE 1

DATE		ACCOUNT TITLES AND EXPLANATION	P.R.	DEBIT	CREDIT
19— Nov.	5	Cash	1	1 5 0 0 00	
		Office Equipment	8	9 5 0 00	
		Sherry Dale, Capital	15		2 4 5 0 00
		Invested in a real estate agency.			
	6	Office Equipment	8	4 2 5 00	
		Cash	1		4 2 5 00
		Purchased office equipment.			

GENERAL LEDGER

Cash

Account No. 1

DATE		EXPLANATION	P.R.	DEBIT	CREDIT	BALANCE
19— Nov.	5		G–1	1 5 0 0 00		1 5 0 0 00
	6		G–1		4 2 5 00	1 0 7 5 00

Office Equipment

Account No. 8

DATE		EXPLANATION	P.R.	DEBIT	CREDIT	BALANCE
19— Nov.	5		G–1	9 5 0 00		9 5 0 00
	6		G–1	4 2 5 00		1 3 7 5 00

Sherry Dale, Capital

Account No. 15

DATE		EXPLANATION	P.R.	DEBIT	CREDIT	BALANCE
19— Nov.	5		G–1		2 4 5 0 00	2 4 5 0 00

Problem V

Problem VI

1. a ledger.
2. journal
3. the difference between the debits and credits entered in it
4. trace the debits and credits
5. increases, decreases
6. to enter in the journal the ledger account number to which the amount was posted.
7. increases, decreases
8. (a) Determine the balance of each account; (b) List in their ledger order the accounts having balances, with the debit balances in one column and the credit balances in another; (c) Add the debit balances; (d) Add the credit balances; (e) Compare the two totals for equality.
9. credited, debited
10. (a) debit (b) credit (c) credit (d) debit (e) credit (f) debit
11. debits, credits, credits, debits
12. entering the balance in the account in red or entering it in black and circling it
13. are not
14. one or more errors have been made
15. some types of errors do not cause debits to be unequal to credits

3 Adjusting the Accounts and Preparing the Statements

Your objectives in studying this chapter should include learning how to:

1. Explain why the life of a business is divided into accounting periods of equal length and why the accounts of a business must be adjusted at the end of each accounting period.

2. Prepare adjusting entries for prepaid expenses, accrued expenses, unearned revenues, accrued revenues, and depreciation.

3. Prepare entries to record cash receipts and cash disbursements of items that were recorded at the end of the previous period as accrued revenues and accrued expenses.

4. Explain the difference between the cash and accrual bases of accounting.

5. Define each asset and liability classification appearing on a balance sheet, classify balance sheet items, and prepare a classified balance sheet.

6. Define or explain the words and phrases listed in the chapter Glossary.

After studying the Appendix to Chapter 3 (Appendix A), you should be able to:

7. Explain why some companies record prepaid and unearned items in income statement accounts and prepare adjusting entries when this procedure is used.

Topical Outline

I. Adjusting the accounting records at the end of an accounting period

A. Time-period concept—the idea that the life of a business is divisible into time periods of equal length for the purpose of preparing periodic financial reports for the business. The specific period a business adopts is its:

1. Fiscal year—a period of any 12 consecutive months used by a business as its annual accounting period. This annual accounting period may be the:

a. Calendar year—January 1 to December 31.
b. Natural business year—the 12-month period that ends when the activities of a business are at their lowest point.

B. Accounts that require adjustments are:

1. Prepaid expenses—expenses that have been paid for in advance of use. These expenses remain assets until they are consumed in the operation of the business.

2. Depreciation—expiration of the usefulness of plant and equipment and allocation of the cost of such assets to expense of the periods during which the assets are used.

3. Accrued expenses—expenses that are incurred during an accounting period but that, prior to end-of-period adjustments, remain unrecorded because payment is not due.

4. Unearned revenues—liabilities created by the receipt of cash from customers in payment for products or services that have not yet been delivered to the customers.

5. Accrued revenues—revenues that are earned during an accounting period but that, prior to end-of-period adjustments, remain unrecorded because payment has not been received.

C. The adjustment process—recording appropriate adjusting entries and assigning to each accounting period that portion of a transaction's effect applicable to the period, based on:

1. The realization principle—requires that revenue be assigned to the accounting period in which it is earned.

2. The matching principle—requires that expenses be reported in the same period as the revenues earned as a result of the expenses.

D. Bases of accounting are the:

1. Cash basis—revenues and expenses are reported in the income statement when cash is received or paid; no adjustments are made for prepaid, unearned, and accrued items.

2. Accrual basis—the adjustment process is used to assign revenues to the periods in which they are earned and to match expenses with revenues.

II. Preparing financial statements

A. The adjusted trial balance—prepared after end-of-period adjustments to the accounts have been made.

B. Classification of balance sheet items

1. Current assets—cash, short-term investments, notes receivable, accounts receivable, merchandise inventory, prepaid expenses, office supplies.

2. Investments—long-term investments in items such as stocks, bonds, promissory notes, land held for future expansion.

3. Plant and equipment—equipment, buildings, land.

     4. Intangible assets—goodwill, patents, trademarks, franchises, copyrights.

     5. Current liabilities—short-term notes payable, accounts payable, wages payable, current portions of long-term liabilities, unearned revenues, interest payable, taxes payable.

     6. Long-term liabilities—notes payable, bonds payable.

     7. Owner's equity—single proprietorship, partnership, corporation.

  C. Balance sheet format

     1. Account form—assets are listed on the left and liability and owner's equity items are listed on the right.

     2. Report form—vertical format, shows the assets above the liabilities and the liabilities above the owner's equity.

III. Appendix A

  A. If prepayments of expenses are debited to expense accounts—

     1. End-of-period adjusting entries must be designed to transfer unused or unexpired amounts to prepaid expense accounts.

     2. Beginning-of-period balances in prepaid expense accounts must be considered when you prepare adjusting entries.

  B. If cash receipts of unearned revenues are credited to revenue accounts—

     1. End-of-period adjusting entries must be designed to transfer remaining unearned amounts to liability accounts.

     2. Beginning-of-period balances in unearned revenue accounts must be considered when you prepare adjusting entries.

Problem I

The following statements are either true or false. Place a (T) in the parentheses before each true statement and an (F) before each false statement.

1. ( ) The effect of a debit to an unearned revenue account and a corresponding credit to a revenue account is to transfer the earned portion of the fee from the liability account to the revenue account.

2. ( ) If the accountant failed to make the end-of-period adjustment to remove from the Unearned Fees account the amount of fees earned, the omission would cause an overstatement of assets.

3. ( ) The economic effect of a revenue generally occurs when it is earned, not when cash is received.

4. ( ) The equity section of a balance sheet is the same for a single proprietorship, a partnership, or a corporation.

5. ( ) Under the cash basis of accounting, revenues are recognized when they are earned and expenses are matched with revenues.

Problem II

You are given several words, phrases or numbers to choose from in completing each of the following statements or in answering the following questions. In each case select the one that best completes the statement or answers the question and place its letter in the answer space provided.

_____ 1. The average time a business takes to invest cash in merchandise or raw materials that are manufactured into finished products, sell the products, and convert the receivables (if sales are on credit) back into cash is the:

    a. accounting period of a business.
    b. fiscal year.
    c. time-period concept.
    d. operating cycle of a business.
    e. natural business year.

_____ 2. Depreciation is:

    a. expenses that are incurred during an accounting period but that, prior to end-of-period adjustments, remain unrecorded because payment is not due.
    b. the expiration of the usefulness of plant and equipment, and the related process of allocating the cost of such assets to expense of the periods during which the assets are used.
    c. an account the balance of which is subtracted from the balance of an associated account to show a more proper amount for the item recorded in the associated account.
    d. a distribution, generally of assets, made by a corporation to its stockholders.
    e. economic benefits or resources without physical substance, the value of which stems from the privileges or rights that accrue to their owner.

Problem II *(continued)*

_____ 3. X Company has 4 employees who are each paid $40 per day for a five-day work week. The employees are paid every Friday. If the accounting period ends on Wednesday, X Company should make the following entry to accrue wages:

    a.   Salary Expense 800
            Salaries Payable   800
    b.   Salary Expense 800
            Cash   800
    c.   Salary Expense 480
            Salaries Payable   480
    d.   Salary Expense 320
            Salaries Payable   320
    e.   No entry should be made until the salaries are actually paid.

_____ 4. Lori Teach owns a sole proprietorship. During April of 1990 Lori's business received $250 cash in advance for future services. The following entry should be made when the money is received:

    a.   Cash 250
            Services Owed   250
    b.   Accounts Receivable 250
            Unearned Revenue   250
    c.   Cash 250
            Unearned Revenue   250
    d.   Unearned Revenue 250
            Earned Revenue   250
    e.   No entry should be made until services are actually rendered.

_____ 5. B & B Corporation had $175,000 of common stock issued and outstanding during all of 1990. It began the year with $50,000 of retained earnings, and it declared and paid $10,000 of cash dividends to its stockholders. B & B earned a $15,000 net income in 1990 and invested $5,000 in G. I. Jane common stock. What is the retained earnings balance at the end of 1990?

    a. $230,000.
    b. $ 45,000.
    c. $ 40,000.
    d. $ 50,000.
    e. $ 55,000.

Problem II *(continued)*

_____ 6. The Epicure Restaurant prepares monthly financial statements. On January 31, the balance in the Supplies account was $1,600. During February, $2,960 of supplies were purchased and debited to Supplies Expense. What is the adjusting entry on February 28 to account for the supplies assuming a February 28 inventory showed that $1,300 of supplies were on hand?

    a. Supplies Expense 300
       Supplies 300
    b. Supplies 300
       Supplies Expense 300
    c. Supplies 3,260
       Cash 3,260
    d. Supplies Expense 3,260
       Supplies 3,260
    e. Some other entry.

_____ 7. Calculate the missing item in the following case:

    The Owner, capital, January 1, 1990 ....$57,000
    Total revenues during 1990 .... ?
    Total expenses during 1990 27,900
    Withdrawals during the year 15,750
    The Owner, capital, December 31, 1990 63,300

    a. $29,100.
    b. $49,950.
    c. $47,550.
    d. $46,350.
    e. $18,450.

Problem III

Many of the important ideas and concepts discussed in Chapter 3 are reflected in the following list of key terms. Test your understanding of these terms by matching the appropriate definitions with the terms. Record the number identifying the most appropriate definition in the blank space next to each term.

_____ Account form balance sheet

_____ Accounting period

_____ Accrual basis of accounting

_____ Accrued expenses

_____ Accrued revenues

_____ Accumulated depreciation

_____ Adjusted trial balance

_____ Adjusting entry

_____ Cash basis of accounting

_____ Classified balance sheet

_____ Common stock

_____ Contra account

_____ Contributed capital

_____ Current assets

_____ Current liabilities

_____ Depreciation

_____ Dividends

_____ Fiscal year

_____ Intangible assets

_____ Interim financial reports

_____ Long-term liabilities

_____ Matching principle

_____ Natural business year

_____ Operating cycle of a business

_____ Paid-in capital

_____ Plant and equipment

_____ Report form balance sheet

_____ Retained earnings

_____ Time-period concept

_____ Unadjusted trial balance

_____ Unclassified balance sheet

1. Expenses that are incurred during an accounting period but that, prior to end-of-period adjustments, remain unrecorded because payment is not due.

2. The portion of a corporation's equity that represents investments in the corporation by its stockholders.

3. Obligations that are not due to be paid within one year or the current operating cycle of the business.

4. A trial balance that shows the account balances after they have been revised to reflect the effects of end-of-period adjustments.

5. Revenues that are earned during an accounting period but that, prior to end-of-period adjustments, remain unrecorded because payment has not been received.

6. A trial balance that is prepared before any adjustments have been recorded.

7. The idea that the life of a business is divisible into time periods of equal length for the purpose of preparing periodic financial reports of the business.

8. The portion of a corporation's equity that represents its cumulative net incomes, less net losses and dividends.

9. A period of any 12 consecutive months used by a business as its annual accounting period.

10. The expiration of the usefulness of plant and equipment, and the related process of allocating the cost of such assets to expense of the periods during which the assets are used.

Problem III *(continued)*

11. Tangible, long-lived assets that are held for use in the production or sale of other assets or services.

12. A journal entry made at the end of an accounting period for the purpose of assigning revenues to the period in which they are earned, assigning expenses to the period in which the expiration of benefit is incurred, and to correct related liability and asset accounts.

13. The accounting requirement that expenses be reported in the same accounting period as are the revenues that were earned as a result of the expenses.

14. The 12-month period that ends when the activities of a business are at their lowest point.

15. The total amount of depreciation recorded against an asset or group of assets during the entire period of time the asset or assets have been owned.

16. A balance sheet prepared with a vertical format that shows the assets above the liabilities and the liabilities above the owner's equity.

17. The accounting system in which revenues are reported in the income statement when cash is received and expenses are reported when cash is paid; no adjustments are made for prepaid, unearned, and accrued items.

18. Another name for contributed capital.

19. Cash or other assets that are reasonably expected to be realized in cash or be sold or consumed within one year or one operating cycle of the business, whichever is longer.

20. The name given to a corporation's stock when it issues only one kind or class of stock.

21. A balance sheet that presents a single list of assets and a single list of liabilities with no attempt to divide them into classes.

22. Economic benefits or resources without physical substance, the value of which stems from the privileges or rights that accrue to their owner.

23. A system of accounting in which the adjustment process is used to assign revenues to the periods in which they are earned and to match expenses with revenues.

24. The average time a business takes to invest cash in merchandise or raw materials that are manufactured into finished products, sell the products, and convert the receivables (if sales are on credit) back into cash.

25. An account the balance of which is subtracted from the balance of an associated account to show a more proper amount for the item recorded in the associated account.

26. The length of time into which the life of a business is divided for the purpose of preparing periodic financial statements.

27. A balance sheet that is arranged so that the assets are listed on the left and the liabilities and owner's equity items are listed on the right.

28. A balance sheet that shows assets and liabilities grouped in meaningful subclasses.

29. A distribution, generally of assets, made by a corporation to its stockholders.

30. Obligations that are due to be paid or liquidated within one year or one operating cycle, whichever is longer.

31. Financial reports of a business that are based on one-month or three-month accounting periods.

Problem IV

On October 1 of the current year, Harold Lloyd began business as a public stenographer. During the month he completed the following transactions:

Oct. 1 Invested $3,000 in the business.
   1 Paid three months' rent in advance on the office space, $1,245.
   1 Purchased office equipment for cash, $925.50.
   2 Purchased on credit office equipment, $700, and office supplies, $75.50.
   31 Completed stenographic work during the month and collected cash, $1,725. (Combined into one entry to conserve space.)
   31 Withdrew $725 for personal living expenses.

After the foregoing entries were recorded in the journal and posted, the accounts of Harold Lloyd appeared as follows:

Cash   Account No. 1

DATE		EXPLANATION	P.R.	DEBIT	CREDIT	BALANCE
Oct.	1		G–1	3 0 0 0 00		3 0 0 0 00
	1		G–1		1 2 4 5 00	1 7 5 5 00
	1		G–1		9 2 5 50	8 2 9 50
	31		G–2	1 7 2 5 00		2 5 5 4 50
	31		G–2		7 2 5 00	1 8 2 9 50

Prepaid Rent   Account No. 2

DATE		EXPLANATION	P.R.	DEBIT	CREDIT	BALANCE
Oct.	1		G–1	1 2 4 5 00		1 2 4 5 00

Office Supplies   Account No. 3

DATE		EXPLANATION	P.R.	DEBIT	CREDIT	BALANCE
Oct.	2		G–1	7 5 50		7 5 50

Office Equipment   Account No. 4

DATE		EXPLANATION	P.R.	DEBIT	CREDIT	BALANCE
Oct.	1		G–1	9 2 5 50		9 2 5 50
	2		G–1	7 0 0 00		1 6 2 5 50

Problem IV *(continued)*

Accumulated Depreciation, Office Equipment   Account No. 5

DATE		EXPLANATION	P.R.	DEBIT	CREDIT	BALANCE

Accounts Payable   Account No. 6

DATE		EXPLANATION	P.R.	DEBIT	CREDIT	BALANCE
Oct.	2		G–1		775 50	775 50

Harold Lloyd, Capital   Account No. 7

DATE		EXPLANATION	P.R.	DEBIT	CREDIT	BALANCE
Oct.	1		G–1		3 000 00	3 000 00

Harold Lloyd, Withdrawals   Account No. 8

DATE		EXPLANATION	P.R.	DEBIT	CREDIT	BALANCE
Oct.	31		G–2	725 00		725 00

Stenographic Revenue   Account No. 9

DATE		EXPLANATION	P.R.	DEBIT	CREDIT	BALANCE
Oct.	31		G–2		1 725 00	1 725 00

Rent Expense   Account No. 10

DATE		EXPLANATION	P.R.	DEBIT	CREDIT	BALANCE

Office Supplies Expense   Account No. 11

DATE		EXPLANATION	P.R.	DEBIT	CREDIT	BALANCE

Problem IV *(continued)*

Depreciation Expense, Office Equipment   Account No. 12

DATE		EXPLANATION	P.R.	DEBIT	CREDIT	BALANCE

On October 31 Harold Lloyd decided to adjust his accounts and prepare a balance sheet and an income statement. His adjustments were:

a.   One month's rent had expired.
b.   An inventory of office supplies showed $40 of unused office supplies.
c.   The office equipment had depreciated $35 during October.

Required:

1.   Prepare and post general journal entries to record the adjustments.
2.   After posting the adjusting entries, complete the adjusted trial balance.
3.   From the adjusted trial balance complete the income statement and balance sheet.

GENERAL JOURNAL   PAGE 2

DATE		ACCOUNT TITLES AND EXPLANATION	P.R.	DEBIT	CREDIT

Problem IV *(continued)*

HAROLD LLOYD																		
Adjusted Trial Balance																		
October 31, 19—																		
Cash																		
Prepaid rent																		
Office supplies																		
Office equipment																		
Accumulated depreciation, office equipment																		
Accounts payable																		
Harold Lloyd, capital																		
Harold Lloyd, withdrawals																		
Stenographic revenue																		
Rent expense																		
Office supplies expense																		
Depreciation expense, office equipment																		
Totals																		

HAROLD LLOYD																		
Income Statement																		
For Month Ended October 31, 19—																		
Revenue:																		
Stenographic revenue																		
Operating expenses:																		
Rent expense																		
Office supplies expense																		
Depreciation expense, office equipment																		
Total operating expenses																		
Net income																		

Problem IV *(continued)*

	HAROLD LLOYD																				
	Balance Sheet																					
	October 31, 19—																					
Assets																						
Current Assets:																						
Cash																						
Prepaid rent																						
Office supplies																						
Total current assets																						
Plant and Equipment:																						
Office equipment																						
Less accumulated depreciation																						
Total plant and equipment																						
Total assets																						
Liabilities																						
Current Liabilities:																						
Accounts payable																						
Total liabilities																						
Owner's Equity																						
Harold Lloyd, capital, October 31, 19—																						
October net income																						
Less withdrawals																						
Excess of income over withdrawals																						
Harold Lloyd, capital, October 1, 19—																						
Total liabilities and owner's equity																						

Problem V

a. Blade Company has one employee who earns $72.50 per day. The company operates with monthly accounting periods, and the employee is paid each Friday night for a work week that begins on Monday. Assume the calendar for October appears as shown on the right and enter the four $362.50 weekly wage payments directly in the T-accounts below. Then enter the adjustment for the wages earned but unpaid on October 31.

OCTOBER						
S	M	T	W	T	F	S
	1	2	3	4	5	6
7	8	9	10	11	12	13
14	15	16	17	18	19	20
21	22	23	24	25	26	27
28	29	30	31			

Problem V *(continued)*

Cash	Wages Payable	Wages Expense

b. Blade Company's October income statement should show $_____ of wages

expense, and its October 31 balance sheet should show a $_____ liability for wages payable. The wages earned by its employee but unpaid on October 31 are an example of an

_____ expense.

c. In the space that follows give the general journal entry to record payment of a full week's wages to the Blade Company employee on November 2.

DATE	ACCOUNT TITLES AND EXPLANATION	P.R.	DEBIT	CREDIT

Problem VI

Riverview Properties operates an apartment building. On December 31, at the end of an annual accounting period, its Revenue from Rents account had a $335,500 credit balance, and the Unearned Rents account had a $3,600 credit balance. The following information was available for the year-end adjustments: (a) The credit balance in the Unearned Rents account resulted from a tenant paying his rent for six months in advance beginning on November 1. (b) Also, a tenant in temporary financial difficulties had not paid his rent for the month of December. The amount due was $475.

Problem VI *(continued)*

Required: Enter the necessary adjustments directly in the T-accounts below.

Rents Receivable		Unearned Rents		Revenue from Rents	
			Nov. 1 3,600		Bal. 335,500

After the foregoing adjustments are entered in the accounts, the company's Revenue from Rents account

has a $_____ balance which should appear on its income statement as revenue

earned during the year. Its Unearned Rents account has a $_____ balance,

and this should appear on the company's balance sheet as a _____

_____. Likewise, the company's Rents Receivable ac-

count has a $_____ balance, and this should appear on its balance sheet

as a _____.

Problem VII

1. Under the cash basis of accounting, revenues are reported as being earned in the accounting period

    in which _____; expenses are charged to the period

    in which _____; and net income for the period is the difference

    between _____ and _____

    _____. Under the accrual basis of accounting, revenues are

    credited to the period in which _____, expenses are

    _____ with revenues, and no consideration is given as to when cash is
    received or disbursed.

2. Current assets consist of cash and assets that are expected to be realized in cash or (complete

    definition) _____

    _____

    _____

    _____.

Problem VIII (This problem applies to Appendix A.)

The following statements are either true or false. Place a (T) in the parentheses before each true statement and an (F) before each false statement.

1. ( ) If a business follows the practice of debiting prepayments of expenses to expense accounts, the adjusting entries for prepaid expenses require debits to prepaid expense accounts.

2. ( ) If a business records receipts of unearned revenues with debits to cash and credits to revenue accounts, no adjusting entries are required at the end of the period.

Problem IX (This problem applies to Appendix A.)

You are given several words, phrases, or numbers to choose from in completing each of the following statements or in answering the following questions. In each case select the one that best completes the statement or answers the question and place its letter in the answer space provided.

_____ 1. Hanover Company prepares monthly financial statements and follows the procedure of crediting revenue accounts when it records cash receipts of unearned revenues. During April, the business received $4,800 for services to be rendered during April and May. On April 30, $2,000 of the amounts received had been earned. What is the adjusting journal entry on April 30 for service fees?

    a. Service Fees Earned 2,000
           Unearned Service Fees   2,000
    b. Unearned Service Fees 2,800
           Service Fees Earned   2,800
    c. Cash 2,000
           Service Fees Earned   2,000
    d. Unearned Service Fees 2,000
           Service Fees Earned   2,000
    e. Service Fees Earned 2,800
           Unearned Service Fees   2,800

_____ 2. Xanadu Company prepared monthly financial statements. On August 31, the balance in the Office Supplies account was $300. During July, $500 of supplies were purchased and debited to Office Supplies Expense. What is the adjusting journal entry on September 30 to account for the supplies assuming a September inventory of supplies showed that $250 were on hand.

    a. Office Supplies 350
           Office Supplies Expense   350
    b. Office Supplies Expense 250
           Office Supplies   250
    c. Office Supplies Expense 50
           Office Supplies   50
    d. Office Supplies Expense 350
           Office Supplies   350
    e. Office Supplies 250
           Office Supplies Expense   250

Solutions for Chapter 3

Problem I

1. T
2. F
3. T
4. F
5. F

Problem II

1. D
2. B
3. C
4. C
5. E
6. A
7. B

Problem III

Account form balance sheet	27	Dividends	29
Accounting period	26	Fiscal year	9
Accrual basis of accounting	23	Intangible assets	22
Accrued expenses	1	Interim financial reports	31
Accrued revenues	5	Long-term liabilities	3
Accumulated depreciation	15	Matching principle	13
Adjusted trial balance	4	Natural business year	14
Adjusting entry	12	Operating cycle of a	
Cash basis of accounting	17	business	24
Classified balance sheet	28	Paid-in capital	18 or 2
Common stock	20	Plant and equipment	11
Contra account	25	Report form balance sheet	16
Contributed capital	2	Retained earnings	8
Current assets	19	Time-period concept	7
Current liabilities	30	Unadjusted trial balance	6
Depreciation	10	Unclassified balance sheet	21

Problem IV

Oct. 31	Rent Expense		415.00	
	Prepaid Rent			415.00
31	Office Supplies Expense		35.50	
	Office Supplies			35.50
31	Depreciation Expense, Office Equipment		35.00	
	Accumulated Depreciation, Office Equipment			35.00

Problem IV (*continued*)

Cash

DATE	DEBIT	CREDIT	BALANCE
Oct. 1	3,000.00		3,000.00
1		1,245.00	1,755.00
1		925.50	829.50
31	1,725.00		2,554.50
31		725.00	1,829.50

Prepaid Rent

DATE	DEBIT	CREDIT	BALANCE
Oct. 1	1,245.00		1,245.00
31		415.00	830.00

Office Supplies

DATE	DEBIT	CREDIT	BALANCE
Oct. 2	75.50		75.50
31		35.50	40.00

Office Equipment

DATE	DEBIT	CREDIT	BALANCE
Oct. 1	925.50		925.50
2	700.00		1,625.50

Accumulated Depr., Office Equipment

DATE	DEBIT	CREDIT	BALANCE
Oct. 31		35.00	35.00

Accounts Payable

DATE	DEBIT	CREDIT	BALANCE
Oct. 2		775.50	775.50

Harold Lloyd, Capital

DATE	DEBIT	CREDIT	BALANCE
Oct. 1		3,000.00	3,000.00

Harold Lloyd, Withdrawals

DATE	DEBIT	CREDIT	BALANCE
Oct. 31	725.00		725.00

Stenographic Revenue

DATE	DEBIT	CREDIT	BALANCE
Oct. 31		1,725.00	1,725.00

Rent Expense

DATE	DEBIT	CREDIT	BALANCE
Oct. 31	415.00		415.00

Office Supplies Expense

DATE	DEBIT	CREDIT	BALANCE
Oct. 31	35.50		35.50

Depr. Expense, Office Equipment

DATE	DEBIT	CREDIT	BALANCE
Oct. 31	35.00		35.00

HAROLD LLOYD
Adjusted Trial Balance
October 31, 19—

Cash	$1,829.50	
Prepaid rent	830.00	
Office supplies	40.00	
Office equipment	1,625.50	
Accumulated depreciation, office equipment		$ 35.00
Accounts payable		775.50
Harold Lloyd, capital		3,000.00
Harold Lloyd, withdrawals	725.00	
Stenographic revenue		1,725.00
Rent expense	415.00	
Office supplies expense	35.50	
Depreciation expense, office equipment	35.00	
Totals	$5,535.50	$5,535.50

Problem IV (*continued*)

HAROLD LLOYD
Income Statement
For Month Ended October 31, 19—

Revenue:		
Stenographic revenue		$1,725.00
Operating expenses:		
Rent expense	$415.00	
Office supplies expense	35.50	
Depreciation expense, office equipment	35.00	
Total operating expenses		485.50
Net income		$1,239.50

HAROLD LLOYD
Balance Sheet
October 31, 19—

Assets

Current Assets:		
Cash	$1,829.50	
Prepaid rent	830.00	
Office supplies	40.00	
Total current assets		$2,699.50
Plant and Equipment:		
Office equipment	$1,625.50	
Less accumulated depreciation	35.00	
Total plant and equipment		1,590.50
Total assets		$4,290.00

Liabilities

Current Liabilities:		
Accounts payable		$ 775.50
Total current liabilities		$ 775.50

Owner's Equity

Harold Lloyd, capital, October 1, 19—		$3,000.00
October net income	$1,239.50	
Less withdrawals	725.00	
Excess of income over withdrawals		514.50
Harold Lloyd, capital, October 31, 19—		3,514.50
Total liabilities and owner's equity		$4,290.00

Problem V

a.

Cash		
	Oct. 5	362.50
	12	362.50
	19	362.50
	26	362.50

Wages Expense		
Oct. 5	362.50	
12	362.50	
19	362.50	
26	362.50	
31	217.50	

Wages Payable		
	Oct. 31	217.50

b. $1,667.50; $217.50; accrued

c. Nov. 2 Wages Expense 145.00
   Wages Payable 217.50
   Cash 362.50

Problem VI

Rents Receivable		
Dec. 31	475	

Unearned Rents			
Dec. 31	1,200	Nov. 1	3,600

Revenue from Rents		
	Bal.	335,500
	Dec. 31	1,200
	31	475

Revenue from Rents, $337,175
Unearned Rents, $2,400, current liability
Rents Receivable, $475, current asset

Problem VII

1. they are received in cash, they are paid, revenue receipts, expense disbursements, earned, matched

2. be sold or consumed within one year or within one operating cycle of the business, whichever is longer

Problem VIII   Problem IX

1. T   1. E
2. F   2. C

4 | The Work Sheet and Closing the Accounts of Proprietorships, Partnerships, and Corporations

Your objectives in studying this chapter should include learning how to:

1. Explain why a work sheet is prepared and be able to prepare a work sheet for a service-type business.

2. Prepare closing entries for a service business and explain why it is essary to close the temporary accounts at the end of each accounting period.

3. Prepare a post-closing trial balance and explain its purpose.

4. Explain the nature of a corporation's retained earnings and its relationship to the declaration of dividends.

5. Prepare entries to record the declaration and payment of a dividend and to close the temporary accounts of a corporation.

6. List the steps in the accounting cycle in the order in which they are completed and perform each step.

7. Define or explain the words and phrases listed in the chapter Glossary.

After studying the Appendix to Chapter 4 (Appendix B), you should be able to:

8. Prepare reversing entries and explain when and why they are used.

Topical Outline

I. The work sheet and adjusting entries

    A. A work sheet is prepared at the end of each accounting period to:

        1. Reflect the effects of adjustments before adjusting entries are made.

        2. Provide the information used in preparing financial statements by sorting adjusted account balances into appropriate income statement and statement of changes in owner's equity and balance sheet columns.

        3. Calculate and prove the mathematical accuracy of net income.

    B. To prepare a work sheet:

        1. List all accounts contained in the unadjusted trial balance.

        2. Make adjusting entries in appropriate columns.

        3. Combine amounts in Unadjusted Trial Balance columns and Adjustment columns and carry these amounts to Adjusted Trial Balance columns.

        4. Add Adjusted Trial Balance columns to prove their equality.

        5. Sort amounts into Statement of Changes in Owner's Equity and Balance Sheet or Income Statement columns.

        6. Determine net income (or loss) by taking the difference between debit and credit totals of Income Statement columns, and balance the Balance Sheet columns by adding net income (or loss).

    C. Journalize and post adjusting entries.

II. Closing entries

    A. Closing entries are made to:

        1. Transfer the effects of revenues, expenses, and withdrawals to the capital account.

        2. Bring the temporary (revenue, expense, withdrawal, and Income Summary) account balances to zero, so that revenues, expenses, and withdrawals in the next accounting period can be properly recorded and closed.

    B. Closing the accounts

        1. Revenue accounts, which have credit balances, are closed by debiting the accounts and crediting Income Summary.

        2. Expense accounts, which have debit balances, are closed by crediting the accounts and debiting Income Summary.

        3. The balance of the Income Summary account is transferred to the proprietor's capital account.

        4. The withdrawals account is closed to the proprietor's capital account.

    C. Accounts that appear in the balance sheet are called real or permanent accounts. Those that are closed at the end of each period are called nominal or temporary accounts.

III. Accounting for partnerships and corporations

    A. Partnership accounting is like accounting for a single proprietorship, except:

        1. Separate withdrawals and capital accounts are kept for each partner.

        2. The Income Summary account is closed with a compound journal entry to allocate each partner's share of income (or loss).

    B. Corporation accounting is also like accounting for a single proprietorship, except:

        1. There are two kinds of stockholders' equity accounts:

            a. Contributed capital accounts (such as Common Stock)
            b. Retained Earnings account

        2. The Income Summary account is closed to the Retained Earnings account.

        3. Dividend declarations are recorded in Dividends Declared, which is closed to the Retained Earnings account.

IV. The accounting cycle—the sequence of accounting procedures followed each accounting period:

    A. Journalizing

    B. Posting

    C. Preparing an unadjusted trial balance

    D. Completing the work sheet

    E. Preparing the statements

    F. Adjusting the ledger accounts

    G. Closing the temporary accounts

    H. Preparing a post-closing trial balance

V. Appendix B

    A. Reversing entries are optional entries prepared after closing entries and dated the first day of the new period.

    B. Reversing entries are usually applied to asset and liability account balances that arose from the accrual of revenues and expenses.

    C. The accrued asset and liability account balances are transferred to related revenue and expense accounts.

    D. When reversing entries are used, subsequent cash receipts (and payments) are recorded in revenue (and expense) accounts.

Problem I

The following statements are either true or false. Place a (T) in the parentheses before each true statement and an (F) before each false statement.

1. ( ) If the Income Statement columns of a work sheet are equal after transferring from the Adjusted Trial Balance columns, then it can be concluded that there is no net income (or loss).

2. ( ) The only reason why the Statement of Changes in Owner's Equity or Balance Sheet columns of a work sheet might be out of balance would be if an error had been made in sorting revenue and expense data from the Adjusted Trial Balance columns of the work sheet.

3. ( ) After all closing entries are posted at the end of an accounting period, the Income Summary account balance is zero.

4. ( ) Throughout the current period, one could refer to the balance of the Income Summary account to determine the amount of net income or loss that was earned in the prior accounting period.

5. ( ) On a work sheet, net income would be understated if a liability was extended into the Income Statement—Credit column.

Problem II

You are given several words, phrases, or numbers to choose from in completing each of the following statements or in answering the following questions. In each case select the one that best completes the statement or answers the question and place its letter in the answer space provided.

_____ 1. Equipment, Wages Expense, and The Owner, Capital would be sorted to which respective columns in completing a work sheet?

     a. Statement of Changes in Owner's Equity or Balance Sheet—Debit; Income Statement—Debit; and Statement of Changes in Owner's Equity or Balance Sheet—Debit.

     b. Statement of Changes in Owner's Equity or Balance Sheet—Debit; Income Statement—Debit; and Statement of Changes in Owner's Equity or Balance Sheet—Credit.

     c. Statement of Changes in Owner's Equity or Balance Sheet—Debit; Income Statement—Credit; and Statement of Changes in Owner's Equity or Balance Sheet—Debit.

     d. Statement of Changes in Owner's Equity or Balance Sheet—Debit; Income Statement—Credit; and Statement of Changes in Owner's Equity or Balance Sheet—Credit.

     e. Statement of Changes in Owner's Equity or Balance Sheet—Credit; Income Statement—Credit; and Statement of Changes in Owner's Equity or Balance Sheet—Credit.

Problem II (continued)

_____ 2. Based on the following T-accounts and their end-of-period balances, what will be the balance of the Joe Cool, Capital account after the closing entries are posted?

Joe Cool, Capital	Joe Cool, Withdrawals	Income Summary
Dec. 31 7,000	Dec. 31 9,600	

Revenue	Rent Expense	Salaries Expense
Dec. 31 29,700	Dec. 31 3,600	Dec. 31 7,200

Insurance Expense	Depr. Expense, Equipment	Accum. Depr., Equipment
Dec. 31 920	Dec. 31 500	Dec. 31 500

a. $12,880 Debit.
b. $12,880 Credit.
c. $24,480 Credit.
d. $14,880 Credit.
e. $10,480 Debit.

_____ 3. The following items appeared on a December 31 work sheet. Based on the following information, what are the totals in the Statement of Changes in Owner's Equity or Balance Sheet columns?

	Unadjusted Trial Balance		Adjustments	
	Debit	Credit	Debit	Credit
Cash	975			
Prepaid insurance	3,600			150
Supplies	180			70
Equipment	10,320			
Accounts payable		1,140		
Unearned fees		4,500	375	
The Owner, capital		9,180		
The Owner, withdrawals	1,650			
Fees earned		5,850		375
				300
Rent expense	1,500			
Salaries expense	2,100		315	
Utilities expense	345			
	20,670	20,670		
Insurance expense			150	
Supplies expense			70	
Depreciation expense, equipment			190	
Accumulated depreciation, equipment				190
Salaries payable				315
Accounts receivable			300	
			1,400	1,400

a. $16,805.
b. $16,505.
c. $14,950.
d. $14,820.
e. Some other amount.

Problem II *(continued)*

_____ 4. In what order are the following steps in the accounting cycle performed?

        1) Preparing an unadjusted trial balance
        2) Journalizing and posting closing entries
        3) Journalizing transactions
        4) Preparing a post-closing trial balance
        5) Preparing the financial statements
        6) Completing the work sheet
        7) Journalizing and posting adjusting entries
        8) Posting the entries to record transactions

    a. (1) , (3) , (8) , (7) , (6) , (2) , (4) , (5)
    b. (3) , (8) , (1) , (6) , (5) , (7) , (2) , (4)
    c. (1) , (3) , (8) , (6) , (7) , (2) , (5) , (4)
    d. (3) , (1) , (8) , (7) , (6) , (5) , (4) , (2)
    e. (3) , (8) , (1) , (7) , (6) , (2) , (4) , (5)

_____ 5. Real accounts are:

    a. accounts that are closed at the end of each accounting period; therefore, the revenue, expense, Income Summary, and withdrawals accounts.
    b. accounts used to record the owner's investment in the business plus any more or less permanent changes in the owner's equity.
    c. accounts the balance of which is subtracted from the balance of an associated account to show a more proper amount for the item recorded in the associated account.
    d. also called temporary accounts.
    e. also called permanent accounts.

Problem III

Many of the important ideas and concepts discussed in Chapter 4 are reflected in the following list of key terms. Test your understanding of these terms by matching the appropriate definitions with the terms. Record the number identifying the most appropriate definition in the blank space next to each term.

_____ Accounting cycle

_____ Closing entries

_____ Date of declaration

_____ Date of payment

_____ Date of record

_____ Deficit

_____ Dividends Declared

_____ Income Summary

_____ Nominal accounts

_____ Permanent accounts

_____ Post-closing trial balance

_____ Real accounts

_____ Reversing entries

_____ Stockholders of record

_____ Temporary accounts

_____ Working papers

_____ Work sheet

Problem III *(continued)*

1. The stockholders of a corporation as reflected in the records of the corporation.

2. A trial balance prepared after all adjusting and closing entries have been posted.

3. The recurring accounting steps that are performed each accounting period and that begin with the recording of transactions and proceed through posting the recorded amounts, preparing a trial balance and completing a work sheet, preparing the financial statements, preparing and posting adjusting and closing entries, and preparing a post-closing trial balance.

4. A temporary account that serves the same function for a corporation as does a withdrawals account for a proprietorship, and which is closed to Retained Earnings at the end of each accounting period.

5. Accounts that are closed at the end of each accounting period; therefore, the revenue, expense, Income Summary, and withdrawals accounts.

6. A negative amount (debit balance) of retained earnings.

7. The date on which a dividend liability of a corporation is satisfied by mailing checks to the stockholders.

8. Another name for permanent accounts.

9. The date on which a dividend is declared by a corporation's board of directors.

10. Entries made at the end of each accounting period to establish zero balances in the temporary accounts and to transfer the temporary account balances to a capital account or accounts or to the Retained Earnings account.

11. The account used in the closing process to summarize the amounts of revenues and expenses, and from which the amount of the net income or loss is transferred to the owner's capital account in a single proprietorship, the partners' capital accounts in a partnership, or the Retained Earnings account in a corporation.

12. A working paper on which the accountant shows the unadjusted trial balance, shows the effects of the adjustments on the account balances, calculates the net income or loss, and sorts the adjusted amounts according to the financial statements on which the amounts will appear.

13. The date on which the stockholders who are listed in a corporation's records are determined to be those who will receive a dividend.

14. The memoranda, analyses, and other informal papers prepared by accountants in the process of organizing the data that goes into the formal financial reports given to managers and other interested parties.

15. Accounts that remain open as long as the asset, liability, or owner's equity items recorded in the accounts continue in existence; therefore, accounts that appear in the balance sheet.

16. Optional entries that transfer the balances in balance sheet accounts which arose as a result of certain adjusting entries (usually accruals) to income statement accounts.

17. Another name for temporary accounts.

Problem IV

Complete the following by filling in the blanks.

1. A work sheet is prepared after all transactions are recorded but before _____

    _____

    _____.

2. Revenue accounts have credit balances; consequently, to close a revenue account and make it show a zero balance, the revenue account is _____ and the Income Summary account is _____ for the amount of the balance.

3. In sorting the amounts in the Adjusted Trial Balance columns of a work sheet to the proper Income Statement or Statement of Changes in Owner's Equity and Balance Sheet columns, two decisions are involved. The decisions are:

    (a) _____ and

    (b) _____.

4. Expense accounts have debit balances; therefore, expense accounts are _____

    _____ and the Income Summary account is _____ in closing the expense accounts.

5. In preparing a work sheet for a concern, its unadjusted ledger account balances are entered in the

    _____ of the work sheet form, after which

    the _____ are entered in the second pair of money columns. Next, the unadjusted trial balance amounts and the amounts in the Adjustments columns are combined to

    secure a(n) _____ in the third pair of money columns.

6. Only balance sheet accounts should have balances appearing on the post-closing trial balance

    because the balances of all temporary accounts are reduced to _____

    _____ in the closing procedure.

Problem IV *(continued)*

7. A work sheet is a tool of the accountant, that is used to:

    (a) _____

    _____,

    (b) _____

    _____,

    (c) _____

    _____.

8. A corporation has two kinds of stockholders' equity accounts, called _____

    _____ and

    _____.

9. Closing entries are necessary because if at the end of an accounting period the revenue and expense accounts are to show only one period's revenues and expenses, they must begin the period

    with _____ balances, and closing entries cause the revenue and expense

    accounts to begin a new period with _____ balances.

10. Closing entries accomplish two purposes: (1) they cause all _____

    _____ accounts to begin the new accounting period with zero balances, and (2) they transfer the net effect of the past period's

    _____, _____, and withdrawal transactions to the owner's capital account.

Problem V

The unfinished year-end work sheet of Homer's Home Shop appears on the next page.

Required:

1. Complete the work sheet using the following adjustments information:
    a. A $725 inventory of shop supplies indicates that $1,037 of shop supplies have been used during the year.
    b. The shop equipment has depreciated $475 during the year.
    c. On December 31, wages of $388 have been earned by the one employee but are unpaid because payment is not due.
2. After completing the work sheet, prepare the year-end adjusting and closing entries.
3. Post the adjusting and closing entries to the accounts that appear in skeletonized form beginning on page 69.
4. After posting the adjusting and closing entries, prepare a post-closing trial balance.

Problem V *(continued)*

HOMER'S HOME SHOP
Work Sheet for Year Ended December 31, 19—

ACCOUNT TITLES	UNADJUSTED TRIAL BALANCE DR.	UNADJUSTED TRIAL BALANCE CR.	ADJUSTMENTS DR.	ADJUSTMENTS CR.	ADJUSTED TRIAL BALANCE DR.	ADJUSTED TRIAL BALANCE CR.	INCOME STATEMENT DR.	INCOME STATEMENT CR.	ST. OF CH. IN O.E. OR BALANCE SHEET DR.	ST. OF CH. IN O.E. OR BALANCE SHEET CR.
Cash	2,875 00									
Accounts receivable	2,000 00									
Shop supplies	1,762 00									
Shop equipment	5,125 00									
Accumulated depreciation, shop equipment		725 00								
Accounts payable		575 00								
Homer Tonely, capital		5,500 00								
Homer Tonely, withdrawals	30,000 00									
Revenue from repairs		55,785 00								
Rent expense	2,500 00									
Wages expense	18,250 00									
Miscellaneous expenses	73 00									
	62,585 00	62,585 00								
Shop supplies expense										
Depreciation expense, shop equipment										
Wages payable										

Problem V *(continued)*

GENERAL JOURNAL

PAGE 1

DATE	ACCOUNT TITLES AND EXPLANATION	P.R.	DEBIT	CREDIT

Problem V *(continued)*

GENERAL LEDGER

Cash

Date	Debit	Credit	Balance
Dec. 31			2,875.00

Homer Tonely, Withdrawals

Date	Debit	Credit	Balance
Dec. 31			30,000.00

Accounts Receivable

Date	Debit	Credit	Balance
Dec. 31			2,000.00

Income Summary

Date	Debit	Credit	Balance

Shop Supplies

Date	Debit	Credit	Balance
Dec. 31			1,762.00

Revenue from Repairs

Date	Debit	Credit	Balance
Dec. 31			55,785.00

Shop Equipment

Date	Debit	Credit	Balance
Dec. 31			5,125.00

Rent Expense

Date	Debit	Credit	Balance
Dec. 31			2,500.00

Accumulated Depr., Shop Equipment

Date	Debit	Credit	Balance
Dec. 31			725.00

Wages Expense

Date	Debit	Credit	Balance
Dec. 31			18,250.00

Accounts Payable

Date	Debit	Credit	Balance
Dec. 31			575.00

Miscellaneous Expenses

Date	Debit	Credit	Balance
Dec. 31			73.00

Wages Payable

Date	Debit	Credit	Balance

Shop Supplies Expense

Date	Debit	Credit	Balance

Homer Tonely, Capital

Date	Debit	Credit	Balance
Dec. 31			5,500.00

Depr. Expense, Shop Equipment

Date	Debit	Credit	Balance

Problem V *(continued)*

HOMER'S HOME SHOP

Post-Closing Trial Balance

December 31, 19—

Cash		
Accounts receivable		
Shop supplies		
Shop equipment		
Accumulated depreciation, shop equipment		
Accounts payable		
Wages payable		
Homer Tonely, capital		
Totals		

Problem VI

Prepare journal entries to record the following events related to Slater Company.

1. Slater Company sold 15,000 shares of $25 par common stock for $375,000.
2. In making closing entries, the net income for the year amounted to $50,000. (Close the Income Summary account.)
3. Slater Company declared $15,500 of dividends to be paid in cash to common stockholders.
4. Slater Company paid the dividends declared in (3).

GENERAL JOURNAL

DATE	ACCOUNT TITLES AND EXPLANATION	P.R.	DEBIT	CREDIT

Problem VII (This problem applies to Appendix B.)

The following statements are either true or false. Place a (T) in the parentheses before each true statement and an (F) before each false statement.

1. (   )   After the adjusting, closing, and reversing entries are posted to an account where there were end-of-period adjustments of accrued items, the account will have an opposite from normal balance.

2. (   )   Reversing entries are used only for accruals of expense items such as Salaries Expense, Tax Expense, and Interest Expense.

3. (   )   If a business records prepaid expenses with a debit to a prepaid expense account, then a reversing entry would be appropriate.

Problem VIII (This problem applies to Appendix B.)

You are given several words, phrases, or numbers to choose from in completing each of the following statements or in answering the following questions. In each case select the one that best completes the statement or answers the question and place its letter in the answer space provided.

_____   1.   The December 31, 1990, adjusting entries for Mary Swan's interior design company included accrual of $760 in secretarial salaries. This amount will be paid on January 5, as part of the normal $1,200 salary for two weeks. The bookkeeper for the company uses reversing entries where appropriate. When the secretary's salary was paid on January 10, 1991, the following entry was made.

| Jan. 10 | Salaries Expense | 1,200 | |
| | Cash | | 1,200 |

What was the January 1, 1991, reversing entry?

a.	Salaries Payable	760	
	Salaries Expense	440	
	Cash		1,200
b.	Salaries Payable	440	
	Salaries Expense		440
c.	Salaries Payable	760	
	Salaries Expense		760
d.	Cash	1,200	
	Salaries Expense		1,200

  e.   The bookkeeper would not make a reversing entry for this transaction.

_____   2.   On December 31, 1990, X Company accrued salaries expense with an adjusting entry. No reversing entry was made and the payment of the salaries during January 1991 was correctly recorded. If X Company had recorded an entry on January 1, 1991, to reverse the accrual, and the subsequent payment was correctly recorded, the effect on the 1991 financial statements of using the reversing entry would have been:

  a.   to increase net income and reduce liabilities.
  b.   to increase 1991 expense and reduce assets.
  c.   to decrease 1991 expense and increase liabilities.
  d.   to decrease 1991 expense and decrease liabilities.
  e.   No effect.

Problem IX (This problem applies to Appendix B.)

Based on the following end-of-period information, prepare reversing entries assuming that adjusting and closing entries have been properly recorded.

1)   Depreciation on office equipment, $3,000.
2) $350 of the $1,400 Prepaid Insurance balance has expired.
3)   Employees have earned salaries of $1,000 that have not been paid. They will be paid $1,750 on the next pay date.
4)   The company has earned $3,050 of service fees that have not been collected or recorded.
5)   The Unearned Service Fees account balance includes $1,000 that has been earned.
6)   An inventory of supplies shows $250 of unused supplies. The balance of supplies on the unadjusted trial balance for the period is $900.
7)   The company pays $1,200 interest on a loan each quarter. The next quarterly payment is due in two months from the end of the current period.

Solutions for Chapter 4

Problem I   Problem II

1. T	1. B
2. F	2. D
3. T	3. A
4. F	4. B
5. F	5. E

Problem III

Accounting cycle	3	Permanent accounts	15
Closing entries	10	Post-closing trial balance	2
Date of declaration	9	Real accounts	8 or 15
Date of payment	7	Reversing entries	16
Date of record	13	Stockholders of record	1
Deficit	6	Temporary accounts	5
Dividends Declared	4	Working papers	14
Income Summary	11	Work sheet	12
Nominal accounts	17 or 5		

Problem IV

1. the adjustments are entered in the accounts

2. debited, credited

3. (a) Is the item a debit or a credit?
   (b) On which statement does it appear?

4. credited, debited

5. first two money columns, or Unadjusted Trial Balance columns; adjustments; adjusted trial balance

6. zero

7. (a) achieve the effect of adjusting the accounts before entering the adjustments in the accounts,
   (b) sort the adjusted account balances into columns according to the statement on which they appear, and
   (c) calculate and prove the mathematical accuracy of the net income or loss.

8. contributed capital accounts, retained earnings accounts

9. zero, zero

10. temporary or nominal, revenue, expense

Problem V

HOMER'S HOME SHOP
Work Sheet for Year Ended December 31, 19—

	Unadjusted Trial Balance		Adjustments		Adjusted Trial Balance		Income Statement		Statement of Ch. in O.E. or Balance Sheet	
	Dr.	Cr.	Dr.	Cr.	Dr.	Cr.	Dr.	Cr.	Dr.	Cr.
Cash	2,875	.....	.....	.....	2,875	.....	.....	.....	2,875	.....
Accounts receivable	2,000	.....	.....	.....	2,000	.....	.....	.....	2,000	.....
Shop supplies	1,762	.....	.....	(a) 1,037	725	.....	.....	.....	725	.....
Shop equipment	5,125	.....	.....	.....	5,125	.....	.....	.....	5,125	.....
Accumulated depreciation, shop equipment	.....	725	.....	(b) 475	.....	1,200	.....	.....	.....	1,200
Accounts payable	.....	575	.....	.....	.....	575	.....	.....	.....	575
Homer Tonely, capital	.....	5,500	.....	.....	.....	5,500	.....	.....	.....	5,500
Homer Tonely, withdrawals	30,000	.....	.....	.....	30,000	.....	.....	.....	30,000	.....
Revenue from repairs	.....	55,785	.....	.....	.....	55,785	.....	55,785	.....	.....
Rent expense	2,500	.....	.....	.....	2,500	.....	2,500	.....	.....	.....
Wages expense	18,250	.....	(c) 388	.....	18,638	.....	18,638	.....	.....	.....
Miscellaneous expenses	73	.....	.....	.....	73	.....	73	.....	.....	.....
	62,585	62,585								
Shop supplies expense			(a) 1,037	.....	1,037	.....	1,037	.....	.....	.....
Depreciation expense, shop equipment			(b) 475	.....	475	.....	475	.....	.....	.....
Wages payable			.....	(c) 388	.....	388	.....	.....	.....	388
			1,900	1,900	63,448	63,448	22,723	55,785	40,725	7,663
Net income							33,062			33,062
							55,785	55,785	40,725	40,725

Dec. 31	Shop Supplies Expense	1,037		
	Shop Supplies		1,037	
31	Depr. Expense, Shop Equipment	475		
	Accumulated Depr., Shop Equipment		475	
31	Wages Expense	388		
	Wages Payable		388	
Dec. 31	Revenue from Repairs	55,785		
	Income Summary		55,785	
31	Income Summary	22,723		
	Rent Expense		2,500	
	Wages Expense		18,638	
	Miscellaneous Expenses		73	
	Shop Supplies Expense		1,037	
	Depr. Expense, Shop Equipment		475	
31	Income Summary	33,062		
	Homer Tonely, Capital		33,062	
31	Homer Tonely, Capital	30,000		
	Homer Tonely, Withdrawals		30,000	

Problem V *(continued)*

GENERAL LEDGER

Cash

Date		Debit	Credit	Balance
Dec.	31			2,875.00

Homer Tonely, Withdrawals

Date		Debit	Credit	Balance
Dec.	31			30,000.00
	31		30,000.00	–0–

Accounts Receivable

Date		Debit	Credit	Balance
Dec.	31			2,000.00

Income Summary

Date		Debit	Credit	Balance
Dec.	31		55,785.00	55,785.00
	31	22,723.00		33,062.00
	31	33,062.00		–0–

Shop Supplies

Date		Debit	Credit	Balance
Dec.	31			1,762.00
	31		1,037.00	725.00

Revenue from Repairs

Date		Debit	Credit	Balance
Dec.	31			55,785.00
	31	55,785.00		–0–

Shop Equipment

Date		Debit	Credit	Balance
Dec.	31			5,125.00

Rent Expense

Date		Debit	Credit	Balance
Dec.	31			2,500.00
	31		2,500.00	–0–

Accumulated Depr., Shop Equipment

Date		Debit	Credit	Balance
Dec.	31			725.00
	31		475.00	1,200.00

Wages Expense

Date		Debit	Credit	Balance
Dec.	31			18,250.00
	31	388.00		18,638.00
	31		18,638.00	–0–

Accounts Payable

Date		Debit	Credit	Balance
Dec.	31			575.00

Miscellaneous Expenses

Date		Debit	Credit	Balance
Dec.	31			73.00
	31		73.00	–0–

Wages Payable

Date		Debit	Credit	Balance
Dec.	31		388.00	388.00

Shop Supplies Expense

Date		Debit	Credit	Balance
Dec.	31	1,037.00		1,037.00
	31		1,037.00	–0–

Homer Tonely, Capital

Date		Debit	Credit	Balance
Dec.	31			5,500.00
	31		33,062.00	38,562.00
	31	30,000.00		8,562.00

Depr. Expense, Shop Equipment

Date		Debit	Credit	Balance
Dec.	31	475.00		475.00
	31		475.00	–0–

Problem V *(continued)*

HOMER'S HOME SHOP
Post-Closing Trial Balance
December 31, 19—

Cash	$ 2,875	
Accounts receivable	2,000	
Shop supplies	725	
Shop equipment	5,125	
Accumulated depreciation, shop equipment		$ 1,200
Accounts payable		575
Wages payable		388
Homer Tonely, capital		8,562
	$10,725	$10,725

Problem VI

1.	Cash	375,000.00	
	Common Stock		375,000.00
2.	Income Summary	50,000.00	
	Retained Earnings		50,000.00
3.	Dividends Declared	15,500.00	
	Common Dividend Payable		15,500.00
4.	Common Dividend Payable	15,500.00	
	Cash		15,500.00

Problem VII   Problem VIII

1.	T	1.	C
2.	F	2.	E
3.	F		

Problem IX

1) No reversing entry required.

2) No reversing entry required.

3)	Salaries Payable	1,000.00	
	Salaries Expense		1,000.00
4)	Service Fees Earned	3,050.00	
	Accounts Receivable		3,050.00

5) No reversing entry required.

6) No reversing entry required.

7)	Interest Payable	400.00	
	Interest Expense		400.00

5 Accounting for a Merchandising Concern

Your objectives in studying this chapter should include learning how to:

1. Explain the nature of each item entering into the calculation of cost of goods sold and gross profit from sales.

2. Analyze and record transactions that involve the purchase and resale of merchandise.

3. Prepare a work sheet and the financial statements for a merchandising business using a periodic inventory system and organized as either a corporation or a single proprietorship.

4. Prepare adjusting and closing entries for a merchandising business organized as either a corporation or a single proprietorship.

5. Define or explain the words and phrases listed in the chapter Glossary.

After studying the appendix to Chapter 5 (Appendix C), you should be able to:

6. Explain the adjusting entry approach to accounting for inventories and prepare a work sheet, adjusting entries and closing entries according to the adjusting entry approach.

Topical Outline

I. Accounting for a merchandising concern differs from accounting for a service enterprise.

    A. Net income of a service organization is fees (or commissions) earned less operating expenses.

    B. Net income of a merchandising concern is sales revenue less cost of goods sold and operating expenses.

    C. Revenue from sales less cost of goods sold equals gross profit from sales—the "profit" before operating expenses are deducted.

II. Revenue from sales is:

    A. Gross sales—total cash and credit sales before any deductions—

    B. Less sales returns and allowances—the gross sales value of merchandise returned by customers and deductions from the sales price granted to customers for unsatisfactory goods—

    C. Less sales discounts—deductions from the invoice price granted to customers in return for early payment.

III. Cost of goods sold and the periodic inventory system

    A. Merchandise inventory at the end of one period is the beginning inventory of the next period.

    B. Cost of merchandise purchased includes the gross purchase price plus transportation-in, less purchases (cash) discounts and less purchases returns and allowances.

    C. Cost of goods sold is calculated as the cost of beginning inventory plus the cost of merchandise purchased less the cost of ending inventory.

    D. Inventory losses from shrinkage, spoilage, and theft are automatically included in the cost of goods sold.

IV. Classified income statement of a merchandising concern has three sections:

    A. Revenue section

    B. Cost of goods sold section

    C. Operating expenses section

V. Preparing a work sheet for a merchandising concern

    A. The titles of the accounts to be used are entered in the Account Titles column.

    B. The unadjusted account balances are entered in the Unadjusted Trial Balance columns.

    C. All necessary adjustments are entered in the Adjustments columns.

    D. The adjusted amounts are sorted to the proper financial statement columns.

    E. Cost of goods sold appears on the work sheet as follows:

        1. Beginning inventory, purchases, and transportation-in amounts appear in the Income Statement debit column.

        2. The amounts of the ending inventory, purchases returns and allowances, and purchases discounts appear in the Income Statement credit column.

    F. The formal financial statements are prepared using the information contained in the completed work sheet.

VI. Adjusting and closing entries

  A. Adjusting entries for merchandising companies include entries similar to those used in a service business.

  B. Closing entries

   1. Before closing entries are posted, the Merchandise Inventory account shows beginning-of-period inventory as a debit balance.

   2. The first closing entry includes a credit to Merchandise Inventory for the amount of the beginning inventory.

   3. The second closing entry includes a debit to Merchandise Inventory for the amount of the ending inventory.

VII. Financial statements in addition to the balance sheet

  A. Income statement—may be designed as:

   1. Classified (multiple-step) statement in which items are grouped in significant categories, or

   2. Single-step statement.

  B. Retained earnings statement of a corporation

   1. Shows beginning retained earnings, plus net income, less dividends declared, which equals ending retained earnings.

   2. May be combined with income statement.

VIII. Debit and credit memoranda

  A. Used by a company to communicate with a customer or supplier.

  B. Tells the customer or supplier that the amount the company expects to receive or to pay is being changed.

IX. Trade discounts

  A. Deductions from list (or catalog) price to arrive at invoice price

  B. Not entered in the accounts of seller or purchaser

X. Appendix C

  A. When the periodic inventory system is used, end-of-period entries to record the ending inventory and transfer the beginning inventory to Income Summary may be done as closing entries or as adjusting entries.

  B. When the adjusting entry approach is used on the work sheet, the transfer of beginning inventory and recording of ending inventory is shown in the Adjustments columns.

  C. On the work sheet, the debit and credit adjustments to Income Summary are individually extended to the Income Statement columns.

  D. The adjusting entry approach and the closing entry approach result in the same amounts being reported on the financial statements.

Problem I

The following statements are either true or false. Place a (T) in the parentheses before each true statement and an (F) before each false statement.

1. ( ) Sales returns and allowances or discounts are not included in the calculation of net sales.

2. ( ) Ending inventory is subtracted from the cost of goods available for sale to determine cost of goods sold.

3. ( ) The only way to determine the current amount of inventory (assuming no shrinkage) in a periodic inventory system is to take a physical count of the merchandise on hand.

4. ( ) It is impossible to tell whether or not there were inventory losses when a periodic inventory system is used.

5. ( ) In a work sheet for a corporation, the balance of the Retained Earnings account remains the same from the Unadjusted Trial Balance—Credit column to the Retained Earnings Statement or Balance Sheet—Credit column.

6. ( ) Advance payments of income taxes are debited to an Income Taxes Expense account.

7. ( ) The net effect of putting beginning inventory, ending inventory, purchases, purchases returns and discounts, and transportation-in costs into the Income Statement columns is to put cost of goods sold into the columns.

8. ( ) The closing entry in which the Income Summary account is credited to close revenue and cost of goods sold accounts that have credit balances, also enters the ending inventory amount in the Merchandise Inventory account.

9. ( ) A debit or credit memorandum may originate with either party to a transaction, but the memorandum gets its name from the action of the selling party exclusively.

Problem II

You are given several words, phrases or numbers to choose from in completing each of the following statements or in answering the following questions. In each case select the one that best completes the statement or answers the question and place its letter in the answer space provided.

_____ 1. A method of accounting for inventories in which cost of goods sold is recorded each time a sale is made and an up-to-date record of goods on hand is maintained is called a:

    a. product inventory system.
    b. perpetual inventory system.
    c. periodic inventory system.
    d. parallel inventory system.
    e. principal inventory system.

_____ 2. Based on the following information, calculate the missing amounts.

Sales	$28,800	Cost of goods sold	?
Beginning inventory	?	Gross profit	$10,800
Purchases	18,000	Expenses	?
Ending inventory	12,600	Net income	3,600

    a. Beginning inventory, $16,200; Cost of goods sold, $12,600; Expenses, $ 1,800
    b. Beginning inventory, $23,400; Cost of goods sold, $10,800; Expenses, $ 7,200
    c. Beginning inventory, $ 9,000; Cost of goods sold, $14,400; Expenses, $ 3,600
    d. Beginning inventory, $12,600; Cost of goods sold, $18,000; Expenses, $ 7,200
    e. Beginning inventory, $19,800; Cost of goods sold, $25,200; Expenses, $14,400

Problem II *(continued)*

_____ 3. What is the effect on the Income Statement at the end of an accounting period in which the ending inventory of the prior period was understated and carried forward incorrectly?

    a. Cost of goods sold is overstated and net income is understated.
    b. Cost of goods sold is understated and net income is understated.
    c. Cost of goods sold is understated and net income is overstated.
    d. Cost of goods sold is overstated and net income is overstated.
    e. The errors of the prior period and the current period offset each other, so there is no effect on the income statement.

_____ 4. The following information is taken from a single proprietorship's income statement. Calculate ending inventory for the business.

Sales	$165,250	Purchases returns	$ 390
Sales returns	980	Purchases discounts	1,630
Sales discounts	1,960	Transportation-in	700
Beginning inventory	16,880	Gross profit from sales	58,210
Purchases	108,380	Net income	17,360

    a. $19,840.
    b. $22,080.
    c. $21,160.
    d. $44,250.
    e. Some other amount.

_____ 5. On July 18, 1990, Double Aught Sales Company sold merchandise on credit, terms 2/10, n/30, $1,080. On July 21, Double Aught issued a $180 credit memorandum to the customer of July 18 who returned a portion of the merchandise purchased. What is the general journal entry to record the July 21 transaction?

a.	Accounts Receivable	180	
	Sales		180
b.	Sales Returns and Allowances	180	
	Accounts Receivable		180
c.	Accounts Receivable	900	
	Sales Returns and Allowances	180	
	Sales		1,080
d.	Sales	180	
	Accounts Receivable		180
e.	Sales Returns and Allowances	180	
	Sales		180

Problem III

Many of the important ideas and concepts discussed in Chapter 5 are reflected in the following list of key terms. Test your understanding of these terms by matching the appropriate definitions with the terms. Record the number identifying the most appropriate definition in the blank space next to each term.

Problem III *(continued)*

_____ Cash discount

_____ Credit memorandum

_____ Credit period

_____ Credit terms

_____ Debit memorandum

_____ Discount period

_____ EOM

_____ FOB

_____ General and administrative expenses

_____ Gross profit from sales

_____ List price

_____ Merchandise

_____ Multiple-step income statement

_____ Periodic inventory system

_____ Perpetual inventory system

_____ Purchases discounts

_____ Retained earnings statement

_____ Sales discounts

_____ Selling expenses

_____ Single-step income statement

_____ Trade discount

_____ Transportation-in

1. Net sales minus cost of goods sold.

2. A method of accounting for inventories in which cost of goods sold is recorded each time a sale is made and an up-to-date record of goods on hand is maintained.

3. A deduction from a catalog or list price that is used to determine the invoice price of goods.

4. Deductions from the invoice price granted to customers in return for early payment, i.e., cash discounts to customers.

5. A memorandum sent to notify its recipient that the business sending the memorandum has in its records debited the account of the recipient.

6. An income statement on which cost of goods sold and the expenses are subtracted in steps to get net income.

7. An abbreviation for the words "end of month" that is sometimes used in expressing the credit terms of a sales agreement.

8. The catalog price of an item from which a trade discount, if offered, is deducted to determine the invoice or gross sales price of the item.

9. A financial statement that reports the changes in a corporation's retained earnings that occurred during an accounting period.

10. The specified amounts and timing of payments that a buyer agrees to make in return for being granted credit to purchase goods or services.

11. The agreed period of time for which credit is granted and at the end of which payment is expected.

12. Costs incurred by a business for transporting merchandise purchases to the business.

13. Deductions from the invoice price of purchased items, which are granted by suppliers in return for early payment, i.e., cash discounts from suppliers.

14. A memorandum sent to notify its recipient that the business sending the memorandum has in its records credited the account of the recipient.

15. A method of accounting for inventories in which the inventory account is brought up to date once each period, at the end of the period, by counting the units of each product on hand, multiplying the count for each product by its cost, and adding the costs of the various products.

16. The period of time during which, if payment is made, a cash discount may be deducted from the invoice price.

Problem III *(continued)*

17. An income statement on which cost of goods sold and operating expenses are added together and subtracted in one step from net sales to get net income.

18. A deduction from the invoice price of goods that is granted if payment is made within a specified period of time.

19. The expenses of preparing and storing merchandise for sale, promoting sales, making sales, and delivering goods to customers.

20. Assets purchased and held for resale.

21. Expenses to support the management and overall operations of a business, such as central office, accounting, personnel, and credit and collections expenses.

22. The abbreviation for "free on board," which is used to denote that goods purchased are placed on board the means of transportation at a specified geographic point with all loading and transportation charges to that point to be paid by the seller.

Problem IV

Below is the Valentine Variety Store work sheet for the year ended December 31, 1990. Sort the adjusted trial balance amounts into the proper Income Statement and Balance Sheet columns and finish the work sheet. The December 31, 1990, inventory is $15,000.

VALENTINE VARIETY STORE
Work Sheet, December 31, 1990

ACCOUNT TITLES	ADJUSTED TRIAL BALANCE		INCOME STATEMENT		ST. OF CH. IN O.E. OR BALANCE SHEET	
	DR.	CR.	DR.	CR.	DR.	CR.
Cash	4,000 00					
Merchandise inventory	13,000 00					
Other assets	8,000 00					
Liabilities		4,000 00				
Violet Valentine, capital		22,300 00				
Violet Valentine, withdrawals	10,000 00					
Sales		80,000 00				
Sales returns	600 00					
Purchases	48,500 00					
Purchases returns		400 00				
Purchases discounts		900 00				
Transportation-in	2,500 00					
Selling expenses	13,000 00					
Gen. and admin. expenses	8,000 00					
	107,600 00	107,600 00				
Net income						

Problem V

After finishing the work sheet, use the information in its Income Statement columns to complete the following income statement.

VALENTINE VARIETY STORE

Income Statement

For the Year Ended December 31, 1990

Revenue:						
Sales						
Less: Sales returns						
Net sales						
Cost of goods sold:						
Merchandise inventory, Dec. 31, 1989						
Purchases						
Less: Purchases returns $_____						
Purchases discounts _____						
Net purchases						
Add: Transportation-in						
Cost of goods purchased						
Goods available for sale						
Merchandise inventory, Dec. 31, 1990						
Cost of goods sold						
Gross profit from sales						
Operating expenses:						
Selling expenses						
General and administrative expenses						
Total operating expenses						
Net income						

Problem VI

Prepare the closing entries for Valentine Variety Store. Do not make explanations, but skip a line after each entry.

PAGE 9

DATE	ACCOUNT TITLES AND EXPLANATION	P.R.	DEBIT	CREDIT

Problem VII

Below is the Merchandise Inventory account of Valentine Variety Store as it appeared before the 1990 closing entries were posted. Note that its $13,000 debit balance shows the amount of the December 31, 1989, inventory which was posted to the account when the closing entries were made at the end of 1989. From the closing entries that were journalized in Part IV, post the appropriate amounts to the Merchandise Inventory account below.

Merchandise Inventory   Account No. 115

DATE		EXPLANATION	P.R.	DEBIT	CREDIT	BALANCE
1989 Dec.	31		G–3	13 000 00		13 000 00

Problem VIII

1. If a company determines cost of goods sold by counting the inventory at the end of the period and subtracting the inventory from the cost of goods available for sale, the system of accounting for

    inventories is called a(n) _____.

2. Trade discounts _____ (are, are not) credited to the Purchases Discounts account.

3. After the work sheet is completed, the amount of the ending inventory is taken into the accounts by

    means of a(n) _____ entry.

4. A store received a credit memorandum from a wholesaler for unsatisfactory merchandise the store

    had returned for credit. The store should record the memorandum with a _____

    (debit, credit) to its Purchases Returns and Allowances account and a _____
    (debit, credit) to its Accounts Payable account.

5. The two common systems of accounting for merchandise inventories are the _____

    _____ inventory system and the _____

    inventory system. The _____ inventory system is the most likely to be
    used in stores that sell a large volume of relatively low-priced items.

Problem IX (This problem applies to Appendix C.)

The following statements are either true or false. Place a (T) in the parentheses before each true statement and an (F) before each false statement.

1. ( ) Both the adjusting entry and closing entry approaches to accounting for merchandise inventories result in the same balances in the Income Summary account.

2. ( ) On the work sheet under the adjusting entry approach, the debit in the Merchandise Inventory account of the Adjustments column is carried directly to the Statement of Retained Earnings or Balance Sheet—Debit column.

3. ( ) If, in the Adjustments columns of a work sheet when the adjusting entry approach is used, Income Summary is debited $15,000 and credited $20,000, then the net $5,000 is carried to the Income Statement—Credit column.

Problem X   (This problem applies to Appendix C.)

The trial balance that follows was taken from the ledger of Sporthaus Lindner at the end of its annual accounting period. Fritz Lindner, the owner of Sporthaus Lindner, did not make additional investments in the business during 1990.

SPORTHAUS LINDNER
Unadjusted Trial Balance
December 31, 1990

Cash	$ 1,840	
Accounts receivable	2,530	
Merchandise inventory	3,680	
Store supplies	2,070	
Accounts payable		$ 4,370
Salaries payable	—	—
Fritz Lindner, capital		5,980
Fritz Lindner, withdrawals	1,380	
Sales		14,260
Sales returns and allowances	1,150	
Purchases	5,750	
Purchases discounts		920
Transportation-in	1,150	
Salaries expense	4,370	
Rent expense	1,610	
Store supplies expense	—	—
Totals	$25,530	$25,530

Use the adjusting entry approach to account for merchandise inventories and prepare adjusting journal entries and closing journal entries for Sporthaus Lindner using the following information:

a. Ending store supplies inventory, $1,150.
b. Accrued salaries payable, $690.
c. Ending merchandise inventory, $4,830.

Problem X *(continued)*

GENERAL JOURNAL

PAGE 1

DATE	ACCOUNT TITLES AND EXPLANATION	P.R.	DEBIT	CREDIT

Solutions for Chapter 5

Problem I

1.	F	6.	T
2.	T	7.	T
3.	F	8.	T
4.	F	9.	F
5.	T		

Problem II

1.	B
2.	D
3.	C
4.	A
5.	B

Problem III

Cash discount	18	Merchandise	20
Credit memorandum	14	Multiple-step income statement	6
Credit period	11	Periodic inventory system	15
Credit terms	10	Perpetual inventory system	2
Debit memorandum	5	Purchases discounts	13
Discount period	16	Retained earnings statement	9
EOM	7	Sales discounts	4
FOB	22	Selling expenses	19
General and administrative expenses	21	Single-step income statement	17
Gross profit from sales	1	Trade discount	3
List price	8	Transportation-in	12

Problem IV

VALENTINE VARIETY STORE
Work Sheet, December 31, 1990

	Adjusted Trial Balance		Income Statement		St. of Ch. in O.E. or Balance Sheet	
	Dr.	Cr.	Dr.	Cr.	Dr.	Cr.
Cash	4,000	....	......	......	4,000	......
Merchandise inventory	13,000	....	13,000	15,000	15,000	......
Other assets	8,000	....	......	......	8,000	......
Liabilities	....	4,000	......	......	......	4,000
Violet Valentine, capital	....	22,300	......	......	......	22,300
Violet Valentine, withdrawals	10,000	....	......	......	10,000	......
Sales	....	80,000	......	80,000	......	......
Sales returns	600	....	600	......	......	......
Purchases	48,500	....	48,500	......	......	......
Purchases returns	....	400	......	400	......	......
Purchases discounts	....	900	......	900	......	......
Transportation-in	2,500	....	2,500	......	......	......
Selling expenses	13,000	....	13,000	......	......	......
General and administrative exp.	8,000	....	8,000	......	......	......
	107,600	107,600	85,600	96,300	37,000	26,300
Net income			10,700	......	......	10,700
			96,300	96,300	37,000	37,000

Problem V

VALENTINE VARIETY STORE
Income Statement
For the Year Ended December 31, 1990

Revenue:

Sales		$80,000	
Less: Sales returns		600	
Net sales			$79,400

Cost of goods sold:

Merchandise inventory, December 31, 1989		$13,000	
Purchases	$48,500		
Less: Purchases returns	$400		
Purchases discounts	900	1,300	
Net purchases		$47,200	
Add: Transportation-in		2,500	
Cost of goods purchased		49,700	
Goods available for sale		$62,700	
Merchandise inventory, December 31, 1990		15,000	
Cost of goods sold			47,700
Gross profit from sales			$31,700

Operating expenses:

Selling expenses		$13,000	
General and administrative expenses		8,000	
Total operating expenses			21,000
Net income			$10,700

Problem VI

Dec. 31	Income Summary		85,600.00	
	Sales Returns			600.00
	Purchases			48,500.00
	Transportation-in			2,500.00
	Selling Expenses			13,000.00
	General and Administrative Expenses			8,000.00
	Merchandise Inventory			13,000.00
31	Sales		80,000.00	
	Purchases Returns		400.00	
	Purchases Discounts		900.00	
	Merchandise Inventory		15,000.00	
	Income Summary			96,300.00
31	Income Summary		10,700.00	
	Violet Valentine, Capital			10,700.00
31	Violet Valentine, Capital		10,000.00	
	Violet Valentine, Withdrawals			10,000.00

Problem VII

		Merchandise Inventory				Account No. 115

DATE		EXPLANATION	P.R.	DEBIT	CREDIT	BALANCE
1989						
Dec.	31		G–3	13 000 00		13 000 00
1990						
Dec.	31		G–8		13 000 00	-0-
	31		G–9	15 000 00		15 000 00

Problem VIII

1. periodic inventory system
2. are not
3. closing
4. credit, debit
5. periodic, perpetual, periodic

Problem IX

1. T
2. T
3. F

Problem X

Adjusting Entries:

Dec. 31	Store Supplies Expense	920	
	Store Supplies		920
31	Salaries Expense	690	
	Salaries Payable		690
31	Income Summary	3,680	
	Merchandise Inventory		3,680
31	Merchandise Inventory	4,830	
	Income Summary		4,830

Closing Entries:

Dec. 31	Income Summary	15,640	
	Sales Returns and Allowances		1,150
	Purchases		5,750
	Transportation-in		1,150
	Salaries Expense		5,060
	Rent Expense		1,610
	Store Supplies Expense		920
31	Sales	14,260	
	Purchases Discounts	920	
	Income Summary		15,180
31	Income Summary	690	
	Fritz Lindner, Capital		690
31	Fritz Lindner, Capital	1,380	
	Fritz Lindner, Withdrawals		1,380

6

Accounting for Cash

Your objectives in studying this chapter should include learning how to:

1. Explain why internal control procedures are needed in a large concern and state the broad principles of internal control.

2. Describe internal control procedures to protect cash received from cash sales, cash received through the mail, and cash disbursements.

3. Explain the operation of a petty cash fund and be able to journalize entries to record petty cash fund transactions.

4. Explain why the bank balance and the book balance of cash are reconciled and be able to prepare such a reconciliation.

5. Tell how recording invoices at net amounts helps gain control over cash discounts taken and be able to account for invoices recorded at net amounts.

6. Define or explain the words and phrases listed in the chapter Glossary.

Topical Outline

I. Internal control procedures—designed to protect assets from fraud and theft

   A. Seven broad principles of internal control are:

      1. Responsibilities should be clearly established.

      2. Adequate records should be maintained.

      3. Assets should be insured and employees bonded.

      4. Record-keeping and custody of assets should be separated.

      5. Responsibility for related transactions should be divided.

      6. Mechanical devices should be used whenever practicable.

      7. Regular and independent reviews should be conducted.

   B. Computers and internal control:

      1. Computers provide rapid access to large quantities of information.

      2. Computers reduce processing errors.

      3. Computers allow more extensive testing of records.

      4. Computers may limit hard evidence of processing steps.

      5. Separation of duties must be maintained.

   C. Internal control for cash should include procedures for protecting:

      1. Cash receipts

         a. Cash from cash sales
         b. Cash received through the mail

      2. Cash disbursements

   D. Voucher system—used to control the incurrence and payment of obligations. With a voucher system, important business papers include:

      1. Purchase requisitions

      2. Purchase orders

      3. Invoices

      4. Receiving reports

      5. Invoice approval forms

      6. Vouchers

II. Accounting for cash

   A. Petty cash fund—used to avoid writing checks for small amounts.

      1. Petty Cash is debited only when the fund is established or increased.

      2. Petty cash receipts are retained by the petty cashier to account for the amounts expended.

      3. When the petty cash fund is reimbursed, an entry is made to debit the expenses or other items paid for with petty cash and to credit Cash for the amount reimbursed to the petty cash fund.

B. Cash Over and Short account—an income statement item showing the cash shortages or overages that result from making change.

C. Reconciling the bank balance

1. A bank reconciliation proves the accuracy of both the depositor's records and those of the bank.

2. Items that may cause a difference between the bank statement balance and a depositor's book balance of cash:

   a. Outstanding checks
   b. Unrecorded deposits
   c. Charges for services and uncollectible items
   d. Collections made by the bank for the depositor
   e. Errors

3. Steps in reconciling the bank balance:

   a. Compare deposits listed on the bank statement with deposits shown in the accounting records.
   b. Determine whether other credits on bank statement (interest, etc.) have been recorded in the books.
   c. Compare canceled checks listed on bank statement with actual checks returned with statement.
   d. Compare previous month's outstanding checks with canceled checks listed on this month's bank statement.
   e. Compare canceled checks listed on bank statement with checks recorded in books since last reconciliation.
   f. Note any unrecorded debits shown on bank statement; e.g., check printing charges, NSF checks, service charges.
   g. Prepare reconciliation.
   h. Make journal entries for any unrecorded debits or credits appearing on the bank statement.

III. Other internal control procedures

A. Recording purchases

1. Gross method—purchases are recorded at the invoice price without deducting cash discounts.

2. Net method—purchases recorded at net amount of invoices (gross amount less cash discount); provides better control over purchases discounts.

Problem I

The following statements are either true or false. Place a (T) in the parentheses before each true statement and an (F) before each false statement.

1. ( ) One of the fundamental principles of internal control states that the person who has access to or is responsible for an asset should not maintain the accounting record for that asset.

2. ( ) Procedures for controlling cash disbursements are as important as those for cash receipts.

3. ( ) When a voucher system is used, duplication of procedures among several departments is instrumental in maintaining control over cash disbursements.

4. ( ) In order to approve an invoice for payment for the purchase of assets, the accounting department of a large company should require copies of the purchase requisition, purchase order, invoice, and receiving report.

5. ( ) After the petty cash fund is established, the Petty Cash account is not debited or credited again unless the size of the fund is changed.

6. ( ) The Cash Over and Short account is usually shown on the income statement as part of miscellaneous revenues if it has a credit balance at the end of the period.

7. ( ) If 20 canceled checks are listed on the current month's bank statement, then no less than 20 checks could have been issued during the current month.

8. ( ) When the net method of recording invoices is used, cash discounts lost are reported as an expense in the income statement; when the gross method is used, cash discounts taken are deducted from purchases in the income statement.

Problem II

You are given several words, phrases or numbers to choose from in completing each of the following statements or in answering the following questions. In each case select the one that best completes the statement or answers the question and place its letter in the answer space provided.

_____ 1. A voucher system:

    a. permits only authorized individuals to incur obligations that will result in cash disbursements.

    b. establishes procedures for incurring such obligations and for their verification, approval, and recording.

    c. permits checks to be issued only in payment of properly verified, approved, and recorded obligations.

    d. requires that every obligation be recorded at the time it is incurred and every purchase be treated as an independent transaction, complete in itself.

    e. does all of the above.

Problem II *(continued)*

_____ 2. Liquidity is:

     a. the portion of a corporation's equity that represents investments in the corporation by its stockholders.

     b. cash or other assets that are reasonably expected to be realized in cash or be sold or consumed within one year or one operating cycle of the business.

     c. a characteristic of an asset indicating how easily the asset can be converted into cash or used to buy services or satisfy obligations.

     d. obligations that are due to be paid or liquidated within one year or one operating cycle of the business.

     e. economic benefits or resources without physical substance, the value of which stems from the privileges or rights that accrue to their owner.

_____ 3. A voucher is a:

     a. business paper used in summarizing a transaction and approving it for recording and payment.

     b. business form used within a business to ask the purchasing department of the business to buy needed items.

     c. document, prepared by a vendor, on which are listed the items sold, the sales prices, the customer's name, and the terms of sale.

     d. form used within a business to notify the proper persons of the receipt of goods ordered and of the quantities and condition of the goods.

     e. document on which the accounting department notes that it has performed each step in the process of checking an invoice and approving it for recording and payment.

_____ 4. Each of the following items would cause Brand X Sales Company's book balance of cash to differ from its bank statement balance.

     A. A service charge made by the bank.

     B. A check listed as outstanding on the previous month's reconciliation and that is still outstanding.

     C. A customer's check returned by the bank marked "NSF."

     D. A deposit which was mailed to the bank on the last day of November and is unrecorded on the November bank statement.

     E. A check paid by the bank at its correct $422 amount but recorded in error in the General Journal at $442.

     F. An unrecorded credit memorandum indicating the bank had collected a note receivable for Brand X Sales Company and deposited the proceeds in the company's account.

     G. A check written during November and not yet paid and returned by the bank.

Which of the above items require entries on the books of Brand X Sales Company?

     a. A. , B. , C. , and E.

     b. A. , C. , E. , and F.

     c. A. , B. , D. , and F.

     d. A. , B. , D. , E. , and G.

     e. C. , D. , E. , and F.

Problem III

Many of the important ideas and concepts discussed in Chapter 6 are reflected in the following list of key terms. Test your understanding of these terms by matching the appropriate definitions with the terms. Record the number identifying the most appropriate definition in the blank space next to each term.

_____ Bank reconciliation

_____ Canceled checks

_____ Cash Over and Short account

_____ Discounts lost

_____ Gross method of recording invoices

_____ Internal control system

_____ Invoice

_____ Invoice approval form

_____ Liquid asset

_____ Liquidity

_____ Net method of recording purchases

_____ Outstanding checks

_____ Purchase order

_____ Purchase requisition

_____ Receiving report

_____ Reconcile

_____ Vendee

_____ Vendor

_____ Voucher

_____ Voucher system

1. A form used within a business to notify the proper persons of the receipt of goods ordered and of the quantities and condition of the goods.

2. A characteristic of an asset indicating how easily the asset can be converted into other types of assets or used to buy services or satisfy obligations.

3. An expense resulting from the failure to take advantage of cash discounts on purchases.

4. Checks that were drawn by the depositor, deducted on the depositor's records, and sent to the payees, but have not yet reached the depositor's bank for payment and deduction.

5. The seller of goods or services.

6. A document, prepared by a vendor, on which are listed the items sold, the sales prices, the customer's name, and the terms of sale.

7. A business paper used in summarizing a transaction and approving it for recording and payment.

8. A method of recording purchases by which offered cash discounts are not deducted from the invoice price in determining the amount to be recorded.

9. An asset, such as cash, that can be easily converted into other types of assets or used to buy services or satisfy obligations.

10. Checks that have been punched or stamped by the bank to show they have been paid.

11. A document on which the accounting department notes that it has performed each step in the process of checking an invoice and approving it for recording and payment.

12. A business form used within a business to ask the purchasing department of the business to buy needed items.

13. An income statement account in which cash overages and cash shortages arising from making change are recorded.

14. The procedures adopted by a business to encourage adherence to prescribed managerial policies, to protect its assets from waste, fraud, and theft, and to ensure accurate and reliable accounting data.

Problem III *(continued)*

15. A set of procedures that are designed to control the incurrence of obligations and cash disbursements.

16. A business form that is sent to a vendor as a written order for the purchase of goods or services.

17. An analysis that explains the difference between the balance of a checking account as recorded in the depositor's records and the balance as shown on the bank statement.

18. To explain or account for the difference between two amounts.

19. A method of recording purchases by which offered cash discounts are deducted from the invoice price in determining the amount to be recorded.

20. The purchaser of goods or services.

Problem IV

Complete the following by filling in the blanks.

1. If a cashier errs while making change and gives a customer too much money back, the resulting

   cash shortage is recorded with a debit to an account called _____

   _____.

2. A(n) _____ form is used by the accounting department in checking and approving an invoice for recording and payment.

3. Cash discounts offered but not taken are _____.

4. If the size of the petty cash fund remains unchanged, the Petty Cash account _____

   _____ (is, is not) debited in the entry to replenish the petty cash fund.

5. Control of a small business is commonly gained through the direct supervision and active

   participation of the _____ in the affairs and activities of the business. However, as a business grows, it becomes necessary for the manager to delegate

   responsibilities and rely on _____
   rather than personal contact in controlling the affairs and activities of the business.

6. A properly designed internal control system encourages adherence to prescribed managerial

   policies; and it also (a) _____

   _____;

   (b) _____

   _____; and (c) _____

   _____.

Problem IV *(continued)*

7. A good system of internal control for cash requires a _____ of duties so that the people responsible for handling cash and for its custody are not the same people who

   _____. It also requires that all cash receipts be

   deposited in the bank _____ and that all payments,

   except petty cash payments, be made by _____.

8. A bank reconciliation is prepared to account for the difference between the _____

   _____ and the

   _____.

9. An accounting system used to control the incurrence and payment of obligations requiring the

   disbursement of cash is a _____.

10. A _____ is commonly used by a selling department to notify the purchasing department of items which the selling department wishes the purchasing department to purchase.

11. The business form commonly used by the purchasing department of a large company to order

    merchandise is called a(n) _____.

12. Good internal control follows certain broad principles. These principles are:

    (a) Responsibilities should be clearly established, and in every situation _____

    _____ should be made responsible for each task.

    (b) Adequate records should be maintained since they provide an important means of protecting

    _____.

    (c) Assets should be _____ and employees _____.

    (d) Record-keeping for assets and _____ of assets should be separated.

    (e) Responsibility for related transactions should be _____ so that the work of one department or individual may act as a check on the work of others.

    (f) Mechanical devices _____ where practicable.

    (g) Regular and independent _____ of internal control procedures should be conducted.

13. After preparing a bank reconciliation, journal entries _____ (should, should not) be made to record those items listed as outstanding checks.

Problem V

On November 5 of the current year Cullen Company drew Check No. 23 for $50 to establish a petty cash fund.

1. Give the general journal entry to record the establishment of the fund.

DATE	ACCOUNT TITLES AND EXPLANATION	P.R.	DEBIT	CREDIT

After making a payment from petty cash on November 25, the petty cashier noted that there was only $2.50 cash remaining in the fund. The cashier prepared the following list of expenditures from the fund and requested that the fund be replenished.

Nov.	9	Express freight on merchandise purchased	$ 9.75
	12	Miscellaneous expense to clean office	10.00
	15	Office supplies	3.50
	18	Delivery of merchandise to customer	8.00
	23	Miscellaneous expense for collect telegram	3.25
	25	Express freight on merchandise purchased	13.00

Check No. 97 in the amount of $47.50 was drawn to replenish the fund.

2. In the General Journal below give the entry to record the check replenishing the petty cash fund.

DATE	ACCOUNT TITLES AND EXPLANATION	P.R.	DEBIT	CREDIT

Problem VI

Information about the following eight items is available to prepare Verde Company's December 31 bank reconciliation.

Two checks (1) No. 453 and (2) No. 457 were outstanding on November 30. Check No. 457 was returned with the December bank statement but Check No. 453 was not. (3) Check No. 478, written on December 26, was not returned with the canceled checks; and (4) Check No. 480 for $96 was incorrectly entered in the Cash Disbursements Journal and posted as though it were for $69. (5) A deposit placed in the bank's night depository after banking hours on November 30 appeared on the December bank statement, but (6) one placed there after hours on December 31 did not. (7) Enclosed with the December bank statement was a debit memorandum for a bank service charge and (8) a check received from a customer and deposited on December 27 but returned by the bank marked "Not Sufficient Funds."

1. If an item in the above list should not appear on the December 31 bank reconciliation, ignore it. However, if an item should appear, enter its number in a set of parentheses to show where it should be added or subtracted in preparing the reconciliation.

Problem VI *(continued)*

VERDE COMPANY
Bank Reconciliation
December 31, 1990

Book balance of cash . . . . $X,XXX   Bank statement balance . . . . $X,XXX
   Add: Add:
      (   )   (   )
      (   )   (   )
      (   )   (   )
   Deduct: Deduct:
      (   )   (   )
      (   )   (   )
      (   )   (   )
Reconciled balance . . . . $X,XXX   Reconciled balance . . . . $X,XXX

2. Certain of the above items require entries on Verde Company's books. Place the numbers of these items within the following parentheses:

(   ),(   ),(   ),(   ),(   ),(   )

Problem VII

On May 8 a company that records purchases at net amounts received a shipment of merchandise having a $3,750 invoice price. Attached to the merchandise was the invoice, which was dated May 6, terms 2/10, n/60, FOB the vendor's warehouse. The vendor, Vee Company, had prepaid the shipping charges on the goods, $125, adding the amount to the invoice and bringing its total to $3,875. The invoice was recorded and filed in error for payment on May 26. Give in general journal form the entries to record the (1) purchase, (2) discovery on May 26 of the discount lost, and (3) payment of the invoice on July 5. Do not give explanations but skip a line between entries.

DATE	ACCOUNT TITLES AND EXPLANATION	P.R.	DEBIT	CREDIT

Problem VIII

1. The ABC Company records all purchases at gross amounts. Give in general journal form the entries to record the following transactions (do not give explanations but skip a line between entries):

June 1 Received shipment of merchandise having $2,000 invoice price, terms 2/10, n/30.
June 2 Received shipment of merchandise having $500 invoice price, terms 1/10, n/60.
June 7 Paid for merchandise which was received on June 1.
July 30 Paid for merchandise which was received on June 2.

DATE		ACCOUNT TITLES AND EXPLANATION	P.R.	DEBIT	CREDIT

2. Show the appropriate general journal entries for the ABC Company if they had recorded purchases at net amounts (do not give explanations but skip a line between entries):

DATE		ACCOUNT TITLES AND EXPLANATION	P.R.	DEBIT	CREDIT

Problem IX

The bank statement dated September 30, 1990, for the Smith Company showed a balance of $2,876.35 which differs from the $1,879.50 book balance of cash on that date. In attempting to reconcile the difference, the accountant noted the following facts:

1) The bank recorded a service fee of $15 which was not recorded on the books of Smith Company.
2) A deposit of $500 was made on the last day of the month but was not recorded by the bank.
3) A check for $176 had been recorded on the Smith Company books as $167. The bank paid the correct amount.
4) A check was written during September but has not been processed by the bank. The amount was $422.85.
5) A check for $1,000 is still outstanding from August.
6) A check for $100 deposited by Smith Company was returned marked "Not Sufficient Funds."
7) A credit memorandum stated that the bank collected a note receivable of $200 for Smith Company and charged Smith a $2 collection fee. Smith Company had not previously recorded the collection.

Prepare, in good form, a bank reconciliation which shows the correct cash balance on September 30, 1990.

Solutions for Chapter 6

Problem I

1.	T	5.	T
2.	T	6.	T
3.	F	7.	F
4.	T	8.	T

Problem II

1.	E
2.	C
3.	A
4.	B

Problem III

Bank reconciliation	17	Net method of recording purchases	19
Canceled checks	10	Outstanding checks	4
Cash Over and Short account	13	Purchase order	16
Discounts lost	3	Purchase requisition	12
Gross method of recording purchases	8	Receiving report	1
Internal control system	14	Reconcile	18
Invoice	6	Vendee	20
Invoice approval form	11	Vendor	5
Liquid asset	9	Voucher	7
Liquidity	2	Voucher system	15

Problem IV

1. Cash Over and Short

2. invoice approval

3. discounts lost

4. is not

5. owner-manager, a system of internal control

6. (a) promotes operational efficiencies; (b) protects the business assets from waste, fraud, and theft; and (c) ensures accurate and reliable accounting data

7. separation, keep the cash records, intact each day, check

8. book balance of cash, bank statement balance

9. voucher system

10. purchase requisition

11. purchase order

12. (a) one person; (b) assets; (c) insured, bonded; (d) custody; (e) divided; (f) should be used (g) reviews

13. should not

Problem V

1. Nov. 5 Petty Cash 50.00
                Cash 50.00
             Established a petty cash fund.

2. Nov. 25 Transportation-In 22.75
             Miscellaneous General Expense 13.25
             Office Supplies 3.50
             Delivery Expense 8.00
                Cash 47.50
             Reimbursed the petty cash fund.

Problem VI

1. Book balance of cash .... $X,XXX   Bank statement balance .... $X,XXX
   Add: Add:
      (   )   (6)
   Deduct: Deduct:
      (4)   (1)
      (7)   (3)
      (8)   (   )

2. (4),(7),(8)

Problem VII

May 8 Purchases 3,675.00
      Transportation-In 125.00
           Accounts Payable—Vee Company 3,800.00
          $3,750 − ($3,750 × .02) = $3,675

  26 Discounts Lost 75.00
           Accounts Payable—Vee Company 75.00

July 5 Accounts Payable—Vee Company 3,875.00
           Cash 3,875.00

Problem VIII

1.
June	1	Purchases	......	2,000.00	
		Accounts Payable	......		2,000.00
	2	Purchases	......	500.00	
		Accounts Payable	......		500.00
	7	Accounts Payable	......	2,000.00	
		Purchases Discounts	......		40.00
		Cash	......		1,960.00
July	30	Accounts Payable	......	500.00	
		Cash	......		500.00

2.
June	1	Purchases ($2,000 × 98%)	......	1,960.00	
		Accounts Payable	......		1,960.00
	2	Purchases ($500 × 99%)	......	495.00	
		Accounts Payable	......		495.00
	7	Accounts Payable	......	1,960.00	
		Cash	......		1,960.00
July	30	Discounts Lost	......	5.00	
		Accounts Payable	......		5.00
	30	Accounts Payable	......	500.00	
		Cash	......		500.00

Problem IX

SMITH COMPANY
Bank Reconciliation
September 30, 1990

Book balance of cash	$1,879.50	Bank statement balance		$2,876.35
Add:		Add:		
Proceeds of note less		Deposit on		
collection fee	198.00	9/30/90		500.00
	$2,077.50			$3,376.35
Deduct:		Deduct:		
NSF check $100.00		Outstanding checks:		
Service fee 15.00		August $1,000.00		
Recording error 9.00	124.00	September 422.85		1,422.85
Reconciled balance	$1,953.50	Reconciled balance		$1,953.50

7 Short-Term Investments and Receivables

Your objectives in studying this chapter should include learning how to:

1. Journalize entries to account for short-term investments; and calculate, record, and report the lower of cost or market of short-term investments in marketable equity securities.

2. Prepare entries to account for credit card sales.

3. Prepare entries to account for credit customers, including allowance method entries and direct write-off method entries to account for bad debts.

4. Calculate the interest on promissory notes and prepare entries to record the receipt of promissory notes and their payment or dishonor.

5. Calculate the discount and proceeds on discounted notes receivable and prepare entries to record the discounting of notes receivable and, if dishonored, their dishonor.

6. Define or explain the words and phrases listed in the chapter Glossary.

Topical Outline

I. Short-term investments

    A. Short-term investments must be readily convertible into cash and held as a source of cash to satisfy the needs of current operations. They are classified as current assets on the balance sheet.

    B. Recorded at cost, which includes any commissions paid.

    C. Short-term investments in marketable equity securities must be reported on the balance sheet at the lower of cost or market.

II. Credit card sales

    A. Receipts from some credit card sales are deposited like checks into a business's bank account for immediate cash credit.

    B. Receipts from other credit card sales are sent to the credit card company for payment. The business has an account receivable from the credit card company until payment is received.

III. Subsidiary Accounts Receivable Ledger

    A. Accounts Receivable account in General Ledger is controlling account for subsidiary ledger.

    B. A separate account for each customer is maintained in the Accounts Receivable Ledger.

IV. Bad debts—accounts of customers who do not pay

    A. A necessary expense associated with selling on credit.

    B. Bad debts expense should be matched with the sales that resulted in the bad debts.

    C. Methods of accounting for bad debts

        1. Allowance method—at the end of each accounting period, bad debts expense is estimated and recorded.

        2. Direct write-off method—uncollectible accounts written off directly to Bad Debts Expense. (This method mismatches revenues and expenses.)

    D. Methods of estimating bad debts expense

        1. Income statement approach—bad debts expense is calculated as a percentage of credit sales.

        2. Balance sheet approach—desired credit balance in Allowance for Doubtful Accounts is calculated:

            a. As a percentage of outstanding receivables (simplified approach).
            b. By aging of accounts receivable.

    E. Recovery of bad debts

        1. Reinstate customer's account (reverse original write-off).

        2. Record collection of reinstated account.

V. Installment accounts and notes receivable

    A. Installment account receivable—an account receivable that allows the customer to make periodic payments over several months and which usually earns interest.

B. Note receivable—a written document promising payment and signed by the customer.

    1. Promissory notes are notes payable to the maker of the note and notes receivable to the payee.

    2. Notes receivable are generally preferred by creditors over accounts receivable.

C. Calculating interest

$$\begin{array}{ccccccc} \text{Principal of} \\ \text{note} \end{array} \times \begin{array}{c} \text{Annual} \\ \text{rate of} \\ \text{interest} \end{array} \times \begin{array}{c} \text{Time of note} \\ \text{expressed} \\ \text{in years} \end{array} = \text{Interest}$$

D. Accounting for notes receivable

    1. Record receipt of note.

    2. Record end-of-period adjustment for accrued interest.

    3. Record receipt of note payments.

    4. If note is dishonored, amount of note should be removed from Notes Receivable account and charged back to the account of maker.

E. Discounting notes receivable—owner endorses and delivers note to the bank for cash.

    1. Discount period—the time the bank holds the note.

    2. Bank discount—the amount of interest the bank charges during the discount period.

    3. Proceeds of the note—the maturity value of the note minus the bank discount.

    4. Contingent liability—usually the person who discounts the note is liable for payment of the note if it is dishonored by maker.

VI. Accounting principles

A. Materiality principle—strict adherence to any accounting principle is not required if lack of adherence will not produce an error large enough to influence the judgment of financial statement readers.

B. Full disclosure principle—financial statements and their accompanying notes must disclose all information of a material nature relating to the financial position and operating results of the company for which they are prepared.

Problem I

The following statements are either true or false. Place a (T) in the parentheses before each true statement and an (F) before each false statement.

1. ( ) Short-term investments are classified as current assets on the balance sheet.

2. ( ) Investments in securities that do not mature within one year or the current operating cycle of the business can be classified as current assets on the balance sheet if they are marketable.

3. ( ) A stock quotation of 14-1/8 means $14.125 per share.

4. ( ) To determine the lower of cost or market of a portfolio of short-term investments in marketable equity securities, compare the individual cost of each security held with its current market value.

5. ( ) The Gain on Short-Term Investments account is closed to Income Summary and reported on the income statement.

6. ( ) When the market value of short-term investments increases above cost, the resulting gain is credited to Gain on Short-Term Investments.

7. ( ) If cash from credit card sales is received immediately when the credit card receipts are deposited at the bank, the credit card expense is recorded at the time the sale is recorded.

8. ( ) Businesses with credit customers must maintain a separate account for each customer.

9. ( ) After all entries are posted, the sum of the balances in the Accounts Receivable Ledger should be equal to the balance of the Accounts Receivable account in the General Ledger.

10. ( ) Under the allowance method of accounting for bad debts, accounts receivable are reported on the balance sheet at the amount of cash proceeds expected from their collection.

11. ( ) At the time an adjusting entry to record estimated bad debts expense is made, the credit side of the entry is to Accounts Receivable.

12. ( ) When an account deemed uncollectible is written off against Allowance for Doubtful Accounts, the estimated realizable amount of Accounts Receivable is decreased.

13. ( ) The income statement approach to estimating bad debts is based on the idea that some percentage of credit sales will be uncollectible.

14. ( ) The balance sheet approach to estimating bad debts is based on the idea that some particular percentage of a company's credit sales will become uncollectible.

15. ( ) Aging of accounts receivable requires the examination of each account in the accounts receivable ledger.

16. ( ) A 90-day note, dated August 17, matures on November 16.

17. ( ) Although the direct write-off method of accounting for bad debts usually mismatches revenues and expenses, it may be allowed in cases where bad debt losses are immaterial in relation to total net sales and net income.

18. ( ) If the principal of a note exceeds the proceeds, the difference is debited to Interest Expense.

Problem II

You are given several words, phrases, or numbers to choose from in completing each of the following statements or in answering the following questions. In each case select the one that best completes the statement or answers the question and place its letter in the answer space provided.

_____ 1. On June 12, Cookie Company purchased 400 shares of Photograph Company common stock at 12-1/8 plus a 1% brokerage fee as a short-term investment. What is the general journal entry to record the transaction?

a.	Short-Term Investments	4,851.00	
	Cash		4,851.00
b.	Cash	4,365.00	
	Short-Term Investments		4,365.00
c.	Short-Term Investments	4,898.50	
	Cash		4,898.50
d.	Cash	4,801.50	
	Short-Term Investments		4,801.50
e.	Short-Term Investments	4,365.00	
	Cash		4,365.00

_____ 2. The cost and market values of Company B's short-term investments in marketable equity securities were as follows on sequential balance sheet dates:

	Cost	Market
On December 31, 1989	$30,000	$28,000
On December 31, 1990	34,000	32,500

What general journal entry is required on December 31, 1990?

a.	Loss on Market Decline of Short-Term Inv.	1,500	
	Allowance to Reduce Short-Term Inv. to Market		1,500
b.	Allowance to Reduce Short-Term Inv. to Market	500	
	Gain on Market Recovery of Short-Term Inv.		500
c.	No entry is required.		
d.	Allowance to Reduce Short-Term Inv. to Market	1,500	
	Loss on Market Decline of Short-Term Inv.		1,500
e.	Loss of Market Decline of Short-Term Inv.	3,500	
	Allowance to Reduce Short-Term Inv. to Market		3,500

_____ 3. Orion Company has decided to write off the account of Jack Irwin against the Allowance for Doubtful Accounts. The $2,100 balance in Irwin's account originated with a credit sale in July of last year. What is the general journal entry to record this write-off?

a.	Allowance for Doubtful Accounts	2,100	
	Accounts Receivable—Jack Irwin		2,100
b.	Accounts Receivable	2,100	
	Allowance for Doubtful Accounts		2,100
c.	Bad Debts Expense	2,100	
	Allowance for Doubtful Accounts		2,100
d.	Accounts Receivable	2,100	
	Accounts Receivable—Jack Irwin		2,100
e.	Bad Debts Expense	2,100	
	Accounts Receivable		2,100

Problem II *(continued)*

_____ 4. Hitech Corporation had credit sales of $3,000,000 in 1990. Before recording the December 31, 1990, adjustments, the company's Allowance for Doubtful Accounts had a credit balance of $1,400. A schedule of the December 31, 1990, accounts receivable by age is summarized as follows:

December 31, 1990 Accounts Receivable	Age of Accounts Receivable	Uncollectible Percent Expected
$285,000	Not due	1.5
87,000	1-45 days past due	8.2
34,000	46-90 days past due	37.0
8,000	over 90 days past due	70.0

Calculate the amount that should appear on the December 31, 1990, balance sheet as allowance for doubtful accounts.

  a. $28,189.
  b. $ 5,600.
  c. $25,314.
  d. $30,989.
  e. $29,589.

_____ 5. Based on the information given in problem 4, what is the general journal entry to record bad debts expense for 1990?

  a. Debit Bad Debts Expense; credit Allowance for Doubtful Accounts.
  b. Debit Accounts Receivable; credit Allowance for Doubtful Accounts.
  c. Debit Bad Debts Expense; credit Accounts Receivable.
  d. Debit Allowance for Doubtful Accounts; credit Bad Debts Expense.
  e. Debit Accounts Receivable; credit Bad Debts Expense.

_____ 6. On June 22, Xrox Corporation accepted a $4,500, 90-day, 12% note dated June 20 from Curtis Sims. On June 30, Xrox discounted the note at the bank at 14%. What amount of interest earned (or interest expense) should Xrox Corporation record?

  a. $135 interest earned.
  b. $9.20 interest expense.
  c. $5 interest expense.
  d. $144.20 interest expense.
  e. $22.50 interest expense.

_____ 7. What were the proceeds from discounting the note in problem 6?

  a. $4,500.00
  b. $4,635.00
  c. $4,472.77
  d. $4,490.80
  e. $4,355.80

Problem III

Many of the important ideas and concepts discussed in Chapter 7 are reflected in the following list of key terms. Test your understanding of these terms by matching the appropriate definitions with the terms. Record the number identifying the most appropriate definition in the blank space next to each term.

_____ Accounts receivable ledger

_____ Aging accounts receivable

_____ Allowance for doubtful accounts

_____ Allowance method of accounting for bad debts

_____ Bad debt

_____ Bank discount

_____ Contingent liability

_____ Controlling account

_____ Direct write-off method of accounting for bad debts

_____ Discount period of a note

_____ Discounting a note receivable

_____ Dishonoring a note

_____ Full-disclosure principle

_____ General ledger

_____ Installment accounts receivable

_____ Lower of cost or market

_____ Maker of a note

_____ Materiality principle

_____ Maturity date of a note

_____ Maturity value of a note

_____ Notice of protest

_____ Payee of a note

_____ Proceeds of a discounted note

_____ Protest fee

_____ Realizable value

_____ Short-term investments

_____ Subsidiary ledger

_____ Temporary investments

1. Selling a note receivable to a bank or other concern, usually with the provision that the seller assumes a contingent liability to pay the note if it is dishonored.

2. One who signs a note and promises to pay it at maturity.

3. A collection of accounts other than general ledger accounts which shows the details underlying the balance of a controlling account in the General Ledger.

4. The accounting requirement that financial statements including the footnotes contain all relevant information about the operations and financial position of the entity and that the information be presented in an understandable manner.

5. An accounting procedure that (1) estimates the bad debts arising from credit sales and reports bad debts expense during the period of the sales, and (2) reports accounts receivable in the balance sheet net of estimated uncollectibles, which is their estimated realizable value.

6. The maturity value of a note minus any interest deducted because of its being discounted before maturity.

7. A potential liability that will become an actual liability if and only if certain events occur.

8. Another name for short-term investments.

9. The fee charged for preparing and issuing a notice of protest.

Problem III *(continued)*

10. A procedure whereby uncollectible accounts are not estimated in advance and are not charged to expense until they prove to be uncollectible.

11. Principal of the note plus any interest due on the note's maturity date.

12. Refusal of a promissory note's maker to pay the amount due upon maturity of the note.

13. The idea that the requirements of any accounting principle may be ignored if the effect on the financial statements is unimportant to financial statement readers.

14. The amount of interest charged by a bank when the bank accepts a discounted note from a customer. Also, the interest deducted in advance any time a bank deducts interest in advance on a loan.

15. An uncollectible receivable.

16. Accounts receivable that allow the customer to make periodic payments over several months and which typically earn interest.

17. The expected proceeds from converting an asset into cash.

18. The one to whom a promissory note is made payable.

19. The estimated amount of accounts receivable that will be uncollectible.

20. A written statement that says a note was duly presented to the maker for payment and payment was refused.

21. The date on which a note and any interest are due and payable.

22. The number of days following the date on which a note is discounted at the bank until the maturity date of the note.

23. A process of classifying accounts receivable in terms of how long they have been outstanding for the purpose of estimating the amount of uncollectible accounts.

24. A subsidiary ledger having an account for each customer.

25. A general ledger account the balance of which is always equal to the sum of the balances in a related subsidiary ledger.

26. Investments such as government or corporate debt obligations and marketable equity securities that can be converted into cash quickly and that are held as a source of cash to satisfy the needs of current operations.

27. A method of reporting whereby the total cost of the entire portfolio of short-term investments in marketable equity securities is compared to the total market value on the date of the balance sheet and the lesser amount is reported in the balance sheet.

28. The collection of financial statement accounts of a business.

Problem IV

On December 12, Lark Company received from Guy Hall, a customer, $300 in cash and a $1,500, 12%, 60-day note dated December 11 in granting a time extension on Hall's past-due account. On December 31, Lark Company recorded the accrued interest on the note, and Guy Hall paid the note and its interest on the following February 9. Complete the general journal entries to record these transactions.

Problem IV *(continued)*

DATE		ACCOUNT TITLES AND EXPLANATION	P.R.	DEBIT	CREDIT
Dec.	12				
		Received cash and a note in granting a time			
		extension on a past-due account.			
	31				
		To record accrued interest on a note			
		receivable.			
Feb.	9				
		Received payment of a note and interest.			

Problem V

On March 1 Lark Company accepted a $1,200, 12%, 60-day note dated that day from a customer, Mary Dale, in granting a time extension on the customer's past-due account. When Lark Company presented the note for payment on April 30, it was dishonored, and on December 20 Lark Company wrote off the debt as uncollectible. Present entries to record the dishonor and the write-off against the company's Allowance for Doubtful Accounts.

DATE		ACCOUNT TITLES AND EXPLANATION	P.R.	DEBIT	CREDIT
Apr.	30				
		To charge the account of Mary Dale for her			
		dishonored $1,200, 12%, 60-day note.			
Dec.	20				
		To write off the uncollectible note of			
		Mary Dale.			

Problem VI

On April 2 Lark Company received from Sam Fox, a customer, a $1,000, 12%, 60-day note dated that day in granting a time extension on the customer's past-due account. Lark Company held the note until April 26 and then discounted it at its bank at 14%. The note was not protested at maturity. Complete the following entries for this note.

Problem VI *(continued)*

DATE		ACCOUNT TITLES AND EXPLANATION	P.R.	DEBIT	CREDIT
Apr.	2				
		Received a note in granting a time extension			
		on a past-due account.			
	26				
		Discounted the Sam Fox note at 14%.			

Problem VII

On June 10 Lark Company received a $2,400, 10%, 60-day note dated that day from Ted Sack, a customer, in granting a time extension on his past-due account. The company held the note until June 16 and then discounted it at its bank at 13%. On August 10 Lark Company received notice protesting the note. It paid the bank the maturity value of the note plus a $15 protest fee. On October 8 Lark Company received a $2,495.92 check from Ted Sack in payment of the maturity value of his dishonored note, the protest fee, and 10% interest on both for 60 days beyond maturity. Complete the following general journal entries to record this series of transactions.

DATE		ACCOUNT TITLES AND EXPLANATION	P.R.	DEBIT	CREDIT
June	10				
		Received a note in granting a time extension			
		on a past-due account.			
June	16				
		Discounted the Ted Sack note at 14%.			
Aug.	10				
		Paid the bank the maturity value of the			
		Ted Sack note plus a protest fee.			
Oct.	8				
		Received payment of the maturity value of			
		the Ted Sack note plus the protest fee and			
		interest on both for 60 days beyond maturity.			

Problem VIII

Marin Company uses the allowance method in accounting for bad debt losses, and over the past several years it has experienced an average loss equal to one fourth of 1% of its credit sales. During 1990 the company sold $928,000 of merchandise on credit, including a $98 credit sale to Gus Bell on March 5, 1990. The $98 had not been paid by the year's end.

1. If at the end of 1990 Marin Company, in providing for estimated bad debt losses, assumes history

    will repeat, it will provide an allowance for 1990 estimated bad debts equal to _____%
    of its $928,000 of 1990 charge sales; and the adjusting entry to record the allowance will appear as follows: (Complete the following entry.)

DATE		ACCOUNT TITLES AND EXPLANATION	P.R.	DEBIT	CREDIT
1990					
Dec.	31				
		To record estimated bad debts.			

2. The debit of the foregoing entry is to the expense account, _____

    _____, which is closed to the

    _____ account at the end of the accounting period, just as any other expense account is closed.

3. The effect of the foregoing adjusting entry on the 1990 income statement of Marin Company is to cause an estimated amount of bad debts expense to be deducted from the $928,000 of revenue

    from 1990 charge sales. This complies with the accounting principle of _____

    _____.

4. The credit of the foregoing adjusting entry is to the contra account _____

    _____

    On the December 31, 1990, balance sheet the balance of this contra account is subtracted from the

    balance of the _____ account to show the amount that is expected to be realized from the accounts receivable.

Problem VIII *(continued)*

5. On March 31, 1991, the Accounts Receivable controlling account and the Allowance for Doubtful Accounts account of Marin Company had the following balances:

Accounts Receivable		Allowance for Doubtful Accounts	
Mar. 31 65,625			Mar. 31 4,475

A balance sheet which was prepared on March 31, 1991, would show that Marin Company expects

to collect $_____ of its accounts receivable.

6. On April 1, 1991, Marin Company decided the $98 account of Gus Bell (sale made on March 5 of the previous year) was uncollectible and wrote it off as a bad debt. (Complete the entry and post to the above T-accounts the portions affecting the accounts.)

DATE		ACCOUNT TITLES AND EXPLANATION	P.R.	DEBIT	CREDIT
1991					
Apr.	1				
		To write off the account of Gus Bell.			

7. If a balance sheet was prepared immediately after the entry writing off the uncollectible account of

Gus Bell was posted, it would show that Marin Company expected to collect $_____

_____ of its accounts receivable. Consequently, the write-off

_____ (did, did not) affect the net balance sheet amount of accounts

receivable. Likewise, the entry writing off the account did not record an expense because the

expense was anticipated and recorded in the _____ entry
made on December 31, 1990, the year of the sale.

Problem IX

Pell Company sells almost exclusively for cash, but it does make a few small charge sales, and it also occasionally has a small bad debt loss which it accounts for by the direct write-off method.

1. Give below the entry made by Pell Company on February 5 to write off the $55 uncollectible account of Joan Bond (the goods were sold during the previous period.)

DATE		ACCOUNT TITLES AND EXPLANATION	P.R.	DEBIT	CREDIT
Feb.	5				

Problem IX *(continued)*

2. Writing off the foregoing bad debt directly to the Bad Debts Expense account violates the

accounting principle of _____

_____. However, due to the accounting principle of

_____ the direct write-off is permissible in this case because the company's bad debt losses are very small in relation to its sales.

Problem X

A company that ages its accounts receivable and increases its allowance for doubtful accounts to an amount sufficient to provide for estimated bad debts had a $75 debit balance in its Allowance for Doubtful Accounts account on December 31. If on that date it estimated that $1,800 of its accounts receivable were uncollectible, it should make a year-end adjusting entry crediting

$_____ to its Allowance for Doubtful Accounts account.

Problem XI

Pierce Company allows its customers to use two credit cards: the University National Bank credit card and the Community Credit Card. Using the information given below, prepare general journal entries for Pierce Company to record the following credit card transactions:

a) University National Bank charges a 3% service fee for sales on its credit card. As a commercial customer of the bank, Pierce Company receives immediate credit when it makes its daily deposit of sales receipts.

May   2   Sold merchandise for $525 to customers who used the University National Bank credit card.

Problem XI *(continued)*

b) Community Credit Card Company charges 4% of sales for use of its card. Pierce Company submits accumulated sales receipts to Community Company and is paid within thirty days.

May   3   Sold merchandise for $675 to customers using the Community Credit Card. Submitted receipts to Community Company for payment.

         30   Received amount due from Community Credit Card Company.

Solutions for Chapter 7

Problem I

1.	T	10.	T	
2.	T	11.	F	
3.	T	12.	F	
4.	F	13.	T	
5.	T	14.	F	
6.	F	15.	T	
7.	T	16.	F	
8.	T	17.	T	
9.	T	18.	T	

Problem II

1.	C
2.	B
3.	A
4.	E
5.	A
6.	B
7.	D

Problem III

Problem IV

Dec.	12	Cash	300.00	
		Notes Receivable	1,500.00	
		Accounts Receivable—Guy Hall		1,800.00
	31	Interest Receivable ($1,500 × .12 × 20/360)	10.00	
		Interest Earned		10.00
Feb.	9	Cash	1,530.00	
		Interest Receivable		10.00
		Interest Earned		20.00
		Notes Receivable		1,500.00

Problem V

Apr. 30	Accounts Receivable—Mary Dale 1,224.00	
	Interest Earned	24.00
	Notes Receivable	1,200.00
Dec. 20	Allowance for Doubtful Accounts 1,224.00	
	Accounts Receivable—Mary Dale	1,224.00

Problem VI

Apr. 2	Notes Receivable 1,000.00	
	Accounts Receivable—Sam Fox	1,000.00
26	Cash 1,005.72	
	Interest Earned	5.72
	Notes Receivable	1,000.00

($1,000 × .12 × 60/360) = $20.00
($1,020 × .14 × 36/360) = 14.28
                          $ 5.72

Problem VII

June 10	Notes Receivable 2,400.00	
	Accounts Receivable—Ted Sack	2,400.00
16	Cash 2,392.42	
	Interest Expense 7.58	
	Notes Receivable	2,400.00

($2,400 × .10 × 60/360) = $40.00
($2,440 × .13 × 54/360) = 47.58
                          $ 7.58

Aug. 10	Accounts Receivable—Ted Sack 2,455.00	
	Cash ($2,440 + $15)	2,455.00
Oct. 8	Cash 2,495.92	
	Interest Earned	40.92
	Accounts Receivable—Ted Sack	2,455.00

Problem VIII

1. one fourth of 1%, or .25%

Dec. 31	Bad Debts Expense 2,320.00	
	Allowance for Doubtful Accounts	2,320.00

2. Bad Debts Expense, Income Summary
3. matching revenues and expenses
4. Allowance for Doubtful Accounts, Accounts Receivable
5. $61,150

Problem VIII *(continued)*

6. Apr. 1 Allowance for Doubtful Accounts 98.00
             Accounts Receivable—Gus Bell 98.00

Accounts Receivable				Allowance for Doubtful Accounts			
Mar. 31	65,625						
		Apr. 1	98	Apr. 1	98	Mar. 31	4,475

7. $61,150, did not, adjusting

Problem IX

1. Feb. 5 Bad Debts Expense 55.00
             Accounts Receivable—Joan Bond 55.00
2. matching revenues and expenses, materiality

Problem X

$1,875

Problem XI

a) May 2 Cash 509.25
            Credit Card Expense ($525 × .03) 15.75
              Sales 525.00

b) May 3 Accounts Receivable—Community Company 675.00
              Sales 675.00

      30 Cash 648.00
            Credit Card Expense ($675 × .04) 27.00
              Accounts Receivable—Community Company 675.00

8 Inventories and Cost of Goods Sold

Your objectives in studying this chapter should include learning how to:

1. Calculate the cost of an inventory based on (a) specific invoice prices, (b) weighted-average cost, (c) FIFO, and (d) LIFO, and explain the financial statement effects of choosing one method over the others.

2. Calculate the lower-of-cost-or-market amount of an inventory.

3. Explain the effect of an inventory error on the income statements of the current and succeeding years.

4. Prepare entries to record merchandise transactions and maintain subsidiary inventory records under a perpetual inventory system.

5. Estimate an inventory by the retail method and by the gross profit method.

6. Define or explain the words and phrases listed in the chapter Glossary.

Topical Outline

I.   Inventory accounting

    A. Merchandise inventory

       1. The tangible property a merchandising business holds for sale.

       2. Usually the largest current asset of a merchandising concern.

    B. Major objective in inventory accounting

       1. The proper determination of income through the process of matching appropriate costs against revenues.

       2. Means assigning costs of inventory for sale during the accounting period either to cost of goods sold or to ending inventory.

II. Periodic inventory system

    A. Cost of ending inventory is determined by:

       1. Determining quantity of each item on hand.

       2. Assigning a cost to the quantities on hand.

    B. Cost of goods sold is calculated by subtracting cost of ending inventory from goods available for sale.

    C. Four ways to assign costs

       1. Specific invoice prices

          a. Each inventory item is matched with its invoice price.
          b. This method is of practical use only with relatively high-priced items of which only a few are sold.

       2. Weighted-average cost

          a. Total cost of beginning inventory and purchases is divided by number of units to find average cost.
          b. This method tends to smooth out price fluctuations.

       3. First-in, first-out (FIFO)

          a. Costs are assigned under the assumption that the oldest goods are sold first. (This pricing method may be assumed even if physical flow of goods does not follow this pattern.)
          b. With FIFO method, inventory on the balance sheet most closely approximates current replacement cost.

       4. Last-in, first-out (LIFO)

          a. Costs are assigned under the assumption that the most recent purchases are sold first.
          b. Use of LIFO method results in better matching of current costs and revenues.
          c. LIFO offers a tax advantage to users during a period of rising prices.

    D. Items included on an inventory

       1. All goods owned by the business and held for sale regardless of the physical location of the goods.

       2. All costs incurred in bringing an article to its existing condition and location.

III. Lower of cost or market

    A. Inventory is normally reported on the balance sheet at market value whenever market is lower than cost.

        1. Market normally means replacement cost.

        2. Merchandise is written down to market because the value of the merchandise to the company has declined.

    B. Lower-of-cost-or-market pricing is applied either:

        1. To the inventory as a whole, or

        2. Separately to each product in the inventory.

    C. Exceptions

        1. Inventory should never be valued at more than its net realizable value (expected sales price less additional costs to sell).

        2. Inventory should never be valued at less than net realizable value minus a normal profit margin.

IV. Accounting principles

    A. Principle of consistency

        1. Requires a persistent application of an accounting method, period after period.

    B. Full-disclosure principle

        1. Requires a full-disclosure of the nature of any change in accounting methods.

    C. Principle of conservatism

        1. When two estimates of amounts to be received or paid in the future are about equally likely, the less optimistic estimate should be used.

        2. Inventory cannot be written up to market when market exceeds cost.

    D. Principle of materiality

        1. In pricing an inventory, incidental costs of acquiring merchandise may be treated as expenses of the period in which incurred.

V. Inventory errors

    A. Periodic inventory system

        1. An error in determining the end-of-period inventory will cause misstatements in cost of goods sold, gross profit, net income, current assets, and owners' equity.

        2. Error will carry forward in succeeding period's cost of goods sold, gross profit, and net income.

        3. Errors in cost of goods sold and net income will be offset by errors in the following period.

VI. Perpetual inventory system

    A. Updates the Merchandise Inventory account after each purchase and each sale.

    B. Does not use a Purchases account; cost of items purchased is debited directly to Merchandise Inventory.

C. Requires two entries to record a sale of merchandise.

D. Merchandise Inventory account serves as a controlling account to a subsidiary Merchandise Inventory Ledger, which contains a separate record for each product in stock.

E. Using LIFO, a perpetual inventory system results in different amounts of cost of goods sold and ending inventory than under a periodic inventory system.

VII. Estimated inventories

A. Retail inventory method

1. Used to estimate ending inventory on the ratios of cost of goods for sale at cost and cost of goods for sale at retail.

2. Satisfactory for interim statements, but a physical inventory should be taken at least once a year.

B. Gross profit method

1. Similar to retail method, but does not require information about retail price of beginning inventory, purchases, and markups.

2. Company must know its normal gross profit margin or rate.

Problem I

The following statements are either true or false. Place a (T) in the parentheses before each true statement and an (F) before each false statement.

1. ( ) The merchandise inventory of a business includes goods sold FOB destination if they are not yet delivered.

2. ( ) When a perpetual inventory system is used, the dollar amount of ending inventory is determined by counting the units of product on hand, multiplying the count for each product by its cost, and adding the costs for all products.

3. ( ) If prices of goods purchased remain unchanged, then all four methods of assigning costs to goods in the ending inventory would yield the same cost figures.

4. ( ) When first-in, first-out inventory pricing is used, the costs of the first items purchased are assigned to the ending inventory, and the remaining costs are assigned to goods sold.

5. ( ) If prices are rising, then using the LIFO method of pricing inventory will result in the highest net income.

6. ( ) Inventory should never be valued at more than net realizable value or less than net realizable value minus a normal profit margin.

7. ( ) Under the periodic inventory system, an error in ending inventory will carry forward and cause misstatements in the succeeding period's cost of goods sold, gross profit, and net income.

8. ( ) The perpetual inventory system uses a Purchases account to record items purchased.

9. ( ) The perpetual and periodic inventory systems never result in the same amounts of sales, cost of goods sold, and end-of-period merchandise inventory.

10. ( ) Lower of cost or market may be applied separately to each product or to the merchandise inventory as a whole.

Problem II

You are given several words, phrases or numbers to choose from in completing each of the following statements or in answering the following questions. In each case select the one that best completes the statement or answers the question and place its letter in the answer space provided.

_____ 1. Trivial Games Company's inventory consists of 80 units of product P, all of which have been damaged. The company bought the inventory for $20 per unit. Replacement cost is $22 per unit. Expected sales price is $30 per unit but this can be realized only if $7 additional cost per unit is paid. Calculate the lower of cost or market for the inventory.

  a. $1,840.
  b. $1,200.
  c. $1,760.
  d. $1,040.
  e. $1,600.

Problem II *(continued)*

_____ 2. Magnum Company began a year and purchased merchandise as follows:

Jan.	1	Beginning inventory	40 units @ $17.00
Feb.	4	Purchased	80 units @ $16.00
May	12	Purchased	80 units @ $16.50
Aug.	9	Purchased	60 units @ $17.50
Nov.	23	Purchased	100 units @ $18.00

The company uses a periodic inventory system and the ending inventory consists of 60 units, 20 from each of the last three purchases. Determine ending inventory assuming costs are assigned on the basis of FIFO.

a. $1,040.
b. $1,000.
c. $1,069.
d. $1,080.
e. $1,022.

_____ 3. Linder Company began a year and purchased merchandise as follows:

Jan.	1	Beginning inventory	40 units @ $17.00
Feb.	4	Purchased	80 units @ $16.00
May	12	Purchased	80 units @ $16.50
Aug.	9	Purchased	60 units @ $17.50
Nov.	23	Purchased	100 units @ $18.00

The company uses a periodic inventory system and the ending inventory consists of 60 units, 20 from each of the last three purchases. Determine ending inventory assuming costs are assigned on the basis of LIFO.

a. $1,040.
b. $1,000.
c. $1,022.
d. $ 980.
e. $1,080.

_____ 4. Box Company began a year and purchased merchandise as follows:

Jan.	1	Beginning inventory	40 units @ $17.00
Feb.	4	Purchased	80 units @ $16.00
May	12	Purchased	80 units @ $16.50
Aug.	9	Purchased	60 units @ $17.50
Nov.	23	Purchased	100 units @ $18.00

The company uses a periodic inventory system and the ending inventory consists of 60 units, 20 from each of the last three purchases. Determine ending inventory assuming costs are assigned on the basis of specific invoice prices.

a. $1,000.
b. $1,022.
c. $1,040.
d. $1,080.
e. $ 990.

Problem II *(continued)*

_____ 5. Crow Company began a year and purchased merchandise as follows:

Jan. 1 Beginning inventory 40 units @ $17.00
Feb. 4 Purchased 80 units @ $16.00
May 12 Purchased 80 units @ $16.50
Aug. 9 Purchased 60 units @ $17.50
Nov. 23 Purchased 100 units @ $18.00

The company uses a periodic inventory system and the ending inventory consists of 60 units, 20 from each of the last three purchases. Determine ending inventory assuming costs are assigned on a weighted-average basis.

a. $1,022.00.
b. $1,040.00.
c. $1,080.00.
d. $1,000.00.
e. $1,042.50.

_____ 6. Atlantis Company uses a periodic inventory system and made an error at the end of year 1 that caused its year 1 ending inventory to be understated by $5,000. What effect does this error have on the company's financial statements?

a. Net income is understated; assets are understated.
b. Net income is understated; assets are overstated.
c. Net income is overstated; assets are understated.
d. Net income is overstated; assets are overstated.
e. Net income is overstated; assets are correctly stated.

_____ 7. Cheese Company sold $224,000 of merchandise at marked retail prices during an accounting period. The records show the following, at retail: beginning inventory = $60,000; net purchases = $214,000; additional markups = $6,000; markdowns = $5,800. At cost: beginning inventory = $40,000; net purchases = $156,000. Use the retail method to estimate the store's ending inventory at cost.

a. $ 35,833.
b. $ 50,200.
c. $191,940.
d. $ 43,260.
e. $ 35,140.

_____ 8. Sanders Company wants to prepare interim financial statements for the first quarter of 1990. The company uses a periodic inventory system and has an average gross profit rate of 30%. Based on the following information, use the gross profit method to prepare an estimate of the March 31 inventory.

January 1, beginning inventory ...... $ 97,000
Purchases 214,000
Purchases returns 2,000
Transportation-in 4,000
Sales 404,000
Sales returns 5,000

a. $ 33,700.
b. $193,300.
c. $119,700.
d. $179,900.
e. $ 26,700.

Problem II *(continued)*

_____ 9. Assume that in addition to estimating the ending inventory by the retail method (refer to question 7), Cheese Company also took a physical inventory at marked selling prices of the inventory items which equaled $48,000. Determine the amount of the company's inventory shrinkage at cost.

  a. $12,860.
  b. $ 2,200.
  c. $ 4,740.
  d. $ 1,540.
  e. $ 2,283.

Problem III

Many of the important ideas and concepts discussed in Chapter 8 are reflected in the following list of key terms. Test your understanding of these terms by matching the appropriate definitions with the terms. Record the number identifying the most appropriate definition in the blank space next to each term.

_____ Conservatism principle

_____ Consignee

_____ Consignor

_____ Consistency principle

_____ FIFO inventory pricing

_____ Gross profit inventory method

_____ Interim statements

_____ Inventory ticket

_____ LIFO inventory pricing

_____ Markdown

_____ Markon

_____ Markup

_____ Net realizable value

_____ Normal markup

_____ Periodic inventory system

_____ Perpetual inventory system

_____ Retail inventory method

_____ Retail method cost ratio

_____ Specific invoice inventory pricing

_____ Weighted-average inventory pricing

1. The expected sales price of an item less any additional costs to sell.

2. The pricing of an inventory under the assumption that the first items received were the first items sold.

3. An inventory pricing system in which the unit prices of the beginning inventory and of each purchase are weighted by the number of units in the beginning inventory and each purchase. The total of these amounts is then divided by the total number of units available for sale to find the unit cost of the ending inventory and of the units that were sold.

4. Another name for markon.

5. The accounting requirement that a company use the same accounting methods period after period so that the financial statements of succeeding periods will be comparable.

6. An increase in the sales price of merchandise above the normal markon given the goods.

7. The ratio of goods available for sale at cost to goods available for sale at retail prices.

8. An owner of goods who ships them to another party who will then sell the goods for the owner.

Problem III *(continued)*

9. A procedure for estimating an ending inventory in which the past gross profit rate is used to estimate cost of goods sold, which is then subtracted from the cost of goods available for sale to determine the estimated ending inventory.

10. The pricing of an inventory where the purchase invoice of each item in the ending inventory is identified and used to determine the cost assigned to the inventory.

11. A form attached to the counted items in the process of taking a physical inventory.

12. An inventory system in which cost of goods sold is recorded after each sale and the Merchandise Inventory account is updated after each purchase and each sale.

13. The pricing of an inventory under the assumption that the last items received were the first items sold.

14. A reduction in the marked selling price of merchandise.

15. The accounting principle that guides accountants to select the less optimistic estimate when two estimates of amounts to be received or paid are about equally likely.

16. An accounting system in which the Merchandise Inventory account is updated only once each accounting period, based on a physical count of the inventory.

17. A method for estimating an ending inventory based on the ratio of the amount of goods for sale at cost to the amount of goods for sale at marked selling prices.

18. One who receives and holds goods owned by another party for the purpose of selling the goods for the owner.

19. Monthly or quarterly financial statements prepared in between the regular year-end statements.

20. The normal amount or percentage of cost that is added to the cost of merchandise to arrive at its selling price.

Problem IV

Complete the following by filling in the blanks.

1. Consistency in the use of an inventory costing method is particularly important if there is to be

_____

_____.

2. If a running record is maintained for each inventory item of the number of units received as units are received, the number of units sold as units are sold, and the number of units remaining after

each receipt or sale, the inventory system is called _____

_____.

3. When a company changes its accounting procedures, the _____

principle requires that the nature of the change, justification for the change, and the effect of the

change on _____ be disclosed in the notes accompanying the financial statements.

Problem IV (continued)

4. Two exceptions to the idea that market means replacement cost are:

    a. _____
    _____.

    b. _____
    _____.

5. Inventories are generally priced at cost. However, a departure from cost may be necessary for

    _____

    _____

    _____.

6. With a periodic inventory system, an error in taking an end-of-period inventory will cause a

    misstatement of periodic net income for _____ (one, two) accounting periods

    because _____

    _____

    _____.

7. When identical items are purchased during an accounting period at different costs, a problem arises as to which costs apply to the ending inventory and which apply to the goods sold. There are at least four commonly used ways of assigning costs to inventory and to goods sold. They are:

    a. _____;

    b. _____;

    c. _____;

    d. _____.

8. A major objective of accounting for inventories is the proper determination of periodic net in-

    come through the process of matching _____ and

    _____. The matching process consists of determining how much of the cost of the goods that were for sale during an accounting period should be deducted from the

    period's _____ and how much should be carried forward as

    _____, to be matched against a future period's revenues.

Problem IV *(continued)*

9. Although changing back and forth from one inventory costing method to another might allow management to report the incomes it would prefer, the accounting principle of _____ _____ requires a company to use the same pricing method period after period unless it can justify the change.

10. Using _____ inventory pricing, a perpetual inventory system and a periodic inventory system may result in different amounts of _____ _____ and _____.

11. In the gross profit method of estimating an ending inventory, an average _____ _____ rate is used to determine estimated cost of goods sold, and the ending inventory is then estimated by subtracting estimated _____ _____ from the cost of goods for sale.

12. In separating cost of goods for sale into cost of goods sold and cost of goods unsold, the procedures for assigning a cost to the ending inventory are also the means of determining _____ because whatever portion of the cost of goods available for sale is assigned to ending inventory, the remainder goes to _____ _____.

13. Cost of an inventory item includes _____ _____ _____ _____.

14. Use of the lower-of-cost-or-market rule places an inventory on the balance sheet at a _____ _____ figure. The argument in favor of this rule provides that any loss should be _____ in the year of the price decline.

15. When recording a sale of merchandise using a _____ (perpetual, periodic) inventory system, two journal entries must be made. One entry records the revenue received for the sale and the second entry debits the _____ account.

Problem V

A company uses a perpetual inventory system and during a year had the following beginning inventory, purchases, and sales of Product Z:

Jan.	1	Inventory	200 units @ $0.50 = $100
Mar.	15	Purchased	400 units @ 0.50 = 200
Apr.	1	Sold	300 units
June	3	Purchased	300 units @ 0.60 = 180
July	1	Sold	200 units
Oct.	8	Purchased	600 units @ 0.70 = 420
Nov.	1	Sold	500 units
Dec.	15	Purchased	500 units @ 0.80 = 400

In the spaces below show the cost that should be assigned to the ending inventory and to the goods sold under the following assumptions:

	Portions Assigned to—	
	Ending Inventory	Cost of Goods Sold
1. A first-in, first-out basis was used to price the ending inventory	$	$
2. A last-in, first-out basis was used to price the ending inventory	$	$

Problem VI

The following end-of-period information about a store's beginning inventory, purchases, markups, markdowns, and sales is available.

	At Cost	At Retail
Beginning inventory	$ 9,600	$12,000
Purchases, net	54,400	68,000
Transportation-in	1,680	
Additional markups		2,100
Markdowns		700
Sales		69,000

The above information is to be used to estimate the store's ending inventory by the retail method.

Problem VI *(continued)*

1. The store had goods for sale during the year calculated as follows:

	At Cost	*At Retail*
Beginning inventory	$_____	$_____
Purchases, net	_____	_____
Transportation-in	_____	_____
Additional markups	_____	_____
Goods for sale	══════	_____

2. The store's cost ratio was:

    $_____ / $_____ = _____

3. Of the goods the store had for sale at market retail prices during the year, the following dollar amounts are gone because of —

    Sales .... $_____

    And because of price markdowns, which in effect reduced the total goods for sale at retail .... _____

    Total sales and markdowns .... $_____

    Which left the store an estimated ending inventory at retail (goods for sale at $ retail less sales and markdowns) .... $══════

4. And when the store's cost ratio is applied to this estimated ending inventory at retail, the estimated ending inventory at cost is $══════

Solutions for Chapter 8

Problem I

1.	T	6.	T
2.	F	7.	T
3.	T	8.	F
4.	F	9.	F
5.	F	10.	T

Problem II

1.	E	6.	A
2.	D	7.	E
3.	B	8.	A
4.	C	9.	D
5.	A		

Problem III

Conservatism principle	15	Markon	20
Consignee	18	Markup	6
Consignor	8	Net realizable value	1
Consistency principle	5	Normal markup	4 or 20
FIFO inventory pricing	2	Periodic inventory system	16
Gross profit inventory method	9	Perpetual inventory system	12
Interim statements	19	Retail inventory method	17
Inventory ticket	11	Retail method cost ratio	7
LIFO inventory pricing	13	Specific invoice inventory pricing	10
Markdown	14	Weighted-average inventory pricing	3

Problem IV

1. comparability in the financial statements prepared period after period

2. a perpetual inventory system

3. full-disclosure, net income

4. (a) market is never more than net realizable value, (b) market is never less than net realizable value minus a normal profit margin

5. goods that have been damaged or have deteriorated and also when replacement costs for inventory items are less than the amounts paid for the items

6. two, the ending inventory of one period becomes the beginning inventory of the next

7. (a) specific invoice prices; (b) weighted-average cost; (c) first-in, first-out; (d) last-in, first-out

8. costs, revenues, revenues, merchandise inventory

9. consistency

10. last-in, first-out; cost of goods sold; ending merchandise inventory

11. gross profit, cost of goods sold

12. cost of goods sold, cost of goods sold

13. the invoice price, less the discount, plus any additional incidental costs necessary to put the item in place and in condition for sale

Problem IV *(continued)*

14. conservative, recognized
15. perpetual, cost of goods sold

Problem V

	Portions Assigned to —	
	Ending Inventory	*Cost of Goods Sold*
1.	$750	$550
2.	550	750

Problem VI

	At Cost	*At Retail*
Goods for sale:		
Beginning inventory	$ 9,600	$12,000
Purchases, net	54,400	68,000
Transportation-in	1,680	
Additional markups		2,100
Goods for sale	$65,680	$82,100
Cost ratio: $65,680/$82,100 = .80		
Sales at retail		$69,000
Markdowns		700
Total sales and markdowns		$69,700
Ending inventory at retail ($82,100 less $69,700)		$12,400
Ending inventory at cost ($12,400 x 80%)	$ 9,920	

9 | Plant and Equipment, Natural Resources, and Intangible Assets

Your objectives in studying this chapter should include learning how to:

1. Tell what is included in the cost of a plant asset, allocate the cost of lump-sum purchases to the separate assets being purchased, and prepare entries to record the plant asset purchases.

2. Explain depreciation accounting including the reasons for depreciation, calculate depreciation by the straight-line and units-of-production methods, and calculate depreciation after revising the estimated useful life of an asset.

3. Describe the use of accelerated depreciation for financial accounting purposes and calculate accelerated depreciation under *(a)* the declining-balance method, *(b)* the sum-of-the-years'-digits method, and *(c)* the Modified Accelerated Cost Recovery System.

4. Explain how subsidiary ledgers and related controlling accounts are used to maintain control over plant assets.

5. Prepare entries to record the disposal of plant assets and the exchange of plant assets under accounting rules and under income tax rules and tell which should be applied in any given exchange.

6. Make the calculations and prepare the entries to account for plant asset repairs and betterments.

7. Prepare entries to account for natural resources and for intangible assets, including entries to record depletion and amortization.

8. Define or explain the words and phrases listed in the chapter Glossary.

Topical Outline

I. Plant and equipment

  A. Includes assets that are used in the production or sale of other assets and that have an expected service life longer than one accounting period.

  B. Cost of a plant asset

  1. Includes all normal and reasonable costs incurred in getting the asset into position and in condition for intended use.

  2. Must be allocated to the accounting periods that benefit from the asset's use.

  3. Must be allocated on a fair basis such as relative appraisal values, if two or more assets are purchased for one price.

  C. Service life of a plant asset—the period of time that it will be used in producing or selling other assets or services.

  D. Salvage value of a plant asset—the net amount that will be realized when the asset is disposed of at the end of its service life. The amount to be depreciated is the asset's cost minus its salvage value.

II. Depreciation

  A. The expiration of an asset's quantity of usefulness.

  B. The cost (less expected salvage value) of the asset must be allocated as an expense to the accounting periods benefited.

  C. Typical methods of allocating depreciation

  1. Straight-line—a method that allocates an equal share of the total estimated amount a plant asset will be depreciated during its service life to each accounting period in that life.

  2. Units-of-production—a method that allocates depreciation on a plant asset based on the relation of the units of product produced by the asset during a given period to the total units the asset is expected to produce during its entire life.

  D. For assets acquired or disposed of during a year, only a partial year's depreciation should be recorded.

  E. Depreciation in the financial statements

  1. The cost of plant assets and their accumulated depreciation must be shown in the statements or in related footnotes.

  2. Depreciation method must be disclosed in a balance sheet footnote or other manner.

  3. Since depreciation is a process of allocating cost, the cost (net of depreciation) is not intended to represent value.

  4. Since depreciation expense is subtracted from revenues in arriving at net income, a company recovers the original cost of its depreciable assets through the sale of its products.

III. Accelerated depreciation

  A. Use of accelerated depreciation in preparing financial statements does not require that such methods also be used for tax purposes.

B. Accelerated depreciation methods

1. Declining-balance—an accelerated depreciation method in which up to twice the straight-line rate of depreciation, without considering salvage value, is applied to the remaining book value of a plant asset to arrive at the asset's annual depreciation charge.

2. Sum-of-the-years' digits—an accelerated depreciation method that allocates depreciation to each year in a plant asset's life on a fractional basis. The denominator of the fractions used is the sum of the years' digits in the estimated service life of the asset, and the numerators are the years' digits in reverse order.

C. Tax depreciation of personal property

1. Tax laws classify depreciable personal property into 3-year, 5-year, 7-year, 10-year, 15-year, and 20-year classes.

2. Straight-line or MACRS accelerated depreciation may be used.

3. MACRS accelerated depreciation involves declining-balance depreciation with a switch to straight-line at the point where the switch further accelerates the depreciation.

4. Since 1980 salvage values have been ignored.

5. A half-year convention usually is assumed for the first year's depreciation of personal property.

D. Tax depreciation of real property

1. Residential rental property is classified in a 27-1/2 year class. All other real estate is classified in a 31-1/2 year class.

2. Straight-line depreciation must be used, with a half-month convention for the first year's depreciation.

3. Salvage values are ignored.

IV. Control of plant assets

A. Each plant asset should be separately identified.

B. Periodic inventories should be taken to verify the existence and continued use of assets.

C. Formal records of plant assets should be maintained.

1. Controlling and subsidiary ledgers should be kept.

2. Materiality principle may be applied for assets costing less than an established minimum amount.

V. Repairs to plant assets

A. Ordinary repairs keep an asset in its normal good state of repair. These costs are recorded as expenses.

B. Extraordinary repairs extend an asset's service life. These costs are normally debited to the asset's Accumulated Depreciation account.

C. A betterment is the replacement of a portion of an asset with an improved portion. This cost is debited to the asset account.

D. A revenue expenditure benefits only the current period and appears on the current income statement as an expense.

E. A capital expenditure (or balance sheet expenditure) benefits future periods and is charged to an asset account.

VI. Accounting for the disposal of plant assets

    A. Discarded asset—remove cost and accumulated depreciation from accounts (in some cases, a loss may be recorded).

    B. Selling a plant asset—remove cost and accumulated depreciation from accounts. If proceeds are greater than book value, record a gain. If proceeds are less than book value, record a loss.

    C. Exchanging plant assets

        1. For accounting purposes, a material book loss should be recognized in the accounts but a book gain should not be recognized.

        2. For tax purposes, neither a gain nor loss should be recognized at the time of exchanging similar plant assets.

VII. Other plant assets

    A. Natural resources—timber, mineral deposits, oil reserves.

    B. Intangible assets—patents, copyrights, leaseholds, goodwill, trademarks.

    C. Costs of natural resources and intangible assets must also be allocated to the accounting periods that benefit from their use.

Problem I

The following statements are either true or false. Place a (T) in the parentheses before each true statement and an (F) before each false statement.

1. ( ) Cost is the basis for recording the acquisition of a plant asset.

2. ( ) The cost of a plant asset constructed by a business for its own use would include depreciation on the machinery used in constructing the asset.

3. ( ) Depreciation is a process of determining the value of assets.

4. ( ) The cost of extraordinary repairs which extend the service life of an asset should be debited to a Repairs Expense account.

5. ( ) The result of a betterment is a more efficient or more productive asset, but not necessarily an asset that has a longer life.

6. ( ) Natural resources appear on the balance sheet at cost less accumulated depreciation.

7. ( ) The depletion cost of any mined but unsold natural resources which are held for sale is carried forward on the balance sheet as a current asset.

8. ( ) Trademarks and organization costs are intangible assets and must be amortized over the asset's useful life (not to exceed 40 years).

9. ( ) The amortization entry for the costs of leasehold improvements would be a debit to an expense account and a credit to Leasehold Improvements.

10. ( ) Based on a given rate of return of 10%, the goodwill of a company that earns $25,000 annually of which $5,000 is above-average earnings, should be estimated at $200,000.

11. ( ) Subsidiary plant asset records are controlled by asset and accumulated depreciation accounts.

12. ( ) The cost of making ordinary repairs on a machine should be classified as a revenue expenditure.

13. ( ) A capital expenditure is a payment of assets that is charged immediately to expense, thus reducing the owners' equity.

14. ( ) If a cost is incurred to modify an existing plant asset for the purpose of making it more efficient or more productive, the cost should be classified as an extraordinary repair.

15. ( ) The cost of all intangible assets must be amortized over 40 years.

16. ( ) For assets purchased after 1980 and before 1987, the tax law provides a new system of accelerated depreciation called the Accelerated Cost Recovery System.

Problem II

You are given several words, phrases or numbers to choose from in completing each of the following statements or in answering the following questions. In each case select the one that best completes the statement or answers the question and place its letter in the answer space provided.

Problem II (continued)

_____ 1. Flintstone Company depreciated a machine that cost $21,600 on a straight-line basis for three years under the assumption it would have a five-year life and a $3,600 trade-in value. At that point, the manager realized that the machine had three years of remaining useful life, after which it would have an estimated $2,160 trade-in value. Determine the amount of depreciation to be charged against the machine during each of the remaining years in its life.

    a. $3,240.
    b. $1,800.
    c. $2,640.
    d. $2,880.
    e. $3,888.

_____ 2. Flintstone Company installed a machine in its factory at a cost of $84,000 on May 1, 1990. The machine's useful life is estimated at 8 years with a $9,000 salvage value. Determine the machine's 1991 depreciation on a declining-balance basis at twice the straight-line rate.

    a. $17,500.
    b. $15,750.
    c. $15,625.
    d. $14,000.
    e. $18,750.

_____ 3. Spacely's Sprockets purchased a machine on September 1, 1990, for $400,000. The machine's useful life was estimated at six years or 500,000 units of product with a $25,000 trade-in value. During its second year, the machine produced 87,000 units of product. Assuming units-of-production depreciation, calculate the machine's second-year depreciation.

    a. $ 69,600.
    b. $108,750.
    c. $ 65,250.
    d. $116,000.
    e. $ 62,500.

_____ 4. A machine that cost $40,000 and had been depreciated $30,000 was traded in on a new machine of like purpose having an estimated 20-year life and priced at $50,000. If a $13,000 trade-in allowance was received on the old machine, at what amount should the new machine be recorded in the accounts?

    a. $37,000.
    b. $40,000.
    c. $47,000.
    d. $50,000.
    e. $53,000.

Problem II *(continued)*

_____ 5. Book value is:

a. the carrying amount for an item in the accounting records. When applied to a plant asset, it is the cost of the asset minus its accumulated depreciation.
b. that portion of the value of a business due to its expected ability to earn a rate of return greater than in its industry.
c. the portion of a plant asset's cost that will be recovered at the end of its service life through a sale or as a trade-in allowance on a new asset.
d. the expected sales price of an item less any additional costs to sell.
e. the price of an item from which a trade discount, if offered, is deducted to determine the invoice or gross sales price of the item.

_____ 6. A change in a calculated amount to be reported in the financial statements that results from new information or subsequent developments and accordingly from better insight or improved judgment is a(n):

a. betterment.
b. adjusted trial balance.
c. change in an accounting estimate.
d. contra account.
e. capital expenditure.

_____ 7. Depletion is:

a. the process of periodically writing off as an expense a share of the cost of an asset, usually an intangible asset.
b. the expiration of the usefulness of equipment and the related process of allocating the cost of such assets to expense of the periods during which the assets are used.
c. the carrying amount for an item in the accounting records.
d. the amount a wasting asset is reduced through cutting, mining, or pumping.
e. a situation in which, because of new inventions and improvements, an old plant asset can no longer produce its product on a competitive basis.

_____ 8. On January 1, 1990, a machine in the three-year class for tax purposes was purchased for $72,000. The machine had a salvage value of $12,000. What is the 1990 depreciation deduction for tax purposes assuming the MACRS (accelerated) method?

a. $36,000.
b. $24,000.
c. $18,000.
d. $15,000.
e. $12,000.

_____ 9. The process of allocating the cost of a patent to expense over time:

a. is called depletion.
b. is sometimes called depreciation.
c. is usually done by the declining-balance method over 50 years.
d. is seldom limited to less than 40 years.
e. should be accomplished in 17 years or less.

Problem II *(continued)*

_____ 10. The Romeo Company exchanged its used bottle-capping machine for a new machine. The old machine cost $14,000, and the new one had a cash price of $19,000. Romeo had taken $12,000 depreciation on the old machine and was allowed a $500 trade-in allowance. What gain or loss should be recorded on the exchange?

    a. No gain or loss.
    b. $ 500 gain.
    c. $1,500 loss.
    d. $1,500 gain.
    e. $4,500 gain.

_____ 11. A machine that cost $40,000 and had been depreciated $30,000 was traded in on a new machine of like purpose having an estimated 20-year life and priced at $50,000. If a $7,000 trade-in allowance was received on the old machine and the loss was considered immaterial, the new machine is recorded in the accounts by the income tax method at:

    a. $40,000.
    b. $47,000.
    c. $50,000.
    d. $53,000.
    e. some other amount.

_____ 12. On January 1, 1990, a machine in the three-year class for tax purposes was purchased for $72,000. The machine had a salvage value of $12,000. What is the 1990 depreciation deduction for tax purposes assuming a three-year straight-line method?

    a. $24,000.
    b. $20,000.
    c. $18,000.
    d. $12,000.
    e. $10,000.

_____ 13. X-Ray Company sold for $6,000 an x-ray machine that originally cost $10,000. The accumulated depreciation on this machine was $4,000. X-Ray Company's gain (loss) on this sale is:

    a. $ -0- .
    b. $ 2,000 .
    c. $ 4,000 .
    d. $ (6,000).
    e. $ 10,000 .

_____ 14. Cherokee Company had a bulldozer destroyed by fire. The bulldozer originally cost $16,000, but insurance paid only $14,200. Accumulated depreciation on this bulldozer was $2,000. The gain (loss) from the fire is:

    a. $ -0- .
    b. $ 200.
    c. $ (200).
    d. $(14,000).
    e. $(16,000).

Problem III

Many of the important ideas and concepts discussed in Chapter 9 are reflected in the following list of key terms. Test your understanding of these terms by matching the appropriate definitions with the terms. Record the number identifying the most appropriate definition in the blank space next to each term.

_____ Accelerated Cost Recovery System (ACRS)

_____ Accelerated depreciation

_____ Amortize

_____ Balance sheet expenditure

_____ Betterment

_____ Book value

_____ Change in an accounting estimate

_____ Capital expenditure

_____ Copyright

_____ Declining-balance depreciation

_____ Deferred income taxes

_____ Depletion

_____ Extraordinary repairs

_____ Fixed asset

_____ Goodwill

_____ Inadequacy

_____ Income tax rules

_____ Intangible asset

_____ Internal Revenue Code

_____ Land improvements

_____ Lease

_____ Leasehold

_____ Leasehold improvements

_____ Lessee

_____ Lessor

_____ Modified Accelerated Cost Recovery System

_____ Obsolescence

_____ Office Equipment Ledger

_____ Ordinary repairs

_____ Patent

_____ Revenue expenditure

_____ Salvage value

_____ Service life

_____ Store Equipment Ledger

_____ Straight-line depreciation

_____ Sum-of-the-years'-digits depreciation

_____ Trademark

_____ Trade name

_____ Units-of-production depreciation

1. Another name for plant asset, no longer widely in use.

2. The portion of a plant asset's cost that will be recovered at the end of its service life through a sale or as a trade-in allowance on a new asset.

3. The situation in which, because of new inventions and improvements, an old plant asset can no longer produce its product on a competitive basis.

4. A depreciation method that allocates depreciation on a plant asset based on the relation of the units of product produced by the asset during a given period to the total units the asset is expected to produce during its entire life.

5. Assets that improve or increase the value or usefulness of land but which have a limited useful life and are subject to depreciation.

Problem III *(continued)*

6. A depreciation method in which up to twice the straight-line rate of depreciation, without considering salvage value, is applied to the beginning-of-period book value of a plant asset to determine the asset's depreciation charge for the period.

7. A subsidiary ledger that contains a separate record for each item of office equipment owned.

8. A depreciation method that allocates an equal share of the total estimated amount a plant asset will be depreciated during its service life to each accounting period in that life.

9. The codification of the United States federal tax laws.

10. A unique, accelerated depreciation method prescribed in the tax law for assets placed in service after 1980 and before 1987.

11. A depreciation method that allocates depreciation to each year in a plant asset's life on a fractional basis. The denominator of the fractions used is the sum-of-the-years' digits in the estimated service life of the asset, and the numerators are the years' digits in reverse order.

12. The carrying amount for an item in the accounting records. When applied to a plant asset, it is the cost of the asset minus its accumulated depreciation.

13. Any depreciation method that results in greater amounts of depreciation expense in the early years of a plant asset's life and lesser amounts in later years.

14. The period of time a plant asset is used in the production and sale of other assets or services.

15. A subsidiary ledger that contains a separate record for each item of store equipment owned.

16. The situation in which a plant asset does not produce enough product to meet current needs.

17. An exclusive right granted by the federal government to manufacture and sell a machine or mechanical device for a period of years.

18. A modification to an existing plant asset to make it more efficient, usually by replacing part of the asset with an improved or superior part.

19. That portion of the value of a business due to its expected ability to earn a rate of return greater than the average in its industry.

20. An expenditure that benefits future periods because the value or asset obtained by the expenditure does not fully expire by the end of the current period.

21. Improvements to leased property made by the lessee.

22. An asset that has no physical existence but has value due to the rights resulting from its ownership and possession.

23. The individual or enterprise that has given up possession of property under the terms of a lease contract.

24. A change in a calculated amount to be reported in the financial statements that results from new information or subsequent developments and accordingly from better insight or improved judgment.

25. A unique name selected by a company for use in marketing its products or services.

26. An expenditure that benefits only the current period because the value or asset obtained by the expenditure will fully expire before the end of the current accounting period.

27. The amount a wasting asset is reduced through cutting, mining, or pumping.

28. An exclusive right granted by the federal government to publish and sell a musical, literary, or artistic work for a period of years.

29. The rights granted to a lessee under the terms of a lease contract.

30. Repairs made to keep a plant asset in its normal good operating condition.

31. A unique symbol designed by a company for use in marketing its products or services.

32. Amounts of income tax the incurrence of which is delayed or put off until later years due to accelerated depreciation or other cause.

Problem III *(continued)*

33. A contract that grants the right to possess and use property.

34. To periodically write off as an expense a share of the cost of an asset, usually an intangible asset.

35. Another name for capital expenditure.

36. An individual or enterprise that has been given possession of property under the terms of a lease contract.

37. Rules that govern how income for tax purposes and income taxes are to be calculated.

38. Major repairs that extend the life of a plant asset beyond the number of years originally estimated.

39. The system of depreciation specified in the tax law for assets placed in service after 1986.

Problem IV

Complete the following by filling in the blanks.

1. The estimated salvage value of a plant asset is the estimated portion of the asset's _____

_____ that is expected to be recovered at the end of its service life.

2. There are several factors that affect the useful life of some assets. These factors include:

    a) _____ ;

    b) _____ ;

    c) _____ .

3. To be classified as a plant asset, an asset must be _____

    _____ ;

    and it must have _____

    _____

4. Amounts of accumulated depreciation shown on a balance sheet _____ (do, do not) represent funds accumulated to buy new assets when present assets wear out and must be discarded.

5. Recording depreciation _____ (is, is not) a process of recording the decline in the market value of a plant asset.

6. The tax advantage of accelerated depreciation is that _____

    _____ .

7. Balance sheet amounts shown for plant assets may bear little relation to the market values of the

    plant assets because balance sheets show for plant assets _____

    _____ rather than market values.

Problem IV (*continued*)

8. Recording depreciation _____ (is, is not) a process of recording the physical deterioration of a plant asset.

9. The cost of a plant asset includes _____

_____

_____.

10. Trucks held for sale by a dealer and land held for future expansion are not classified as plant assets

because _____

_____.

11. If a company breaks even on its operations, it will eventually recover the cost of its plant assets

through _____

_____.

12. The book value of a plant asset is its "value" as shown by the books and consists of its cost minus

its _____

_____.

13. Since a plant asset contributes to the production or sale of other assets for a period longer than one accounting period, if revenues and expenses are to be matched, the cost of the plant asset's

quantity of usefulness must be _____

_____

_____.

14. The amount of accumulated depreciation deducted on a balance sheet from a plant asset's cost

represents that portion of the cost that has been charged off to _____

_____ during the asset's life.

15. When a business buys a plant asset, it in effect buys a quantity of usefulness that will be consumed during the service life of the asset; and depreciation of the asset, as the phrase is used in

accounting, is nothing more than an expiration of the asset's _____

_____. Furthermore, recording depreciation

on the asset is the process of _____

_____

_____.

Problem V

A machine was purchased for $7,000, terms 2/10, n/60, FOB vendor's factory. The invoice was paid within the discount period along with $175 of freight charges. The machine was installed on a special concrete base by the employees of the company that bought it. The concrete base and special power connections for the machine cost $575, and the wages of the employees during the period in which they installed the machine amounted to $425. The employees accidentally dropped the machine while moving it onto its special base, causing damages to the machine which cost $125 to repair. As a result of all this, the cost of the machine for accounting purposes was

$_____.

Problem VI

A machine cost $8,000 and was estimated to have an eight-year service life and an $800 salvage value. It was further estimated that the machine would produce 40,000 units of product during its life. If the machine produced 9,000 units during its first year, the depreciation charge for the year was:

1. $_____ calculated on a straight-line basis.

2. $_____ calculated by the units-of-production method.

3. $_____ calculated by the declining-balance method at twice the straight-line rate.

4. $_____ calculated by the sum-of-the-years'-digits method.

Problem VII

A machine that cost $45,000 and had been depreciated $20,000 was traded in on a new machine that had a cash price of $35,000. After taking into account the trade-in allowance, the balance was paid in cash. Present a general journal entry to record the trade under each of the following unrelated assumptions:

(a) The trade-in allowance was $28,000.

(b) The trade-in allowance was $24,500. Since the loss was not considered material, the income tax method of recording the transaction should be used.

Problem VII *(continued)*

(c)   The trade-in allowance was $21,000 and the loss was considered to be material.

Problem VIII

In January 1989, a company purchased a heavy, general-purpose truck for $50,000. The truck is expected to last 9 years and have a salvage value of $10,000. For tax purposes, the tractor is in the five-year class of assets, and the company is considering two depreciation alternatives: (a) straight line over five years, or (b) MACRS depreciation. Complete the table by showing the amount of depreciation to be taken each year under each of the alternatives.

Year	Straight-line	MACRS Depreciation for Year	Undepreciated Cost at End of Year—MACRS
1989	_____	_____	_____
1990	_____	_____	_____
1991	_____	_____	_____
1992	_____	_____	_____
1993	_____	_____	_____
1994	_____	_____	_____

Problem IX

Farmer Company paid $208,000 for real estate plus $4,320 in closing costs. The real estate included land appraised at $64,000; land improvements appraised at $25,600; and a building appraised at $166,400. The plan is to use the building as a factory. Prepare a calculation showing the allocation of cost to the assets purchased and present the journal entry to record the purchase.

Solutions for Chapter 9

Problem I

1.	T	9.	T
2.	T	10.	F
3.	F	11.	T
4.	F	12.	T
5.	T	13.	F
6.	F	14.	F
7.	T	15.	F
8.	T	16.	T

Problem II

1.	D	8.	B
2.	A	9.	E
3.	C	10.	C
4.	C	11.	D
5.	A	12.	D
6.	C	13.	A
7.	D	14.	B

Problem III

Accelerated Cost Recovery System (ACRS)	10	Lease	33
Accelerated depreciation	13	Leasehold	29
Amortize	34	Leasehold improvements	21
Balance sheet expenditure	35 or 20	Lessee	36
Betterment	18	Lessor	23
Book value	12	Modified Accelerated Cost Recovery System	39
Change in an accounting estimate	24	Obsolescence	3
Capital expenditure	20	Office Equipment Ledger	7
Copyright	28	Ordinary repairs	30
Declining-balance depreciation	6	Patent	17
Deferred income taxes	32	Revenue expenditure	26
Depletion	27	Salvage value	2
Extraordinary repairs	38	Service life	14
Fixed asset	1	Store Equipment Ledger	15
Goodwill	19	Straight-line depreciation	8
Inadequacy	16	Sum-of-the-years'-digits depreciation	11
Income tax rules	37	Trademark	31
Intangible asset	22	Trade name	25
Internal Revenue Code	9	Units-of-production depreciation	4
Land improvements	5		

Problem IV

1. cost

2. a) wear and tear
   b) inadequacy
   c) obsolescence

3. used in the production or sale of other assets, a useful life longer than one accounting period

4. do not

5. is not

6. it defers the payment of income taxes

7. undepreciated costs

Problem IV *(continued)*

8. is not

9. all normal and reasonable expenditures necessary to get the asset in place and ready for use

10. they are not presently being used to produce or sell other assets

11. the sale of its product

12. accumulated depreciation

13. allocated to the several accounting periods during which it will be used

14. depreciation expense

15. quantity of usefulness, allocating the cost of the asset's quantity of usefulness to the accounting periods that will benefit from its use.

Problem V

$(.98 \times \$7,000) + \$175 + \$575 + \$425 = \$8,035$

Problem VI

1. $(\$8,000 - \$800)/8 = \$900$
2. $[(\$8,000 - \$800)/40,000] \times 9,000 = \$1,620$
3. $\$8,000 \times 25\% = \$2,000$
4. $(\$8,000 - \$800)(8/36) = \$1,600$

Problem VII

(a)	Machinery	32,000.00	
	Accumulated Depreciation, Machinery	20,000.00	
	Cash ($35,000 − $28,000)		7,000.00
	Machinery		45,000.00
(b)	Machinery	35,500.00	
	Accumulated Depreciation, Machinery	20,000.00	
	Cash ($35,000 − $24,500)		10,500.00
	Machinery		45,000.00
(c)	Machinery	35,000.00	
	Accumulated Depreciation, Machinery	20,000.00	
	Loss on Exchange of Machinery	4,000.00	
	Cash ($35,000 − $21,000)		14,000.00
	Machinery		45,000.00

Problem VIII

Year	Straight-line	MACRS Depreciation for Year	Undepreciated Cost at End of Year—MACRS
1989	$ 5,000	.20 × $50,000 = $10,000	$50,000 − $10,000 = $40,000
1990	10,000	.40 × 40,000 = 16,000	40,000 − 16,000 = 24,000
1991	10,000	.40 × 24,000 = 9,600	24,000 − 9,600 = 14,400
1992	10,000	.40 × 14,400 = 5,760	14,400 − 5,760 = 8,640
1993	10,000	($8,640/3) × 2 = 5,760	8,640 − 5,760 = 2,880
1994	5,000	($8,640/3) × 1 = 2,880	2,880 − 2,880 = −0−

Problem IX

	Appraised value	Percent of total	Apportioned cost
Land	$ 64,000	25%	$ 53,080
Land improvements	25,600	10	21,232
Building	166,400	65	138,008
	$256,000	100%	$212,320

Land	53,080.00	
Land Improvements	21,232.00	
Building	138,008.00	
Cash		212,320.00

Current and Long-Term Liabilities

10

Your objectives in studying this chapter should include learning how to:

1. Explain the difference between current and long-term liabilities.

2. Explain the meaning of definite and estimated liabilities.

3. Explain the difference between liabilities and contingent liabilities.

4. Record transactions that involve liabilities such as property taxes payable, product warranties, and short-term notes payable.

5. Calculate the present value of a sum of money that will be received a number of periods in the future or will be received periodically.

6. Prepare entries to account for long-term, noninterest-bearing notes payable and for capital and operating leases.

7. Prepare entries to account for payroll liabilities.

8. Define or explain the words and phrases listed in the chapter Glossary.

Topical Outline

I. Definition and classification of liabilities

   A. Liabilities—obligations resulting from past transactions that require the future payment of assets or the future performance of services.

   B. Current liabilities—debts or other obligations, the liquidation of which is expected to require the use of existing current assets or the creation of other current liabilities; they are due within one year or the current operating cycle of the business, whichever is longer.

   C. Long-term liabilities—obligations that will not require the use of existing current assets because they do not mature within one year or one operating cycle.

   D. Definite liabilities—liabilities may be indefinite with respect to:

      1. Identity of the creditor.

      2. Due date of the debt.

      3. Amount to be paid (in which case the liability is called an estimated liability).

   E. Estimated liabilities—obligations for which the amounts to be paid are uncertain but can be reasonably estimated. Examples are:

      1. Property taxes payable.

      2. Product warranty liabilities.

   F. Contingent liabilities—are not existing obligations and are not recorded as liabilities. They become obligations only if some future, uncertain event actually occurs. Examples are:

      1. Potential legal claims.

      2. Debt guaranties.

II. Short-term notes payable

   A. Examples

      1. Note given to secure a time extension on an account—provides a written promise to pay and specifies a rate of interest that will apply to the debt.

      2. Note given to secure borrowing from a bank

         a. Loan—cash proceeds equal to the face value of the note; the note is a promise to repay the face value of the note plus interest.

         b. Discount—cash proceeds equal to the face value of the note less interest that is deducted in advance; the note is a promise to repay the face value of the note.

   B. End-of-period adjustments

      1. Accrued interest expense on outstanding notes payable should be recorded at the end of the accounting period.

      2. Interest on a discounted note must be allocated to the periods benefited.

III. Present value

   A. The concept: a dollar received in the future is worth less than a dollar received today because the dollar received today can be invested to earn more than a dollar in the future.

B. Present value tables—used instead of a formula to solve present value problems.

   1. "Present value of $1" table used for problem based on single payments.

   2. "Present value of $1 received periodically for a number of periods" table used for problem based on a number of equal payments.

   3. Interest rates are normally expressed in annual amounts.

   4. Discount periods can be any length of time; if less than a year, annual interest rate must be adjusted for the discount period.

IV. Exchanging a note for a plant asset

A. Two elements may or may not be stipulated in the note:

   1. A dollar amount equivalent to the bargained cash price of the asset.

   2. An interest factor to compensate the supplier for the use of the funds that otherwise would have been received in a cash sale.

B. Asset should be recorded at its cash price or at the present value of the note, whichever is more clearly determinable.

C. A discount on notes payable is created if the note does not have a stated interest rate or if the interest rate is unreasonably low. The discount is amortized over the life of the note.

V. Liabilities from leasing

A. Capital lease (or financing lease)—must meet any one of four criteria:

   1. Ownership of the leased asset is transferred to the lessee at the end of the lease period.

   2. The lease gives the lessee the option of purchasing the leased asset at less than fair value at some point during or at the end of the lease period.

   3. The period of the lease is 75 percent or more of the estimated service life of the leased asset.

   4. The present value of the minimum lease payments is 90 percent or more of the fair value of the leased asset.

B. Operating lease—any lease that does not meet any one of the preceding criteria.

C. Accounting for leases

   1. Capital lease—treated as a purchase transaction. The present value of the lease payments constitutes the cost of the asset and is debited to an asset account.

   2. Operating lease—annual rental payments for leased asset, as well as payments for taxes, insurance and repairs, are charged to expense.

VI. Payroll liabilities

A. Federal Insurance Contribution Act (FICA) taxes—also known as social security taxes, are levied on the employer and the employee in equal amounts.

B. Federal income taxes levied on employees must be withheld by employers.

C. Other deductions from wages—charitable contributions, health insurance premiums, union dues.

D. State and federal unemployment taxes are levied on employers.

E. Employee fringe benefit costs are expenses that must be accrued along with other payroll costs.

Problem I

The following statements are either true or false. Place a (T) in the parentheses before each true statement and an (F) before each false statement.

1. ( )   An example of an estimated liability is prepaid property taxes.

2. ( )   Contingent liabilities are generally not recorded in the books as liabilities.

3. ( )   When a borrower records the receipt of a discounted note payable, Interest Expense or Discount on Notes Payable is debited for the amount of interest deducted from the face amount of the note by the lender.

4. ( )   The borrower is required to pay the lender the face amount of the note when a discounted note matures.

5. ( )   The concept of present value is based on the idea that the right to receive $1 a year from now is worth more than $1 today.

6. ( )   Receiving $500 on June 30 and $500 on December 31 has the same present value as receiving $1,000 on December 31.

7. ( )   If a note requires quarterly payments and the borrower could obtain a 12% annual rate of interest in borrowing money, a 3% quarterly interest rate should be used to determine the present value of the note.

8. ( )   A discount on a note payable is a contra liability and also the interest element of the transaction.

9. ( )   The carrying amount of a payable decreases each year by the amount of discount amortized that year.

10. ( )   If a portion of a long-term note payable comes due within 12 months, that portion must be reported on the balance sheet as a current liability.

11. ( )   Depending on the terms of a lease obligation, the lease may or may not be recorded as a liability.

12. ( )   Depreciation expense is recorded on a machine that was obtained under a capital lease.

13. ( )   A capital lease should be recorded on the lease date at the present value of the lease payments.

14. ( )   According to law, a W-2 form showing wages earned and taxes withheld must be given each employee within one month after the year-end.

15. ( )   Federal unemployment taxes are withheld from employees' wages at the rate of 0.6% on the first $45,000 earned.

16. ( )   Social security (FICA) taxes are levied equally on the employee and the employer.

17. ( )   Employee (fringe) benefit costs represent expenses to the employer in addition to the direct costs of salaries and wages.

18. ( )   Each time a payroll is recorded, a General Journal entry should also be made to record the employer's FICA and state and federal unemployment taxes.

19. ( )   Since federal income taxes withheld from an employee's wages are expenses of the employee, not the employer, they should not be treated as liabilities of the employer.

20. ( )   Since Jon Company has very little employee turnover, the company has received a very favorable merit rating. As a result, Jon Company should expect to pay substantially smaller amounts of FICA taxes than normal.

Problem II

You are given several words, phrases or numbers to choose from in completing each of the following statements or in answering the following questions. In each case select the one that best completes the statement or answers the question and place its letter in the answer space provided.

_____ 1. Interest charged and deducted by a bank at the time a loan is made is a(n):

    a. automatic discount.
    b. sales discount.
    c. capital discount.
    d. amortized discount.
    e. bank discount.

_____ 2. During the life of a lease, the carrying amount of the lease is:

    a. the remaining lease liability minus the unamortized discount on the lease financing.
    b. the annual payment under a lease agreement.
    c. the remaining lease liability plus the unamortized discount on the lease financing.
    d. the original amount of the lease liability.
    e. the original amount of the lease liability minus the discount on the lease financing (the present value of the lease on the date of the lease).

_____ 3. Falcon Company has entered a 14-year lease agreement on a new boat that has a fair value of $180,000 and an estimated service life of 20 years. The terms of the lease provide that Falcon Company will make equal payments of $21,750 at the end of each year of the lease, and that upon expiration of the lease the vessel must be returned to the lessor without recourse. The prevailing interest rate is 20%, and the present value of $1 received annually for 14 years, discounted at 10% is 7.3667. The lease is a(n):

    a. present value lease.
    b. capital lease.
    c. discount lease.
    d. operating lease.
    e. None of the above.

_____ 4. On November 1, 1989, Profitable Company borrowed $50,000 by giving a 90-day, 12% note payable. The company has an annual, calendar-year accounting period and does not make reversing entries. What amount should be debited to Interest Expense on January 30, 1990?

    a. $6,000.
    b. $1,500.
    c. $1,000.
    d. $ 500.
    e. $ –0– .

_____ 5. Indigo Company is offered a contract whereby it will be paid $15,000 every six months for the next five years. The first payment will be received six months from today. What will the company be willing to pay for this contract if it expects a 16% annual return on the investment? [Use the appropriate present value table in the chapter in the text.]

    a. $ 49,114.50
    b. $ 72,498.00
    c. $100,651.50
    d. $ 98,229.00
    e. $ 59,890.50

Problem III

Many of the important ideas and concepts that are discussed in Chapter 10 are reflected in the following list of key terms. Test your understanding of these terms by matching the appropriate definitions with the terms. Record the number identifying the most appropriate definition in the blank space next to each term.

_____ Bank discount

_____ Capital lease

_____ Carrying amount of a lease

_____ Carrying amount of a note

_____ Employee fringe benefits

_____ Estimated liability

_____ Federal unemployment tax (FUTA)

_____ FICA taxes

_____ Financing lease

_____ Individual earnings record

_____ Long-term liabilities

_____ Merit rating

_____ Operating lease

_____ Payroll tax

_____ Present value

_____ Present value table

_____ Product warranty

_____ State unemployment tax

1. A lease that does not meet any of the criteria of the FASB that would make it a capital lease.

2. The remaining lease liability minus the unamortized discount on the lease financing.

3. Interest charged and deducted by a bank at the time a loan is made.

4. An obligation that definitely exists but for which the amount to be paid is uncertain.

5. A table that shows the present values of one amount to be received at various future dates when discounted at various interest rates, or that shows the present values of a series of equal payments to be received for a varying number of periods when discounted at various interest rates.

6. Payments by an employer, in addition to wages and salaries, that are made to acquire benefits for employees, such as insurance coverage and retirement income programs.

7. A promise to a customer that obligates the seller or manufacturer for a limited period of time to pay for items such as replacement parts or repair costs if the product breaks or fails to perform.

8. An evaluation of an employer by a state, which reflects the employer's experience in maintaining steady employment for its employees or, alternatively, laying them off from time to time. A good rating reduces the employer's unemployment tax rate.

9. Obligations that will not require the use of existing current assets in their liquidation because they do not mature within one year or one operating cycle, whichever is longer.

10. The face amount of a note minus the unamortized discount on the note.

11. Federal Insurance Contributions Act taxes, otherwise known as social security taxes.

12. A tax levied by a state, the proceeds from which are used to pay benefits to unemployed workers.

Problem III *(continued)*

13. The amount of money that could be currently invested at a given interest rate to accumulate a total value equal to a given amount to be received or paid at some future date.

14. A record of an employee's hours worked, gross pay, deductions, net pay, and certain personal information about the employee.

15. A lease that meets any of four criteria established by the FASB, the implication of which is that the lease has essentially the same economic consequences as if the lessee had secured a loan and purchased the leased asset.

16. A tax levied on employers and based on the amount of a payroll or the amount of each employee's gross pay.

17. Another name for a capital lease.

18. A federal tax levied on employers, the proceeds of which are used primarily to finance administrative expenses of the states' unemployment programs.

Problem IV

Complete the following by filling in the blanks.

1. Use the present value tables in the text to calculate the following present values:

   a. $1 to be received 12 years hence at 10%. $_____

   b. $2,000 to be received 14 years hence, at 8%. $_____

   c. $1 to be received at the end of each year for 20 years, at 14%.

      $_____

   d. $1,000 to be received at the end of each period for 10 periods, at 16%.

      $_____

2. Two important examples of estimated liabilities are:

   (a) _____, and

   (b) _____.

3. If a company discounts its $2,000 note payable at the bank, the cash proceeds of the note which the company receives is (less than, equal to, more than) _____ $2,000.

4. When the rate of interest on an investment is 9% compounded annually, the present value of $1,000 to be received three years hence is the amount of money that must be invested today that together with the 9% compound interest earned on the investment will equal

   $_____ at the end of three years. The amount is

   $1,000 × _____ = _____.

Problem IV *(continued)*

5. When the account Discount on Notes Payable is shown on the balance sheet, does it increase or decrease the carrying amount of Notes Payable? _____

6. Certain leases have essentially the same economic consequences as if the lessee secured a loan and purchased the leased asset. These leases are known as _____

    _____.

7. If the interest rate is changed from 5% to 8%, will the present value of $1 to be received in one year be increased or decreased? _____

8. Long-term liabilities are obligations that will not require the use of _____

    _____ in their liquidation.

Problem V

A company prepares monthly financial statements and estimates property taxes based on last year's tax rate. The assessed valuation of property owned by the company is $120,000. Last year's tax levy was $0.80 per $100.

(a) Present a general journal entry to record the property tax for January.

DATE	ACCOUNT TITLES AND EXPLANATION	P.R.	DEBIT	CREDIT

(b) In August the current year's levy is determined to be $1.00. Present the general journal entry to pay the annual tax at the end of August and to record the expense for August.

DATE	ACCOUNT TITLES AND EXPLANATION	P.R.	DEBIT	CREDIT

Problem VI

Glitz Company estimates that future costs to satisfy its product warranty obligation amount to 3% of sales. In January, the company sold merchandise for $50,000 cash and paid $1,200 to repair products returned for warranty work. Present general journal entries to record these transactions.

DATE		ACCOUNT TITLES AND EXPLANATION	P.R.	DEBIT	CREDIT

Problem VII

A company whose accounting periods end each December 31 discounted its own $10,000, noninterest-bearing note at its bank for 60 days at 12% on December 16, 1990. Complete the following entries involving this note.

DATE		ACCOUNT TITLES AND EXPLANATION	P.R.	DEBIT	CREDIT
1990					
Dec.	16				
		Discounted a note.			
	31				
		To record interest expense on			
		discounted note.			
1991					
Feb.	14				
		To pay note.			
	14				
		To record interest on discounted note.			

Problem VIII

Assume that on January 2, 1990, a day on which the prevailing interest rate was 12%, a company exchanged a $15,000, five-year, noninterest-bearing note payable for a machine, the cash price of which was not readily determinable.

1. The present value of the note on the day of exchange and the amount at which the machine should be recorded is calculated:

   $15,000 × _____ = $_____.

2. The entry to record the exchange is:

DATE	ACCOUNT TITLES AND EXPLANATION	P.R.	DEBIT	CREDIT

3. The amount of discount to be amortized at the end of the first year in the five-year life of the note is calculated:

   $_____ × 12% = $_____.

4. The discount amortization entry at the end of the first year is:

DATE	ACCOUNT TITLES AND EXPLANATION	P.R.	DEBIT	CREDIT

5. The note should appear on the company's balance sheet at the end of its first year as follows:

Problem IX

On December 31, 1989, Nord Company signed a 10-year lease agreement under which it promised to pay $30,000 per year in return for the use of some equipment. Assume the lease should be classified as a capital lease, and an interest rate of 12% is reasonable.

1. Prepare a general journal entry to record the lease.

DATE		ACCOUNT TITLES AND EXPLANATION	P.R.	DEBIT	CREDIT

2. Prepare a general journal entry to record the first $30,000 lease payment on December 31, 1990.

DATE		ACCOUNT TITLES AND EXPLANATION	P.R.	DEBIT	CREDIT

3. Prepare a general journal entry to record depreciation expense on December 31, 1990. Use straight-line depreciation and no salvage value.

DATE		ACCOUNT TITLES AND EXPLANATION	P.R.	DEBIT	CREDIT

4. Prepare a general journal entry to amortize the discount on lease financing for 1990.

DATE		ACCOUNT TITLES AND EXPLANATION	P.R.	DEBIT	CREDIT

Problem X

The following information as to earnings and deductions for the pay period ended November 15 was taken from a company's payroll records:

Employee's Name	Earnings to End of Previous Week	Gross Pay This Week	Federal Income Taxes	Hospital Insurance Deducted
Rita Hawn	$25,700	$ 800	$155.00	$ 35.50
Dolores Hopkins	930	800	134.00	35.50
Robert Allen	44,900	1,000	193.00	42.00
Calvin Ingram	18,400	740	128.00	42.00
		$3,340	$610.00	$155.00

Required:

1. Calculate the employees' FICA taxes withheld at an assumed 7.5% rate on the first $45,000 paid each employee, and prepare a general journal entry to accrue the payroll under the assumption that all of the employees work in the office.

2. Prepare a general journal entry to record the employer's payroll taxes resulting from the payroll. Assume a state unemployment tax rate of 2% on the first $7,000 paid each employee and a federal unemployment tax rate of 0.8% on the first $7,000 paid each employee.

DATE	ACCOUNT TITLES AND EXPLANATION	P.R.	DEBIT	CREDIT

Solutions for Chapter 10

Problem I

1.	F	11.	T
2.	T	12.	T
3.	T	13.	T
4.	T	14.	T
5.	F	15.	F
6.	F	16.	T
7.	T	17.	T
8.	T	18.	T
9.	F	19.	F
10.	T	20.	F

Problem II

1. E
2. A
3. D
4. D
5. C

Problem III

Bank discount	3
Capital lease	15
Carrying amount of a lease	2
Carrying amount of a note	10
Employee fringe benefits	6
Estimated liability	4
Federal unemployment tax (FUTA)	18
FICA taxes	11
Financing lease	17
Individual earnings record	14
Long-term liabilities	9
Merit rating	8
Operating lease	1
Payroll tax	16
Present value	13
Present value table	5
Product warranty	7
State unemployment tax	12

Problem IV

1. a. $0.3186
   b. $2,000 × 0.3405 = $681
   c. $6.6231
   d. $1,000 × 4.8332 = $4,833.20

2. a. property taxes
   b. product warranties

3. less than

4. $1,000, $1,000 × 0.7722 = $772.20

5. decrease

6. capital leases (or financing leases)

7. decreased

8. existing current assets

Problem V

(a)

Jan. 31 Property Taxes Expense 80.00
       Estimated Property Taxes Payable 80.00
       [($120,000/$100) × $0.80]/12 = $80

(b)

Aug. 31 Property Taxes Expense 240.00
       Prepaid Property Taxes (Sept.-Dec.) 400.00
       Estimated Property Taxes Payable (7 × $80) 560.00
       Cash 1,200.00
       ($120,000/$100) × $1.00 = $1,200
       ($1,200/12) × 4 = $400

Problem VI

Jan. — Cash 50,000.00
       Sales 50,000.00

     — Warranty Expense ($50,000 × .03) 1,500.00
       Estimated Warranty Liability 1,500.00

     — Estimated Warranty Liability 1,200.00
       Cash 1,200.00

Problem VII

1990

Dec. 16 Cash 9,800.00
       Discount on Notes Payable 200.00
       Notes Payable 10,000.00

    31 Interest Expense 50.00
       Discount on Notes Payable 50.00

1991

Feb. 14 Notes Payable 10,000.00
       Cash 10,000.00

    14 Interest Expense 150.00
       Discount on Notes Payable 150.00

Problem VIII

1. $15,000 \times 0.5674 = $8,511$

2. Jan. 2   Machinery 8,511.00
              Discount on Notes Payable 6,489.00
                  Long-Term Notes Payable 15,000.00

3. $8,511 \times 12\% = $1,021.32$

4. Dec. 31   Interest Expense 1,021.32
                  Discount on Notes Payable 1,021.32

5. Long-term liabilities:
        Long-term notes payable $15,000.00
        Less unamortized discount based on the 12% interest rate
        prevailing on the date of issue .... <u>5,467.68*</u> $ 9,532.32

    *$6,489.00 - $1,021.32 = $5,467.68$

Problem IX

1.   1989
        Dec. 31   Equipment 169,506.00
                  Discount on Lease Financing 130,494.00
                      Long-Term Lease Liability 300,000.00
                      ($30,000 \times 5.6502 = $169,506$)

2.   1990
        Dec. 31   Long-Term Lease Liability 30,000.00
                      Cash 30,000.00

3.   31   Depreciation Expense, Equipment 16,950.60
                      Accumulated Depr., Equipment 16,950.60
                      ($169,506/10 = $16,950.60$)

4.   31   Interest Expense 20,340.72
                      Discount on Lease Financing 20,340.72
                      ($169,506 \times 12\% = $20,340.72$)

Problem X

Nov.	15	Office Salaries Expense	3,340.00	
		FICA Taxes Payable		183.00
		Employees' Federal Income Taxes Payable		610.00
		Employees' Hospital Insurance Payable		155.00
		Accrued Payroll Payable		2,392.00

($800 + $800 + $100 + $740)(.075) = $183.00

	15	Payroll Taxes Expense	205.40	
		FICA Taxes Payable		183.00
		State Unemployment Taxes Payable		16.00
		Federal Unemployment Taxes Payable		6.40

$800 × .02 = $16
$800 × .008 = $6.40

11 Installment Notes Payable and Bonds

Your objectives in studying this chapter should include learning how to:

1. Calculate and record the payments on an installment note payable.

2. Describe the various characteristics of differing bond issues and prepare entries to record bonds that are issued between interest dates.

3. Calculate the price of a bond issue that sells at a discount, and prepare entries to account for bonds issued at a discount.

4. Prepare entries to account for bonds issued at a premium.

5. Explain the purpose and operation of a bond sinking fund and prepare entries for sinking fund operations and for the retirement of bonds.

6. Describe the procedures used to account for investments in bonds.

7. Define or explain the words and phrases listed in the chapter Glossary.

Topical Outline

I. Installment notes payable

    A. Borrower pays back debt by making a series of periodic payments, either in the form of:

        1. Equal payments, where interest and principal amounts vary, and total amount of payment stays the same, or

        2. Payments that vary in total amount and consist of accrued interest to date plus equal amounts of principal.

    B. Difference between notes payable and bonds

        1. Usually a single creditor (e.g., a bank) is involved when a business or individual borrows by signing a note payable.

        2. A bond issue generally includes a large number of bonds sold to many different lenders. Bonds may be owned by a number of people before they mature.

II. Bonds

    A. Difference between stocks and bonds

        1. A share of stock represents an equity or ownership right in a corporation. (Stockholders are owners.)

        2. A bond represents a debt or liability of the corporation issuing the bond. (Bondholders are creditors.)

    B. Reasons for issuing bonds

        1. Issuance of bonds instead of stock often results in increased earnings for common stockholders.

        2. Bond interest must be paid whether or not there are earnings, but interest payments are expenses and are tax-deductible.

    C. Rights of bondholders

        1. To receive periodic interest payments.

        2. To receive the face value of the bond when it matures.

    D. Types of bonds

        1. Serial bonds—an issue of bonds with varying maturity dates, so that the entire bond issue is repaid in installments over a period of years.

        2. Sinking fund bonds—paid at maturity from a special fund created for that purpose.

        3. Registered bonds—ownership is recorded with the issuing corporation.

        4. Coupon bonds—have interest coupons that must be presented to receive interest payments.

        5. Debentures—unsecured bonds.

    E. Issuing bonds

        1. Issuing corporation sells bonds to an investment firm (the underwriter), which resells bonds to the public.

        2. Bond indenture—written, legal document that states the rights and obligations of the issuing company and the bondholders.

3. A trustee (usually a bank or trust company) oversees the fulfillment of contract obligation to the bondholders.

4. Contract rate of bond interest—rate of interest applied to the par value (face amount) of bonds to determine annual cash payment to bondholders.

5. Market rate of bond interest—interest rate that a corporation is willing to pay and investors are willing to take for use of their money to buy that corporation's bonds.

    a. Bond discount—the bond will sell for an amount less than face value if the market rate of bond interest is greater than the contract rate of bond interest.
    b. Bond premium—the bond will sell for an amount greater than face value if the market rate of bond interest is less than the contract rate of bond interest.

6. Bonds sold between interest dates—interest that has accrued on the bonds since the previous interest payment date is customarily charged and collected from purchasers.

F. Accounting for bonds after issuance

1. Bond discount or bond premium must be amortized.

    a. Straight-line method—equal portion of the discount or premium is amortized each period.
    b. Interest method—amount of discount or premium amortized changes each period.

2. End-of-accounting-period adjustments for accrued interest must be made.

G. Additional features of bonds

1. Callable bonds—may be redeemed at the issuing corporation's option, usually upon the payment of a redemption premium. (Not all bonds have this provision.)

2. Bond sinking fund—to provide investors with greater security, a corporation may agree to make periodic cash deposits with a sinking fund trustee. Fund is used to pay bondholders when the bonds become due.

H. Investments in bonds

1. Purchasers of bonds may not hold them to maturity, but may sell them to other investors.

2. Purchasers record bonds at cost, including any brokerage fees.

3. Any discount or premium on bonds held as long-term investments should be amortized using procedures similar to those for bonds payable.

4. A bond investment is shown as a current asset at cost (with no discount or premium amortization) only if the bonds are held as short-term, temporary investments.

III. Mortgages

A. Bonds or notes payable are either secured or unsecured.

B. Many notes payable and bond issues are secured by a mortgage.

C. Mortgage—the legal agreement that helps protect a lender by giving the lender the right to be paid from the cash proceeds from the sale of the borrower's mortgaged assets, if the borrower fails to make payments required by a note payable or bond indenture.

D. Terms of mortgage are written in a separate legal document—a mortgage contract—which normally grants the lender (the mortgage holder) the right to foreclose if the borrower fails to pay.

Problem I

The following statements are either true or false. Place a (T) in the parentheses before each true statement and an (F) before each false statement.

1. ( ) Interest expense on installment notes is calculated each period as the interest rate multiplied by the beginning-of-period principal balance.

2. ( ) Bondholders do not share in either management or earnings of the issuing corporation.

3. ( ) Bondholders are creditors of the issuing corporation.

4. ( ) If bonds are sold at par value, the entry to record the sale has a debit to Cash and a credit to Bonds Payable.

5. ( ) Investors will be willing to pay more than par (buy at a premium) for bonds when the market rate of interest is higher than the contract rate of interest.

6. ( ) To determine the price of bonds, the present value of the future cash flows is calculated by discounting the amounts to be received in the future at the contract rate of interest.

7. ( ) If the market rate of interest is 12%, it is 4% semiannually.

8. ( ) The straight-line method of amortizing bond premium allocates an equal portion of the premium to each interest period.

9. ( ) To calculate the amount of interest expense each period using the interest method, the beginning-of-period carrying amount of the bonds must be multiplied by the market rate of interest at the time the bonds were issued.

10. ( ) When the straight-line method is used to amortize bond premium or bond discount, interest expense as a percentage of carrying amount is the same each period the bonds are outstanding.

11. ( ) Callable bonds are bonds that can be redeemed at the option of the investor.

12. ( ) Sinking fund earnings are revenues.

Problem II

You are given several words, phrases or numbers to choose from in completing each of the following statements or in answering the following questions. In each case select the one that best completes the statement or answers the question and place its letter in the answer space provided.

_____ 1. A legal document that states the rights of the lender and the obligations of the borrower with respect to assets that are pledged as security for a bond or note payable is a:

    a. registered bond.
    b. bond certificate.
    c. bond indenture.
    d. mortgage contract.
    e. debenture.

Problem II *(continued)*

_____ 2. How is the interest expense for each period calculated when the interest method is used to amortize bond discount?

    a. The par value of the bonds is multiplied by the contract rate of bond interest.

    b. The par value of the bonds is multiplied by the market rate of bond interest which applied to the bonds at the time the bonds were issued.

    c. The beginning-of-period carrying amount of the bonds is multiplied by the market rate of bond interest which applied to the bonds at the time the bonds were issued.

    d. The beginning-of-period carrying amount of the bonds is multiplied by the contract rate of bond interest.

    e. The total amount of discount at the time of issue is divided by the number of periods to maturity and added to the cash payment of interest.

_____ 3. On June 30, 1990, the DEF Corporation sold bonds with a face value of $100,000. The contract rate of bond interest was 9% with interest payments on December 31 and June 30. The bonds mature in 10 years. When the bonds were sold, the market rate of bond interest was 12%. How much money did the DEF Corporation receive when it sold the bonds? (Use the present value tables in Chapter 10 of the text and round amounts to the nearest whole dollar.)

    a. $119,252.

    b. $110,042.

    c. $100,000.

    d. $ 82,795.

    e. $ 83,052.

_____ 4. What is the entry to record the payment of interest on December 31, 1990, for DEF Corporation in question number 3? DEF uses the interest method of amortizing bond discount or premium.

a.	Interest Expense	4,500.00	
	Cash		4,500.00
b.	Interest Expense	4,968.00	
	Cash		4,500.00
	Discount on Bonds Payable		468.00
c.	Interest Expense	6,000.00	
	Cash		6,000.00
d.	Interest Expense	4,500.00	
	Premium on Bonds Payable	1,500.00	
	Cash		6,000.00
e.	Interest Expense	4,500.00	
	Cash		4,230.00
	Discount on Bonds Payable		270.00

_____ 5. Commonly used payment patterns on installment notes include:

    a. installment payments consisting of equal amounts of interest and equal amounts of principal.

    b. installment payments of accrued interest plus equal amounts of principal.

    c. installment payments that are equal in total amount and consist of changing amounts of interest and principal.

    d. a and c.

    e. b and c.

Problem II *(continued)*

_____ 6. A callable bond is:

      a. a bond that is not registered and is made payable to whoever holds the bond.

      b. a bond for which the name and address of the owner are recorded with the issuing corporation.

      c. an issue of bonds that mature at different points in time so that the entire bond issue is repaid gradually over a period of years.

      d. a bond that requires the issuing corporation to make deposits to a separate fund of assets during the life of the bonds for the purpose of repaying the bondholders at maturity.

      e. a bond that may be redeemed or repaid before its maturity date at the option of the issuing corporation.

Problem III

Many of the important ideas and concepts discussed in Chapter 11 are reflected in the following list of key terms. Test your understanding of these terms by matching the appropriate definitions with the terms. Record the number identifying the most appropriate definition in the blank space next to each term.

_____ Bearer bond

_____ Bond

_____ Bond indenture

_____ Bond sinking fund

_____ Callable bond

_____ Carrying amount of bonds payable

_____ Contract rate of bond interest

_____ Coupon bond

_____ Debenture

_____ Discount on bonds payable

_____ Face amount of a bond

_____ Interest method of amortizing bond discount or premium

_____ Installment notes

_____ Market rate for bond interest

_____ Mortgage

_____ Mortgage contract

_____ Par value of a bond

_____ Premium on bonds payable

_____ Registered bond

_____ Serial bonds

_____ Sinking fund bonds

_____ Straight-line method of amortizing bond discount or premium

1. The contract between the issuing corporation and the bondholders that states the rights and obligations of both parties.

2. The difference between the par value of a bond and the price at which it is issued when issued at a price below par.

3. The interest rate that a corporation is willing to pay and investors are willing to take for the use of their money to buy that corporation's bonds.

4. A method that calculates interest expense by multiplying the beginning-of-period carrying value of the bonds by the market rate of interest at the date of issuance and then subtracts the cash payment of interest from interest expense to determine the periodic amortization of discount or premium.

5. A legal document that states the rights of the lender and the obligations of the borrower with respect to assets that are pledged as security for a bond or note payable.

Problem III *(continued)*

6. A bond that is not registered and is made payable to whoever holds the bond (the bearer).

7. The par value of bonds payable less any unamortized discount or plus any unamortized premium.

8. A legal agreement that helps protect a lender by giving the lender the right to be paid from the cash proceeds from the sale of specified assets that belong to the borrower.

9. The difference between the par value of a bond and the price at which it is issued when issued at a price above par.

10. Bonds that require the issuing corporation to make deposits to a separate fund of assets during the life of the bonds for the purpose of repaying the bondholders at maturity.

11. An issue of bonds that mature at different points in time so that the entire bond issue is repaid gradually over a period of years.

12. A bond that is issued with interest coupons attached to the bond certificate, so that as each interest payment date approaches, the bondholder detaches a coupon and submits it to the issuing corporation as a demand for payment.

13. A bond that may be redeemed or repaid before its maturity date at the option of the issuing corporation.

14. A rate of interest specified in the bond indenture as the rate that is applied to the par value of the bonds to determine the annual amount of cash payments to the bondholders.

15. The face amount of the bond, which is the amount the borrower agrees to repay at maturity and the amount on which interest payments are based.

16. An unsecured bond.

17. The bond's par value.

18. A method that allocates to each accounting period an equal amount of discount or premium.

19. Promissory notes that require a series of payments which consist of interest plus a portion of the original amount borrowed.

20. A bond for which the name and address of the owner are recorded with the issuing corporation.

21. A long-term liability of a corporation or governmental unit, usually issued in denominations of $1,000, that requires periodic payments of interest and final payment of par value when it matures.

22. A separate pool of assets that is established by deposits from the issuing corporation of a bond issue and from earnings on investments of the assets, and which is established for the purpose of providing the cash to repay the bondholders when the bonds mature.

Problem IV

Complete the following by filling in the blanks.

1. A bond sinking fund offers a measure of security to bondholders, since it is a fund of assets

accumulated to _____

_____.

Problem IV *(continued)*

2. Two important rights given to the owner of a bond are:

   a) _____

   _____, and

   b) _____

   _____.

3. A bond sinking fund would normally be shown in the section of the balance sheet entitled

   _____.

4. Often a corporation cannot obtain debt financing without providing security to the creditors by the

   issuance of a _____.

5. An advantage of securing capital through the sale of bonds as opposed to securing it through the

   sale of stock is that bondholders do not share in either _____

   _____ or _____.

6. When marketable bonds are purchased as a temporary investment, the bond investment appears on

   the balance sheet as a _____.

7. The rate of interest a corporation agrees to pay on a bond issue is called the _____

   _____ rate. This rate is applied to the _____
   value of the bonds to determine the amount of interest that must be paid.

8. In the interest of the bondholders and as protection for the issuing corporation's financial position,

   a _____ may restrict the
   dividends a corporation may pay while its bonds are outstanding.

9. A disadvantage of securing capital through the sale of bonds is that the bondholders are

   _____ and must be paid whether or not there are earnings.

10. If a corporation offers to sell a bond issue on which the contract rate of interest is below the market

    rate, the bonds will sell at a _____; and if it offers to
    sell bonds on which the contract rate is above the market rate, the bonds will sell at a

    _____.

11. A $1,000 bond with a contract rate of bond interest of 9% would provide semiannual interest

    payments of $_____.

12. Bonds that may be redeemed at the issuing company's option are known as _____

    _____ bonds.

Problem IV (continued)

13. When a corporation sells bonds between interest dates, it collects accrued interest from the purchasers. As a result the corporation does not have to keep a record of the purchasers and the

_____ on which they bought bonds, for it can pay a full period's interest to all purchasers for the period in which they bought bonds, and every purchaser receives the amount of

interest he has _____ and gets back the accrued interest paid at the time of purchase.

14. The accounting procedure for dividing a discount and charging a fair share to each period in the

life of the applicable bond issue is called _____

_____ .

15. The terms of installment notes payable require one of two payment plans:

a) _____

_____ , or

b) _____

_____ .

Problem V

On May 1, 1990, JJR Corporation purchased 125 $1,000, 9%, 10-year bonds dated December 31, 1989, at a price of 95 plus a $500 brokerage fee and accrued interest from LLB Co. as a short-term investment.

Make the journal entries to record the purchase of the bonds and to record the receipt of interest on June 30, 1990 (assuming interest is paid semiannually on June 30 and December 31).

DATE		ACCOUNT TITLES AND EXPLANATION	P.R.	DEBIT	CREDIT
1990 May	1				
		Purchased 125 $1,000, 9%, ten-year bonds			
		dated December 31, 1989, at a price of 95			
		plus a $500 brokerage fee and accrued			
		interest.			
June	30				
		To record receipt of interest on bonds			
		purchased May 1 from LLB Co.			

Problem VI

On December 15, 1989, Candida Corporation deposited a bond indenture with the trustee of its bondholders authorizing it to issue $1,000,000 of 10.2%, 20-year bonds dated January 1, 1990, and upon which interest is payable each June 30 and December 31. The bonds were issued at par plus accrued interest on February 1, 1990.

1. Complete the 1990 entries for this bond issue.

DATE		ACCOUNT TITLES AND EXPLANATION	P.R.	DEBIT	CREDIT
1990 Feb.	1				
		Sold $1,000,000 of 10.2%, 20-year bonds at			
		par plus one month's accrued interest.			
June	30				
		Paid the semiannual interest on the bonds.			
Dec.	31				
		Paid the semiannual interest on the bonds.			

2. Post to the T-account below the portions of the above entries that affect bond interest expense and then complete the statement that follows.

Bond Interest Expense

Candida Corporation's 1990 income statement should show $_____ of bond interest expense and its 1991 income statement should show $_____ of bond interest expense.

Problem VII

On January 1, 1990, a day on which the market rate of interest for Bullock Company's bonds was 10%, Bullock Company sold bonds having a $100,000 par value, a 5-year life, and on which interest was to be paid semiannually at a 9% annual rate.

1. The buyer of these bonds received two rights:

    (a) the right to receive $_____ in interest at the end of each six-month interest period throughout the five-year life of the bond issue, and

    (b) the right to receive $_____ at the end of the bond issue's life.

2. To determine the present value of the rights received and to determine the price to pay for the

    rights, the buyer of the bonds should discount the rights at the _____% (semiannual) market rate for bond interest prevailing on the day of the purchase.

3. The calculations for determining the present value of the bond buyer's two rights, using the tables in Chapter 10 in the text are:

    Present value of $100,000 to be received _____ periods hence,

    discounted at _____% per period ($100,000 x

    _____) .... $_____

    Present value of $_____ to be received periodically for

    _____ periods, discounted at _____% ($_____

    × _____) .... _____

    Price to pay for the bonds .... $_____

4. Bullock Corporation's entry to record the sale of the bonds at their present value is:

DATE	ACCOUNT TITLES AND EXPLANATION	P.R.	DEBIT	CREDIT
1990 Jan. 1				
	Sold bonds at a discount.			

Problem VII (*continued*)

5. At the end of the first semiannual interest period Bullock Corporation calculated the number of dollars of interest to be paid its bondholders as follows:

    $_____ × _____\% = \$_____

6. The company then began its calculation of the amount of interest expense to be recorded for the first semiannual interest period and the amount of discount to be amortized by first determining the beginning-of-the-period carrying amount for the bonds with this calculation:

    $_____ − \$_____ = \$_____

7. Using the interest method, the company then calculated the amount of interest expense to be recorded at the end of the first semiannual interest period as follows:

    $_____ × _____\% = \$_____

8. Next, the company determined the amount of discount to be amortized with this calculation:

    $_____ − \$_____ = \$_____

9. After making these calculations, Bullock Corporation recorded the interest paid its bondholders and the discount amortized with this entry:

DATE		ACCOUNT TITLES AND EXPLANATION	P.R.	DEBIT	CREDIT
1990 June	30				
		Paid the semiannual interest on the bonds			
		and amortized a portion of the discount.			

Problem VIII

On December 31, 1989, HX Company borrowed $60,000 by signing a 14% installment note that is to be repaid with six annual payments, the first of which is due on December 31, 1990.

a) Prepare a general journal entry to record the borrowing of the money.

DATE		ACCOUNT TITLES AND EXPLANATION	P.R.	DEBIT	CREDIT

Problem VIII (continued)

b) Assume that the payments are to consist of accrued interest plus equal amounts of principal. Prepare general journal entries to record the first and second installment payments.

DATE		ACCOUNT TITLES AND EXPLANATION	P.R.	DEBIT	CREDIT

c) Contrary to the assumption in (b) above, assume now that the note requires each installment payment to be $15,464. Prepare general journal entries to record the first and second installment payments. (Round all amounts to the nearest whole dollar.)

DATE		ACCOUNT TITLES AND EXPLANATION	P.R.	DEBIT	CREDIT

Solutions for Chapter 11

Problem I

1. T	7. F
2. T	8. T
3. T	9. T
4. T	10. F
5. F	11. F
6. F	12. T

Problem II

1. D
2. C
3. D
4. B
5. E
6. E

Problem III

Bearer bond	6
Bond	21
Bond indenture	1
Bond sinking fund	22
Callable bond	13
Carrying amount of bonds payable	7
Contract rate of bond interest	14
Coupon bond	12
Debenture	16
Discount on bonds payable	2
Face amount of a bond	17 or 15
Interest method of amortizing bond discount or premium	4
Installment notes	19
Market rate for bond interest	3
Mortgage	8
Mortgage contract	5
Par value of a bond	15
Premium on bonds payable	9
Registered bond	20
Serial bonds	11
Sinking fund bonds	10
Straight-line method of amortizing bond discount or premium	18

Problem IV

1. repay the bondholders at maturity
2. a) the right to receive periodic interest payments
   b) the right to receive the face amount of the bond when it matures
3. long-term investments
4. mortgage
5. management, earnings
6. current asset
7. contract, par
8. bond indenture
9. creditors
10. discount, premium
11. $45
12. callable
13. dates, earned

Problem IV *(continued)*

14. amortizing a discount

15. a) payments of accrued interest plus equal amounts of principal
    b) payments that are equal in total amount, consisting of changing amounts of interest and principal

Problem V

1990

May 1	Investment in LLB Co. Bonds	119,250.00	
	Bond Interest Receivable	3,750.00	
	Cash		123,000.00
	(125 × $1,000 × 95%) + $500 = $119,250		
	$125,000 × 4.5% × 4/6 = $3,750		
June 30	Cash	5,625.00	
	Bond Interest Receivable		3,750.00
	Bond Interest Earned		1,875.00
	$125,000 × 4.5% = $5,625		

Problem VI

1.

Feb. 1	Cash	1,008,500.00	
	Bond Interest Expense		8,500.00
	Bonds Payable		1,000,000.00
	($1,000,000 × .102)/12 = $8,500		
June 30	Bond Interest Expense	51,000.00	
	Cash		51,000.00
	($1,000,000 × .102)/2 = $51,000		
Dec. 31	Bond Interest Expense	51,000.00	
	Cash		51,000.00

2.

Bond Interest Expense

June 30	51,000.00	Feb. 1	8,500.00
Dec. 31	51,000.00		

$93,500, $102,000

Problem VII

1. (a) $4,500, (b) $100,000

2. 5

Problem VII *(continued)*

3. Present value of $100,000 to be received 10 periods hence, discounted at 5%
    per period ($100,000 × .6139) $61,390
    Present value of $4,500 to be received periodically for 10 periods, discounted
    at 5% ($4,500 × 7.7217) 34,748*
    Price to pay for the bonds $96,138*

    *rounded to the nearest whole dollar

4. Jan.   1 Cash 96,138.00
                Discount on Bonds Payable 3,862.00
                    Bonds Payable 100,000.00

5. $100,000 × 0.045 = $4,500

6. $100,000 − $3,862 = $96,138

7. $96,138 × 0.05 = $4,807 (rounded to the nearest whole dollar)

8. $4,807 − $4,500 = $307

9. June 30 Interest Expense 4,807.00
                Discount on Bonds Payable 307.00
                Cash 4,500.00

Problem VIII

a)   1989
     Dec. 31 Cash 60,000.00
                 Notes Payable 60,000.00

b)   1990
     Dec. 31 Interest Expense ($60,000 × .14) 8,400.00
                 Notes Payable 10,000.00
                 Cash 18,400.00

     1991
     Dec. 31 Interest Expense ($50,000 × .14) 7,000.00
                 Notes Payable 10,000.00
                 Cash 17,000.00

c)   1990
     Dec. 31 Interest Expense ($60,000 × .14) 8,400.00
                 Notes Payable 7,064.00
                 Cash 15,464.00

     1991
     Dec. 31 Interest Expense ($60,000 − $7,064) × .14 .... 7,411.00
                 Notes Payable 8,053.00
                 Cash 15,464.00

12 Partnerships and Corporations

Your objectives in studying this chapter should include learning how to:

1. Explain mutual agency and unlimited liability, record investments in a partnership, and allocate the net incomes or net losses of a partnership to the partners.

2. Explain the advantages, disadvantages, and organization of corporations, explain the concept of minimum legal capital, and record the issuance of par value stock and no-par stock.

3. Record transactions that involve stock subscriptions and explain the effects of subscribed stock on corporation assets and stockholders' equity.

4. State the differences between common and preferred stocks, and allocate dividends between the common and preferred stocks of a corporation.

5. Explain convertible preferred stock and convertible bonds and record their conversions into common stock.

6. Describe the meaning and significance of the par, redemption, book, and market values of corporate stock.

7. Define or explain the words and phrases listed in the chapter Glossary.

Topical Outline

I.   Partnerships

     A.   Primary advantage—the ease with which a partnership is formed.

     B.   Important characteristics:

         1.   Mutual agency—each partner may bind the partnership to contracts within the normal scope of business.

         2.   Unlimited liability—each partner is responsible for payment of all the debts of the partnership if the other partners are unable to pay their shares.

     C.   Partnership accounting

         1.   Equity accounts

             a.   Capital account for each partner.
             b.   Withdrawals account for each partner.

         2.   Measurement and division of earnings

             a.   Partners have no legal right to salary, so there is no salary *expense* for partners.
             b.   In the absence of an agreement, partnership earnings and losses are shared equally among the partners.
             c.   Partners can agree to salary and interest *allowances* when distributing profits to reward unequal contribution of services or capital.

II.   Corporations

     A.   Advantages:

         1.   Separate legal entity—a corporation, through its agents, may conduct business affairs with the same rights, duties, and responsibilities as a person.

         2.   Lack of stockholders' liability.

         3.   Ease of transferring ownership rights.

         4.   Continuity of life—a perpetual life is possible for a successful corporation.

         5.   No mutual agency—an individual, acting as a stockholder, cannot bind the corporation to contracts.

         6.   Ease of capital assembly—the advantages of the corporate form make it easier for a corporation to raise large amounts of capital.

     B.   Disadvantages:

         1.   Increased governmental regulation.

         2.   Taxation—corporate income is taxed; and when income is distributed to shareholders as dividends, it is taxed a second time.

     C.   Organization costs—normally debited to an asset account and amortized over a period not to exceed 40 years.

D. Common stock

1. Corporations may issue no more stock than is authorized by its charter.

2. Par value—an arbitrary value placed on a share of stock which in many states establishes a minimum legal capital.

3. Premium on stock—the amount of capital contributed by stockholders above the stock's par value.

4. Discount on stock—the difference between the par value of stock and the amount below par value contributed by stockholders. Stock is seldom issued at a discount, since the discount could create a contingent liability for the shareholders.

5. Stated value—an amount that is credited to the no-par stock account at the time the stock is issued.

6. Subscriptions—in some instances, stock can be purchased on an installment basis.

7. Rights of common stockholders:

   a. The right to vote in stockholders' meetings.
   b. The right to sell or otherwise dispose of their stock.
   c. The right (known as the preemptive right) of first opportunity to purchase any additional shares of common stock issued by the corporation.
   d. The right to share pro rata with other common stockholders in any dividends distributed to common stockholders.
   e. The right to share in any assets remaining after creditors are paid if the corporation is liquidated.

E. Preferred stock

1. Preferred stock—so called because of preferences granted to its owners.

   a. Preference as to payment of dividends.
   b. Preference in distribution of assets in a liquidation.

2. Cumulative or noncumulative preferred stock

   a. Cumulative—any undeclared dividends accumulated annually until paid.
   b. Noncumulative—the right to receive dividends is forfeited in any year that dividends are not declared.

3. Participating or nonparticipating preferred stock

   a. Participating preferred stock—provides the right to share in dividends above the fixed amount or percentage which is preferred.
   b. Nonparticipating preferred stock—dividends to stock are limited to a fixed maximum amount.

F. Convertible preferred stock and convertible bonds

1. Initially issuing convertible bonds or preferred stock offers investors more security than common stock.

2. The carrying amount of the converted preferred stock or bonds becomes the book value of the capital contributed for the new shares of common stock.

G. Stock values

1. Redemption value—the amount a corporation agrees to pay to redeem a share of its preferred stock.

2. Market value—the amount at which a share of stock may be bought or sold.

3. Book value—the equity represented by one share of stock in the issuing corporation's net assets.

    a. Common stock—total stockholders' equity (less the book value of preferred stock, if any) divided by number of common shares outstanding.
    b. Preferred stock—redemption value (or par value if there is no redemption value) plus any cumulative dividends in arrears divided by number of preferred shares outstanding.
    c. Generally has little bearing upon liquidation value or market value.

Problem I

The following statements are either true or false. Place a (T) in the parentheses before each true statement and an (F) before each false statement.

1. ( ) Jay and Faye are partners in the operation of an insurance agency. Business has been slow, and without consulting Faye, Jay entered into a contract with Rays Limited to purchase three satellite dishes to be sold by the partnership. Faye repudiated the contract. Rays Limited should be able to hold the partnership liable on the contract.

2. ( ) Partnership accounting is exactly like that of a single proprietorship except for transactions affecting the partners' equities.

3. ( ) Although a partner does not work for either a salary or interest, to be fair in the distribution of partnership earnings, it is often necessary to recognize that the earnings do include a return for services and a return on investments.

4. ( ) Par value has nothing to do with a stock's worth.

5. ( ) Final authority in the management of corporation affairs rests with its board of directors.

6. ( ) The life of a corporation may be unlimited.

7. ( ) To transfer and sell his or her interest in a corporation, a stockholder must secure permission from the corporation's secretary.

8. ( ) The chief executive officer of a corporation is usually elected by the stockholders at one of their annual meetings.

9. ( ) The president of a corporation is responsible to its board of directors for management of the corporation's affairs.

10. ( ) A discount on stock is the difference between market value and the amount at which stock is issued when the stock is issued at a price below its par value.

Problem II

You are given several words, phrases or numbers to choose from in completing each of the following statements or in answering the following questions. In each case select the one that best completes the statement or answers the question and place its letter in the answer space provided.

_____ 1. The amount of capital contributed by stockholders above the stock's par value is the:

    a. contributed capital.
    b. stock dividend.
    c. minimum legal capital.
    d. premium on stock.
    e. discount on stock.

_____ 2. Vector Corporation has outstanding 3,000 shares of $100 par value, 7% cumulative and nonparticipating preferred stock and 10,000 shares of $10 par value common stock. Dividends have not been paid on the preferred stock for the current and one prior year. The corporation has recently prospered, and the board of directors has voted to pay out $49,000 of the corporation's retained earnings in dividends. If the $49,000 is paid out, how much should the preferred and common stockholders receive per share?

    a. $14.00 per share preferred, $0.70 per share common.
    b. $ 7.00 per share preferred, $2.80 per share common.
    c. $12.25 per share preferred, $1.23 per share common.
    d. $ 1.14 per share preferred, $4.56 per share common.
    e. $16.33 per share preferred, $-0- per share common.

Problem II *(continued)*

_____ 3. Vector Corporation has outstanding 3,000 shares of $100 par value, 7% noncumulative and nonparticipating preferred stock and 10,000 shares of $10 par value common stock. Dividends have not been paid on the preferred stock for the current and one prior year. The corporation has recently prospered, and the board of directors has voted to pay out $49,000 of the corporation's retained earnings in dividends. If the $49,000 is paid out, how much should the preferred and common stockholders receive per share?

    a. $ 1.14 per share preferred, $4.56 per share common.
    b. $ 9.33 per share preferred, $2.10 per share common.
    c. $ 7.00 per share preferred, $2.80 per share common.
    d. $14.00 per share preferred, $0.70 per share common.
    e. $12.25 per share preferred, $1.23 per share common.

_____ 4. Participating preferred stock is:

    a.   a preferred stock that may be exchanged for shares of its issuing corporation's common stock at the option of the stockholder.
    b.   preferred stock on which undeclared dividends accumulate annually until paid.
    c.   a preferred stock for which the right to receive dividends is forfeited in any year in which dividends are not declared.
    d.   preferred stock which the issuing corporation, at its option, may retire by paying to the stockholders the redemption value of the stock plus any dividends in arrears.
    e.   preferred stock that has the right to share in dividends above the fixed amount or percentage that is preferred.

_____ 5. Stated value of no-par stock is:

    a.   one share's equity in the issuing corporation's net assets as recorded in the corporation's accounts.
    b.   an amount, established by a corporation's board of directors, that is credited to the no-par stock account at the time the stock is issued.
    c.   the difference between the par value of stock and the amount below or above par value contributed by stockholders.
    d.   the market value of the stock on the date of issuance.
    e.   another name for redemption value.

Problem III

Many of the important ideas and concepts discussed in Chapter 12 are reflected in the following list of key terms. Test your understanding of these terms by matching the appropriate definitions with the terms. Record the number identifying the most appropriate definition in the blank space next to each term.

Problem III *(continued)*

_____ Book value of a share of stock

_____ Call price of preferred stock

_____ Callable preferred stock

_____ Common stock

_____ Common Stock Subscribed

_____ Convertible bond

_____ Convertible preferred stock

_____ Cumulative preferred stock

_____ Discount on stock

_____ Dividend in arrears

_____ Financial leverage

_____ General partner

_____ General partnership

_____ Limited partners

_____ Limited partnership

_____ Minimum legal capital

_____ Mutual agency

_____ Noncumulative preferred stock

_____ No-par stock

_____ Organization costs

_____ Par value

_____ Partnership

_____ Partnership contract

_____ Participating preferred stock

_____ Preemptive right

_____ Preferred stock

_____ Premium on stock

_____ Proxy

_____ Redemption value of preferred stock

_____ Stated value of no-par stock

_____ Stock subscription

_____ Unlimited liability of partners

1. The agreement between partners that sets forth the terms under which the affairs of a partnership will be conducted.

2. An amount, established by a corporation's board of directors, that is credited to the no-par stock account at the time the stock is issued.

3. Preferred stock which the issuing corporation, at its option, may retire by paying to the stockholders the redemption value of the stock plus any dividends in arrears.

4. A partner who assumes unlimited liability for the debts of the partnership.

5. An amount, as defined by state law, that stockholders must invest in a corporation or be contingently liable to its creditors.

6. The right of common stockholders to protect their proportionate interests in a corporation by having the first opportunity to purchase additional shares of common stock issued by the corporation.

7. Another name for redemption value.

8. A class of stock that does not have an arbitrary (par) value placed on the stock at the time the stock is first authorized.

9. The difference between the par value of stock and the amount below par value contributed by stockholders.

10. A legal document that gives an agent of a stockholder the right to vote the stockholder's shares.

11. A stockholders' equity account in which a corporation records the par or stated value of unissued common stock which investors have contracted to purchase.

12. A partnership in which all partners have unlimited liability for partnership debts.

13. An unincorporated association of two or more persons to carry on a business as co-owners for profit.

Problem III *(continued)*

14. Costs of bringing a corporation into existence, such as legal fees, promoters' fees, and amounts paid the state to secure a charter.

15. The legal characteristic of a partnership that makes each general partner responsible for paying all the debts of the partnership if the other partners are unable to pay their shares.

16. A preferred stock that may be exchanged for shares of its issuing corporation's common stock at the option of the stockholder.

17. Preferred stock on which undeclared dividends accumulate annually until paid.

18. One share's equity in the issuing corporation's net assets as recorded in the corporation's accounts.

19. Stock the owners of which are granted a priority status over common stockholders in one or more ways such as in the payment of dividends or in the distribution of assets in a liquidation.

20. An arbitrary value placed on a share of stock at the time the stock is authorized.

21. Partners who have no personal liability for debts of the limited partnership beyond the amounts they have invested in the partnership.

22. The amount a corporation must pay in addition to dividends in arrears if and when it exercises its right to retire a share of callable preferred stock previously issued by the corporation.

23. A dividend to cumulative preferred stock which remains unpaid after the date for payment called for in the corporate charter.

24. Preferred stock that has the right to share in dividends above the fixed amount or percentage that is preferred.

25. The legal characteristic of a partnership whereby each partner is an agent of the partnership and is able to bind the partnership to contracts within the normal scope of the partnership business.

26. A bond that may be exchanged for shares of its issuing corporation's stock at the option of the bondholder.

27. A contractual commitment by an investor to purchase unissued shares of stock and become a stockholder.

28. Stock of a corporation that has only one class of stock, or if there is more than one class, the class that has no preferences relative to the corporation's other classes of stock.

29. A preferred stock for which the right to receive dividends is forfeited in any year in which dividends are not declared.

30. A partnership that has two classes of partners, limited partners and one or more general partners.

31. Increasing the return to common stock as a result of paying preferred stock or bonds a given dividend or interest rate which is less than the rate earned from using the assets paid to the corporation by the preferred stockholders or bondholders.

32. The amount of capital contributed by stockholders above the stock's par value.

Problem IV

Complete the following by filling in the blanks.

1. Blake and Dillon are partners who have always shared incomes and losses equally. Hester has sued the partners on a partnership debt and obtained a $12,000 judgment. The partnership and Dillon have no assets; consequently, Hester is attempting to collect the entire $12,000 from Blake. Blake has sufficient assets to pay the judgment but refuses, claiming she is liable for only one half the

    $12,000. Hester _____ (can, cannot) collect the entire $12,000 from Blake

    because _____

    _____.

2. Four advantages of a partnership over the single proprietorship and corporation forms of organization are:

    (a) _____

    _____;

    (b) _____

    _____;

    (c) _____

    _____;

    (d) _____

    _____.

3. A _____ (limited, general) partnership has two classes of partners.

4. Since a partnership is a voluntary association, an individual _____ (can, cannot) be forced against his will to become a partner; and since a partnership is based on a contract, its

    life is _____.

5. The phrase mutual agency when applied to a partnership means _____

    _____

    _____.

6. Organization costs are classified on the balance sheet as a(n) _____

    _____ asset. However, due to income tax rules organiza-

    tion costs are commonly written off over the first _____ years of a corporation's life.

Problem IV *(continued)*

7. Laws establishing minimum legal capital requirements were written to protect _____ _____, with the protection resulting from making illegal the payment of any dividends that reduce stockholders' equity below _____.

8. When stock is issued at a price above its par value, the difference between par and the price at which the stock is issued is called a _____.

9. Advantages claimed for no-par stock are:

    (a) It may be issued at any price without _____.
    (b) Uninformed persons buying such stock are not misled as to the stock's worth by a _____ printed on the certificates.

10. Laws setting minimum legal capital requirements normally require stockholders to invest, in a corporation, assets equal in value to minimum legal capital or be contingently liable to _____ for the deficiency.

11. A preferred stock is so called because of the preferences granted its owners. The two most common preferences are a preference as to _____ _____ _____ and a preference _____ _____.

12. In many jurisdictions when a corporation issues par value stock, it establishes for itself a _____ equal to the par value of the issued stock.

13. In addition to its separate legal existence, other advantages of a corporation as a form of business organization are _____ _____ _____ _____ _____.

Problem IV *(continued)*

14. A corporation is said to be a separate legal entity; this phrase means that in a legal sense a

corporation is _____

_____.

Problem V

Flip and Flop began a partnership by investing $14,000 and $10,000, respectively, and during its first year the partnership earned a $21,000 net income. Complete the tabulation below to show, under the several assumptions, the share of each partner in the $21,000 net income.

	Flip's Share	*Flop's Share*
1. The partners failed to agree as to the method of sharing	$_____	$_____
2. The partners had agreed to share in their beginning-of-year investment ratio	$_____	$_____
3. The partners had agreed to share by giving an $8,200 per year salary allowance to Flip and a $9,000 per year salary allowance to Flop, plus 10% interest on their beginning-of-year investments, and the remainder equally	$_____	$_____

4. Assume that the partnership of Flip and Flop earned $14,000 rather than $21,000 and that the partners had agreed to share incomes and losses by giving salary allowances of $8,200 and $9,000 respectively, 10% interest on beginning investments, and the remainder equally. Flip's share of the

$14,000 would be $_____, and Flop's share would be

$_____.

5. Also, if Flip and Flop share incomes and losses as immediately above, and the partnership incurred a $3,800 loss rather than a profit, Flip's share of the loss would be

$_____ and Flop's share would be $_____.

Problem VI

The stockholders' equity section from Sonar Corporation's balance sheet shows the following:

CAPITAL STOCK AND RETAINED EARNINGS

Preferred stock, $100 par value, 8% cumulative and non-participating, issued and outstanding 2,000 shares	$200,000	
Common stock, $10 par value, issued and outstanding 25,000 shares	250,000	
Total contributed capital		$450,000
Retained earnings		230,000
Total stockholders' equity		$680,000

Problem VI *(continued)*

1. If there are no dividends in arrears, the book value per share of the corporation's preferred stock is

    $_____, and the book value per share of its common stock is

    $_____.

2. If a total of two years' dividends are in arrears on the preferred stock, the book value per share of the preferred stock is $_____, and the book value per share of the common stock is $_____.

Problem VII

A corporation accepted subscriptions to 25,000 shares of its $5 par value common stock at $5.50 per share. The subscription contracts called for 20% down payments with the balance in 30 days. The explanations for several entries involving this stock follow. Complete the entries.

DATE		ACCOUNT TITLES AND EXPLANATION	P.R.	DEBIT	CREDIT
Sept.	5				
		Accepted subscriptions to 25,000 shares of common stock at $5.50 per share.			
	5				
		Received $27,500 from the common stock subscribers as down payments on their shares.			
Oct.	5				
		Received payment in full of the balance due on the September 5 common stock subscriptions.			
	5				
		Issued the common stock of the fully paid subscribers.			

Solutions for Chapter 12

Problem I

1. F	6. T
2. T	7. F
3. T	8. F
4. T	9. T
5. T	10. F

Problem II

1. D
2. A
3. C
4. E
5. B

Problem III

Book value of a share of stock	18
Call price of preferred stock	7 or 22
Callable preferred stock	3
Common stock	28
Common Stock Subscribed	11
Convertible bond	26
Convertible preferred stock	16
Cumulative preferred stock	17
Discount on stock	9
Dividend in arrears	23
Financial leverage	31
General partner	4
General partnership	12
Limited partners	21
Limited partnership	30
Minimum legal capital	5
Mutual agency	25
Noncumulative preferred stock	29
No-par stock	8
Organization costs	14
Par value	20
Partnership	13
Partnership contract	1
Participating preferred stock	24
Preemptive right	6
Preferred stock	19
Premium on stock	32
Proxy	10
Redemption value of preferred stock ..	22
Stated value of no-par stock	2
Stock subscription	27
Unlimited liability of partners	15

Problem IV

1. can, each partner is unlimitedly liable for the debts of the partnership

2. (a) Brings more money and skills together than a single proprietorship
   (b) Is easier to organize than a corporation
   (c) Does not have the corporation's governmental supervision or extra taxation burden
   (d) Allows partners to act freely and without the necessity of stockholders' and directors' meetings, as is required in a corporation

3. limited

4. cannot, limited

5. each partner is an agent of the partnership and can bind it to contracts

6. intangible, five

7. corporation creditors, minimum legal capital

8. premium

9. (a) discount liability
   (b) par value

Problem IV *(continued)*

10. corporation creditors

11. the payment of dividends, in the distribution of assets if the corporation is liquidated

12. minimum legal capital

13. lack of stockholder liability, ease of transferring ownership rights, continuity of life, no mutual agency, and ease of capital assembly

14. an individual body, separate and distinct from its stockholders

Problem V

1. $10,500, $10,500

2. $12,250, $8,750

3. $10,300, $10,700

4. $6,800, $7,200

5. ($2,100), ($1,700)

Problem VI

1. $100, $19.20

2. $116, $17.92

Problem VII

Sept. 5	Subscriptions Receivable, Common Stock	137,500.00	
	Common Stock Subscribed		125,000.00
	Premium on Common Stock		12,500.00
5	Cash	27,500.00	
	Subscriptions Receivable, Common Stock		27,500.00
Oct. 5	Cash	110,000.00	
	Subscriptions Receivable, Common Stock		110,000.00
5	Common Stock Subscribed	125,000.00	
	Common Stock		125,000.00

13 Additional Corporate Transactions; Reporting Income and Retained Earnings; Earnings per Share

Your objectives in studying this chapter should include learning how to:

1. Record cash dividends, stock dividends, and stock splits and explain their effects on the assets and stockholders' equity of a corporation.

2. Record purchases and sales of treasury stock and retirements of stock and describe their effects on stockholders' equity.

3. Describe restrictions and appropriations of retained earnings and the disclosure of such items in the financial statements.

4. Explain how the income effects of discontinued operations, extraordinary items, changes in accounting principles, and prior period adjustments are reported.

5. Calculate earnings per share for companies with simple capital structures and explain the difference between primary and fully diluted earnings per share.

6. Define or explain the words and phrases listed in the chapter Glossary.

Topical Outline

I. Dividends, retained earnings, and contributed capital

   A. Cash dividend—reduces in equal amounts both cash and stockholders' equity. In order to pay a cash dividend:

      1. A corporation (in most states) must have retained earnings, and

      2. A corporation must also have sufficient cash.

   B. Generally, contributed capital may not be returned to stockholders as dividends. However, in some states, dividends may be debited or charged to certain contributed capital accounts.

   C. Stock dividend—a distribution of a corporation's own stock to its stockholders without any consideration being received in return from the stockholders.

      1. Small stock dividend—up to 25 percent of the previously outstanding shares; the market value of the shares to be distributed is capitalized.

      2. Stock dividend over 25 percent of the previously outstanding shares; only the legally required minimum amount of retained earnings must be capitalized.

      3. When common stock dividends are declared, the par amount is credited to a contributed capital account (Common Stock Dividends Distributable) and any premium is also recorded. The par amount is transferred to Common Stock when the shares are distributed.

II. Stock splits—involve calling in the outstanding shares of stock and replacing them with a larger number of shares which have a lower par value.

   A. Usual purpose is to reduce the market price of the stock to facilitate trading in the stock.

   B. In recording a stock split only a memorandum entry is required.

   C. The total par value of outstanding shares does not change, and retained earnings is not capitalized.

III. Treasury stock—a corporation's own stock that has been issued and then reacquired.

   A. When a corporation purchases its own stock, it reduces in equal amounts both its assets and its stockholders' equity.

   B. Retained earnings equal to the cost of treasury stock are restricted.

   C. Reissuing treasury stock

      1. When sold above cost, the amount received in excess of cost is credited to Contributed Capital, Treasury Stock Transactions.

      2. When sold below cost, the "loss" is debited to Retained Earnings unless there is a contributed capital account from treasury stock transactions, in which case, the "loss" is debited to that account.

   D. Retirement of stock

      1. When stock is purchased for retirement, all capital items related to the shares being retired are removed from the accounts.

      2. A "gain" on the transaction should be credited to contributed capital.

      3. A "loss" on the transaction should be debited to Retained Earnings.

IV. Income and loss items not directly related to continuing operations

    A. Discontinued operations

        1. Results of operations of a discontinued business segment should be reported in a separate section of the income statement.

        2. Income or loss from operating the segment is separated from the gain or loss on disposal.

        3. Each gain or loss is reported net of related income tax effects.

    B. Extraordinary items

        1. Must be both unusual and infrequent.

        2. Reported (net of related income taxes) below discontinued operations.

        3. Items that are unusual or infrequent (but not both) are reported in the income statement within the category of income from continuing operations.

    C. Changes in accounting principles

        1. Notwithstanding the consistency principle, changes in accounting principles are acceptable if justified as improvements in financial reporting.

        2. Cumulative effect on prior years' incomes is reported (net of taxes) below extraordinary items.

    D. Prior period adjustments

        1. Essentially limited to corrections of errors made in prior periods.

        2. Reported in statement of retained earnings as an adjustment to the beginning retained earnings balance.

V. Earnings per share—one of the most commonly reported figures in the financial press.

    A. For companies with simple capital structures, it is calculated as net income (minus preferred dividend requirements, if the company has nonconvertible preferred shares outstanding) divided by the weighted-average number of common shares outstanding.

    B. For companies with complex capital structures, two types of earnings per share calculations are often required:

        1. Primary earnings per share

        2. Fully diluted earnings per share

    C. Generally accepted accounting principles require that earnings per share data be shown on the face of published income statements for:

        1. Income from continuing operations.

        2. Gains or losses from discontinued operations.

        3. Extraordinary items.

        4. Cumulative effect of changes in accounting principles.

        5. Net income.

Problem I

The following statements are either true or false. Place a (T) in the parentheses before each true statement and an (F) before each false statement.

1. ( ) A small stock dividend should be recorded by capitalizing retained earnings equal to the book value of the stock to be distributed.

2. ( ) In most states, a corporation must have current net income in order to pay a cash dividend.

3. ( ) Since a stock dividend is "payable" in stock rather than in assets, it is not a liability of its issuing corporation.

4. ( ) A stock split has no effect on total stockholders' equity, the equities of the individual stockholders, or on the balances of any of the contributed or retained capital accounts.

5. ( ) Appropriations of retained earnings reduce total retained earnings.

6. ( ) In most jurisdictions a corporation may purchase treasury stock only to the extent of its retained earnings available for dividends.

7. ( ) The appropriation of retained earnings sets aside cash or funds for a special purpose.

8. ( ) A cash dividend reduces a corporation's cash and its stockholders' equity, but a stock dividend does not affect either cash or total stockholders' equity.

9. ( ) The cumulative effect on prior years' incomes of a change in accounting principle is reported on the statement of retained earnings.

10. ( ) For companies with simple capital structures, earnings per share is calculated by dividing net income minus preferred dividends, if any, by the weighted-average number of common shares outstanding.

Problem II

You are given several words, phrases or numbers to choose from in completing each of the following statements or in answering the following questions. In each case select the one that best completes the statement or answers the question and place its letter in the answer space provided.

_____ 1. Bartlett Company had 20,000 shares of common stock outstanding at the beginning of 1990. On April 1, the company sold 20,000 additional shares of its common stock, and on November 1 the company declared a 2 for 1 stock split. For the purpose of determining earnings per share, calculate the weighted-average number of common shares outstanding during the year.

    a. 60,000.00
    b. 80,000.00
    c. 70,000.00
    d. 41,666.66
    e. 83,333.33

Problem II (continued)

_____ 2. The Poseidon Company issued $10 par value common stock for $15, with the premium being credited to Contributed Capital in Excess of Par Value, Common Stock. Later, 500 shares of this stock was repurchased and retired at a cost of $17. The entry to record the retirement is as follows:

a. Common Stock 5,000.00
   Contributed Capital in Excess of Par Value, Common Stock 2,500.00
   Retained Earnings 1,000.00
   Cash 8,500.00

b. Common Stock 5,000.00
   Contributed Capital in Excess of Par Value, Common Stock 2,500.00
   Contributed Capital from the Retirement of Common Stock 1,000.00
   Cash 8,500.00

c. Common Stock 5,000.00
   Contributed Capital in Excess of Par Value, Common Stock 3,500.00
   Cash 8,500.00

d. Common Stock 5,000.00
   Contributed Capital in Excess of Par Value, Common Stock 2,500.00
   Cash 6,500.00
   Contributed Capital from the Retirement of Com. St. 1,000.00

e. Treasury Stock 8,500.00
   Cash 8,500.00

_____ 3. Captan Company has a depreciable asset that cost $500,000 (no salvage value) and has decided to switch from straight-line depreciation to declining-balance depreciation at twice the straight-line rate. The company depreciated the asset for 1 year based on straight-line depreciation and a 5-year life. The company is subject to a 40% income tax rate. Calculate (a) the amount of depreciation expense to be reported in the current year (year 2) and (b) the cumulative effect of the change in accounting principle, net of taxes, on the prior year's income.

a. (a) $200,000; (b) $120,000.
b. (a) $200,000; (b) $100,000.
c. (a) $120,000; (b) $ 60,000.
d. (a) $120,000; (b) $ 72,000.
e. (a) $200,000; (b) $200,000.

_____ 4. Earnings per share statistics that are calculated as if all dilutive securities had already been converted are called:

a. primary earnings per share.
b. secured earnings per share.
c. simple earnings per share.
d. convertible earnings per share.
e. fully diluted earnings per share.

_____ 5. The statement of changes in stockholders' equity is:

a. a financial statement that discloses the inflows and outflows of cash during the period.
b. a financial report showing the assets, liabilities, and equity of an enterprise on a specific date.
c. a financial statement showing revenues earned by a business, the expenses incurred in earning the revenues, and the resulting net income or net loss.
d. a financial statement that reconciles the beginning and ending balances of each stockholders' equity account by listing all changes that occurred during the year.
e. None of the above.

Problem III

Many of the important ideas and concepts discussed in Chapter 13 are reflected in the following list of key terms. Test your understanding of these terms by matching the appropriate definitions with the terms. Record the number identifying the most appropriate definition in the blank space next to each term.

_____ Antidilutive securities

_____ Appropriated retained earnings

_____ Changes in accounting estimates

_____ Common stock equivalent

_____ Complex capital structure

_____ Dilutive securities

_____ Earned surplus

_____ Earnings per share

_____ Extraordinary gain or loss

_____ Fully diluted earnings per share

_____ Infrequent gain or loss

_____ Liquidating dividends

_____ Primary earnings per share

_____ Prior period adjustments

_____ Restricted retained earnings

_____ Segment of a business

_____ Simple capital structure

_____ Small stock dividend

_____ Statement of changes in stockholders' equity

_____ Stock dividend

_____ Stock split

_____ Treasury stock

_____ Unusual gain or loss

1. A financial statement that reconciles the beginning and ending balances of each stockholders' equity account by listing all changes that occurred during the year.

2. Adjustments to previously made assumptions about the future such as salvage values and the length of useful lives of buildings and equipment.

3. Distributions of corporate assets to stockholders which are charged to contributed capital accounts, therefore representing amounts that had been originally contributed by the stockholders.

4. A gain or loss that is abnormal and unrelated or only incidentally related to the ordinary activities and environment of the business.

5. Convertible securities the assumed conversion of which would have the effect of decreasing earnings per share.

6. Retained earnings that are not available for dividends because of law or binding contract.

7. The act of a corporation to call in its stock and issue more than one new share in the place of each share previously outstanding.

8. Convertible securities the assumed conversion of which would have the effect of increasing earnings per share.

9. A gain or loss that is both unusual and infrequent.

10. A security that is convertible into common stock and for which, according to detailed rules applied at the time of issuance, eventual conversion appears very probable.

11. A capital structure that does not include any rights or options to purchase common shares or any securities that are convertible into common stock.

Problem III *(continued)*

12. Earnings per share statistics that are calculated as if those outstanding common stock equivalents which are dilutive had already been converted.

13. The amount of net income (or components of income) that accrues to common shares divided by the weighted-average number of common shares outstanding.

14. Issued stock that was reacquired and is currently held by the issuing corporation.

15. Retained earnings voluntarily earmarked for a special use as a way of informing stockholders that assets from earnings equal to the appropriations are not available for dividends.

16. A stock dividend that amounts to 25% or less of the issuing corporation's previously outstanding shares.

17. Items that are reported in the current statement of retained earnings as corrections to the beginning retained earnings balance; limited primarily to corrections of errors that were made in past years.

18. A capital structure that includes outstanding rights or options to purchase common stock or securities that are convertible into common stock.

19. Operations of a company that involve a particular line of business or class of customer, providing the assets, activities, and financial results of the operations can be distinguished from other parts of the business.

20. A gain or loss that is not expected to occur again, given the operating environment of the business.

21. A synonym for retained earnings, no longer in general use.

22. A distribution by a corporation of shares of its own stock to its stockholders without any consideration being received in return.

23. Earnings per share statistics that are calculated as if all dilutive securities had already been converted.

Problem IV

Complete the following by filling in the blanks.

1. When a corporation purchases treasury stock, a portion of its retained earnings equal to the cost of the treasury stock becomes _____ and unavailable for _____ .

2. If treasury stock is reissued at a price above cost, the amount received in excess of cost is credited to _____ .
   If treasury stock is sold below cost the difference between cost and the sale price is debited to either _____ or _____ .

3. A stock dividend enables a corporation to give its shareholders some evidence of their interest in its retained earnings without reducing the corporation's _____ .

Problem IV *(continued)*

4. Retained earnings are appropriated or "earmarked" as a means of informing the stockholders that

    _____

    _____.

5. Treasury stock differs from unissued stock in that treasury stock may be reissued at a discount

    without _____.

6. Issued stock that has been reacquired by the issuing corporation is called _____

    _____.

7. If the book value of a share of common stock before the declaration and distribution of a 20% stock dividend was $90, the declaration and distribution of the dividend changed the book value

    to $_____.

8. If a corporation has sufficient retained earnings to pay a dividend, it must also have sufficient

    _____ before it pays that dividend.

9. A small stock dividend contains a number of shares up to _____% of the previously outstanding shares.

10. Changes in accounting estimates _____ (are, are not) prior period adjustments.

11. The results of discontinued operations are separated from the results of other activities on the

    income statement in order to _____

    _____

    _____.

12. Earnings per share statistics that are calculated as if all dilutive securities had already been

    converted are called _____

    _____.

Problem V

On August 10 Mainline Corporation purchased for cash 2,000 shares of its own $25 par value common stock at $27 per share. On October 3 it sold 1,000 of the shares at $30 per share. Complete the entries below to record the purchase and sale of the stock.

DATE		ACCOUNT TITLES AND EXPLANATION	P.R.	DEBIT	CREDIT
Aug.	10				
		Purchased 2,000 shares of treasury stock.			
Oct.	3				
		Sold 1,000 shares of treasury stock.			

Problem VI

The May 31 balance sheet of Eastwood Corporation carried the following stockholders' equity section:

Stockholders' Equity

Common stock, $10 par value, 25,000 shares authorized, 20,000 shares issued $200,000
Retained earnings   44,000
Total contributed and retained capital $244,000

On the balance sheet date, with the common stock selling at $12 per share, the corporation's board of directors voted a 2,000-share stock dividend distributable on June 30 to the June 20 stockholders of record.

1.   In the space below give without explanations the entries to record the declaration and distribution of the dividend.

DATE		ACCOUNT TITLES AND EXPLANATION	P.R.	DEBIT	CREDIT

Problem VI *(continued)*

2.   Harold Jax owned 2,000 shares of the corporation's common stock before the declaration and distribution of the stock dividend; as a result, his portion of the dividend was

_____ shares. The total book value of Jax's 2,000 shares before the

dividend was $_____; the total book value of his shares after the dividend

was $_____; consequently, Jax gained $_____ in the book value of his interest in the corporation.

Problem VII

Retained earnings and shares issued and outstanding for Endel Corporation are as follows:

	Retained Earnings	Shares Issued & Outstanding
December 31, 1989	$475,000	35,000
December 31, 1990	$447,000	38,500

On April 3, 1990, the board of directors declared a $0.775 per share dividend on the outstanding stock. On August 7, while the stock was selling for $17.50 per share, the corporation declared a 10% stock dividend on the outstanding shares to be issued on November 7. Under the assumption that there were no transactions affecting retained earnings other than the ones given, determine the 1990 net income of Endel Corporation.

Problem VIII

Explain where each of the following items should appear in the financial statements of Odyssey Corporation.

1)   The company maintains a stock investment portfolio as part of its business activities to enhance earnings. This year, for the first time in seven years, it sold stock for a gain of $27,000.

2)   After depreciating equipment for three years based on an expected six-year life, the company decided this year that the value of the equipment would last five more years. As a result, the depreciation for the current year is $18,000 instead of $30,000.

1)

2)

Solutions for Chapter 13

Problem I

1.	F	6.	T
2.	F	7.	F
3.	T	8.	T
4.	T	9.	F
5.	F	10.	T

Problem II

1.	C
2.	A
3.	C
4.	E
5.	D

Problem III

Antidilutive securities	8	Primary earnings per share	12
Appropriated retained earnings	15	Prior period adjustments	17
Changes in accounting estimates	2	Restricted retained earnings	6
Common stock equivalent	10	Segment of a business	19
Complex capital structure	18	Simple capital structure	11
Dilutive securities	5	Small stock dividend	16
Earned surplus	21	Statement of changes in stockholders' equity	1
Earnings per share	13		
Extraordinary gain or loss	9	Stock dividend	22
Fully diluted earnings per share	23	Stock split	7
Infrequent gain or loss	20	Treasury stock	14
Liquidating dividends	3	Unusual gain or loss	4

Problem IV

1. restricted, dividends

2. Contributed Capital, Treasury Stock Transactions; Contributed Capital, Treasury Stock Transactions; Retained Earnings

3. cash or other assets

4. assets equal in amount to the appropriation will not be paid out in dividends

5. discount liability

6. treasury stock

7. 75

8. cash

9. 25

10. are not

11. allow statement readers to better evaluate and judge the continuing operations of the business

12. fully diluted earnings per share

Problem V

Aug. 10	Treasury Stock, Common	54,000.00	
	Cash		54,000.00
Oct. 3	Cash	30,000.00	
	Treasury Stock, Common		27,000.00
	Contributed Capital, Treasury Stock Transactions		3,000.00

Problem VI

1.

May 31	Stock Dividends Declared	24,000.00	
	Common Stock Dividend Distributable		20,000.00
	Contributed Capital in Excess of Par Value, Common Stock		4,000.00
June 30	Common Stock Dividend Distributable	20,000.00	
	Common Stock		20,000.00

2.   200; $24,400; $24,400; $0

Problem VII

Retained earnings as of December 31, 1989		$475,000
Reductions in retained earnings due to transactions:		
Dividends declared:		
April 3, on 35,000 shares	$27,125	
Retained earnings capitalized in stock dividend	61,250	
Total reductions		88,375
Retained earnings balance before transfer of net income from Income Summary account		$386,625
Retained earnings, December 31, 1990, after transfer of net income from Income Summary account		$447,000
Deduct retained earnings balance before transfer of net income from Income Summary account		386,625
Net income		$ 60,375

Problem VIII

1) This gain is neither unusual nor infrequent. As a result, it should be reported in the income statement as part of income from continuing operations.

2) This change from an expected useful life of six to eight years is a change in an accounting estimate. The $18,000 should be reported in the income statement as part of income from continuing operations.

14

Statement of Cash Flows

Your objectives in studying this chapter should include learning how to:

1. Explain the differences between operating, investing, and financing activities, and identify the proper classification of a company's cash inflows and outflows.

2. Calculate cash inflows and outflows by inspecting the noncash account balances of a company and related information about its transactions.

3. Prepare a working paper for a statement of cash flows in which cash flows from operating activities are reported according to the direct method.

4. Prepare a statement of cash flows in which cash flows from operating activities are reported according to the direct method, and prepare a schedule of noncash investing and financing activities.

5. Define or explain the words and phrases listed in the chapter Glossary.

Your objectives in studying the appendix to Chapter 14 (Appendix D) should include learning how to:

6. Calculate the net cash provided or used by operating activities according to the indirect method.

7. Prepare a working paper for a statement of cash flows in which the net cash flows from operating activities are calculated by the indirect method.

Topical Outline

I. Content and design of the statement of cash flows

    A. Its purpose is to provide decision makers with information about a company's cash receipts and cash payments during a reporting period.

    B. The statement reconciles the beginning and ending balances of cash plus cash equivalents.

    C. A cash equivalent is a highly liquid, short-term investment that generally meets two criteria:

        1. It is readily convertible to known amounts of cash.

        2. It matures within three months of its purchase date.

    D. The statement is prepared by the direct method or the indirect method.

        1. The direct method is encouraged by the FASB and results in the separate listing of major cash inflows and outflows from operating activities. This method is followed throughout the chapter.

        2. The indirect method, discussed in the appendix to the chapter, adjusts net income to determine cash provided or used by operating activities.

    E. There are three categories into which cash receipts and cash payments are classified:

        1. Cash flows from operating activities.

        2. Cash flows from investing activities.

        3. Cash flows from financing activities.

    F. Operating activities generally involve the production or purchase of merchandise and the sale of goods and services to customers. They also include administrative aspects of the business. Operating activities include:

        1. Cash inflows such as cash receipts from customers and the receipt of dividends and interest.

        2. Cash outflows such as payments to suppliers for merchandise, to employees for wages, to creditors for interest, and to government for taxes.

    G. Investing activities basically involve the purchase or sale of long-term investments, plant assets, and other long-term productive assets. They also include the purchase or sale of short-term investments which are not cash equivalents. Investing activities include:

        1. Cash inflows from selling productive assets (excluding merchandise), from collecting loan principal, from selling investments in debt and equity securities of other companies, and similar activities.

        2. Cash outflows for the purchase of productive assets, for the purchase of debt and equity securities of other companies, and for loans to other parties.

    H. Financing activities usually involve a company's transactions with its owners and long-term creditors. They may also pertain to short-term cash borrowing, even if the cash is then used to buy merchandise. Financing activities include:

        1. Cash inflows from the sale of capital stock, the issuance of notes and bonds payable, and long-term and short-term borrowing.

        2. Cash outflows from dividend payments; the repayment of loans, notes, and bonds; and the purchase of treasury stock.

II.   Noncash investing and financing activities

    A.   Are reported in a narrative discussion or in a supporting schedule. They are not shown on the statement of cash flows.

    B.   Include transactions that do not involve cash but may also include transactions that involve partial payments or receipts of cash.

    C.   Examples include the conversion of debt to equity securities, the purchase of plant assets by issuing equity or debt securities, and the exchange of a noncash asset for another noncash asset.

III. Preparing a statement of cash flows

    A.   Analyzing the Cash account does not provide enough information.

    B.   May be done by inspecting all noncash balance sheet accounts, the income statement, and related information.

        1.   Determine the major classes of cash receipts and payments from operating activities, investing activities, and financing activities.

        2.   Reconcile or explain the period's change in each noncash balance sheet account.

    C.   May be done by using a working paper approach.

IV.   Preparing a direct method working paper

    A.   The working paper has four money columns.

    B.   Columns one and four contain the beginning and ending balances of each balance sheet account. Columns two and three are for the analyses that reconcile the change in each balance sheet account.

    C.   Separate sections on the working paper present *(a)* balance sheet items with debit balances, *(b)* balance sheet items with credit balances, *(c)* all income statement items, *(d)* cash flows from operating activities, *(e)* cash flows from investing activities, *(f)* cash flows from financing activities, and *(g)* noncash investing and financing activities.

    D.   Information for sections *(d)-(g)* is developed in three steps in the Analysis of Changes columns:

        1.   Enter each income statement amount and its related noncash balance sheet effect (e.g., sales and accounts receivable, cost of goods sold and merchandise inventory, and net income and retained earnings).

        2.   The amount needed at this time to fully reconcile a current asset or current liability account usually involves a cash inflow or outflow. These cash effects are entered in sections *(d)*, *(e)*, or *(f)*.

        3.   The noncurrent assets and liabilities usually are reconciled by investing and financing transactions. If cash is involved as an inflow or outflow, the activities are described in sections *(e)* or *(f)*. Noncash investing and financing activities are described in section *(g)*.

V.   Appendix D: The indirect method of calculating net cash provided (or used) by operating activities

    A.   The reconciliation of net income and net cash provided (or used) by operating activities begins with the period's net income.

B. Net income is adjusted to accomplish three purposes:

1. To reflect the cash flow effects of increases or decreases in all noncash current asset and current liability account balances.

2. To exclude the income effects of noncash revenues and expenses.

3. To exclude from net income any gains and losses from investing and financing activities.

C. A working paper approach may be used to organize and analyze the information to prepare a statement of cash flows by the indirect method, including the supplemental disclosures of noncash investing and financing activities.

1. The working paper has four money columns.

2. Columns one and four contain the beginning and ending balances of each balance sheet account. Columns two and three are for reconciling the changes in each balance sheet account.

3. Separate sections on the working paper present *(a)* balance sheet items with debit balances; *(b)* balance sheet items with credit balances; *(c)* cash flows from operating activities, starting with net income; *(d)* cash flows from investing activities; *(e)* cash flows from financing activities; and *(f)* noncash investing and financing activities.

4. Information for sections *(c)-(f)* is developed in four steps in the Analysis of Changes columns:

   a. By adjusting net income for the changes in all noncash current asset and current liability account balances. This reconciles the changes in these accounts.
   b. By eliminating from net income the effects of all noncash revenues and expenses. This begins the reconciliation of noncurrent assets.
   c. By eliminating from net income any gains or losses from investing and financing activities. This involves the reconciliation of noncurrent assets and noncurrent liabilities and perhaps the recording of disclosures in sections *(c)-(g)*.
   d. By entering any remaining items, such as dividend payments, which are necessary to reconcile the changes in all balance sheet accounts.

Problem I

Many of the important ideas and concepts discussed in the chapter are reflected in the following list of key terms. Test your understanding of these terms by matching the appropriate definitions with the terms. Record the number identifying the most appropriate definition in the blank space next to each term.

_____ Cash equivalent

_____ Direct method of calculating net cash provided or used by operating activities

_____ Financing activities

_____ Indirect method of calculating net cash provided or used by operating activities

_____ Investing activities

_____ Operating activities

_____ Statement of cash flows

1. Transactions of a business that involve borrowing cash on a short-term basis or that are with the owners or long-term creditors of the business.

2. Activities that involve the production or purchase of merchandise and the sale of goods and services to customers, including expenditures to administer the business.

3. A calculation of the net cash provided or used by operating activities that lists the major classes of operating cash receipts, such as receipts from customers, and subtracts the major classes of operating cash disbursements, such as cash paid for merchandise.

4. A financial statement that reports the cash inflows and outflows for an accounting period, and that classifies those cash flows

as operating activities, investing activities, and financing activities.

5. A calculation that begins with net income and then adjusts the net income amount by adding and subtracting items that are necessary to reconcile net income to the net cash provided or used by operating activities.

6. An investment that is readily convertible to a known amount of cash and that is sufficiently close to its maturity date so that its market value is relatively insensitive to interest rate changes.

7. Transactions that involve making and collecting loans or that involve purchasing and selling plant assets, other productive assets, or investments (other than cash equivalents).

Problem II

Opposite each transaction, place an "X" in the box below the caption that best describes its disclosure category on a statement of cash flows or supplemental schedule in the case of noncash investing and financing activities.

Problem II *(continued)*

Transaction	Operating Activity	Investing Activity	Financing Activity	Noncash Investing & Financing Activity
1. Paid wages and salaries.				
2. Cash sale of used equipment.				
3. Received a cash dividend.				
4. Issued a long-term bond payable for cash.				
5. Cash sale of merchandise.				
6. Purchased land in exchange for common stock.				
7. Paid a cash dividend.				
8. Paid interest expense.				
9. Purchased stock in another company for cash.				
10. Repaid a six-month note payable.				

Problem III

Analyze the information presented in each question below and determine the missing amounts.

1. Accounts receivable decreased from $25,000 at the beginning of the period to $18,000 at the end of the period. Sales revenue was $280,000. Assume all sales were on account. There were no uncollectible accounts written off during the period. How much cash was collected from customers during the period?

   _____

2. Merchandise inventory increased from $90,000 at the beginning of the period to $100,000 at the end of the period. Cost of goods sold was $160,000. How much merchandise inventory was purchased during the period?

   _____

3. The Accounts Payable balance decreased during the period from $30,000 to $26,000. Disregard your answer to question 2 and assume purchases of merchandise during the period totaled $120,000. Assume all purchases were on account. How much cash was paid to merchandise suppliers during the period?

   _____

Problem III *(continued)*

4. The balance of Accumulated Depreciation increased during the period from $200,000 to $220,000. Also, machinery originally costing $10,000 with accumulated depreciation of $8,000 was sold during the period. What was the amount of the period's depreciation expense?

5. Refer back to question 1. Instead of assuming all sales revenues of $280,000 were on account, assume cash sales totaled $100,000 and credit sales totaled $180,000. How much cash was collected from customers during the period?

Problem IV

Iker Company's 1990 and 1989 balance sheets are presented below along with its 1990 income statement.

IKER COMPANY
Balance Sheet
December 31, 1990, and 1989

Assets

	1990		1989	
Cash		$ 8,000		$ 5,000
Accounts receivable		15,000		12,000
Merchandise inventory		30,000		33,000
Equipment	$40,000		$38,000	
Less accumulated depreciation	16,000	24,000	18,000	20,000
Total assets		$77,000		$70,000

Liabilities and Stockholders' Equity

	1990	1989
Accounts payable	$21,000	$17,000
Accrued liabilities	4,000	5,000
Common stock, $5 par value	35,000	30,000
Retained earnings	17,000	18,000
Total liabilities and stockholders' equity	$77,000	$70,000

IKER COMPANY
Income Statement
For Year Ended December 31, 1990

Sales		$80,000
Cost of goods sold		30,000
Gross profit on sales		$50,000
Operating expenses	$20,000	
Depreciation expense	10,000	
Loss from sale of plant assets	5,000	35,000
Net income		$15,000

Problem IV *(continued)*

Additional information about the company's activities in 1990 is as follows:

1. Sold used equipment costing $20,000 with accumulated depreciation of $12,000 for $3,000 cash.
2. Purchased equipment costing $22,000 by paying $17,000 cash and issuing 1,000 shares of common stock.
3. Paid cash dividends of $16,000.

Required:

a. Use the indirect method to reconcile Iker Company's net income with its net cash flows provided (or used) by operating activities.

Problem IV *(continued)*

b. Below is Iker Company's 1990 working paper for a statement of cash flows. Complete the working paper assuming the direct method is required.

IKER COMPANY
Working Paper for Statement of Cash Flows (Direct Method)
For Year Ended December 31, 1990

	DECEMBER 31, 1989	ANALYSIS OF CHANGES DEBIT	CREDIT	DECEMBER 31, 1990
Balance sheet—Debits:				
Cash	5 0 0 0 00			8 0 0 0 00
Accounts receivable	1 2 0 0 0 00			1 5 0 0 0 00
Merchandise inventory	3 3 0 0 0 00			3 0 0 0 0 00
Equipment	3 8 0 0 0 00			4 0 0 0 0 00
	8 8 0 0 0 00			9 3 0 0 0 00
Balance sheet—Credits:				
Accumulated depreciation	1 8 0 0 0 00			1 6 0 0 0 00
Accounts payable	1 7 0 0 0 00			2 1 0 0 0 00
Accrued liabilities	5 0 0 0 00			4 0 0 0 00
Common stock, $5 par value	3 0 0 0 0 00			3 5 0 0 0 00
Retained earnings	1 8 0 0 0 00			1 7 0 0 0 00
	8 8 0 0 0 00			9 3 0 0 0 00
Income statement:				
Statement of cash flows:				
Operating activities:				
Investing activities:				
Financing activities:				
Noncash investing and financing activities:				

Solutions for Chapter 14

Problem I

Cash equivalent 6

Direct method of calculating
net cash provided or used
by operating activities 3

Financing activities 1

Indirect method of calculating
net cash provided or used by
operating activities 5

Investing activities 7

Operating activities 2

Statement of cash flows 4

Problem II

Transaction	Classification
1. Paid wages and salaries	Operating activity
2. Cash sale of used equipment	Investing activity
3. Received a cash dividend	Operating activity
4. Issued a long-term bond payable for cash	Financing activity
5. Cash sale of merchandise	Operating activity
6. Purchased land in exchange for common stock	Noncash investing and financing activity
7. Paid a cash dividend	Financing activity
8. Paid interest expense	Operating activity
9. Purchased stock in another company for cash	Investing activity
10. Repaid a six-month note payable	Financing activity

Problem III

1. Cash collections from customers:	$280,000 + $ 25,000 − $18,000	= $287,000
2. Merchandise purchases:	$160,000 + $100,000 − $90,000	= $170,000
3. Cash payments for merchandise:	$120,000 + $ 30,000 − $26,000	= $124,000
4. Depreciation expense:	$220,000 − $200,000 + $ 8,000	= $ 28,000
5. Cash collections from customers:	$100,000 + $180,000 + $25,000 − $18,000	= $287,000

Problem IV

a.

IKER COMPANY
Reconciliation of Net Income to Net Cash
Provided by Operating Activities
For Year Ended December 31, 1990

Net income		$15,000
Adjustments:		
Less increase in accounts receivable	$ (3,000)	
Add decrease in merchandise inventory	3,000	
Add increase in accounts payable	4,000	
Less decrease in accrued liabilities	(1,000)	
Add depreciation expense	10,000	
Add loss from sale of equipment	5,000	
Total adjustments		18,000
Net cash flows provided by operating activities		$33,000

Problem IV *(continued)*

IKER COMPANY
Working Paper for Statement of Cash Flows (Direct Method)
For Year Ended December 31, 1990

	DECEMBER 31, 1989	ANALYSIS OF CHANGES				DECEMBER 31, 1990
		DEBIT		CREDIT		
Balance sheet—Debits:						
Cash	5,000					8,000
Accounts receivable	12,000	(a1)	80,000	(a2)	77,000	15,000
Merchandise inventory	33,000	(b2)	27,000	(b1)	30,000	30,000
Equipment	38,000	(g1)	22,000	(e)	20,000	40,000
	88,000					93,000
Balance sheet—Credits:						
Accumulated depreciation	18,000	(e)	12,000	(d)	10,000	16,000
Accounts payable	17,000	(b3)	23,000	(b2)	27,000	21,000
Accrued liabilities	5,000	(c2)	21,000	(c1)	20,000	4,000
Common stock, $5 par value	30,000			(g2)	5,000	35,000
Retained earnings	18,000	(h)	16,000	(f)	15,000	17,000
	88,000					93,000
Income statement:						
Sales				(a1)	80,000	
Cost of goods sold		(b1)	30,000			
Operating expenses		(c1)	20,000			
Depreciation expense		(d)	10,000			
Loss from sale of equipment		(e)	5,000			
Net income		(f)	15,000			
Statement of cash flows:						
Operating activities:						
Receipts from customers		(a2)	77,000			
Payments for merchandise				(b3)	23,000	
Payments for operating expenses				(c2)	21,000	
Investing activities:						
Proceeds from sale of equipment		(e)	3,000			
Payment for purchase of equipment				(g1)	17,000	
Financing activities:						
Payment of cash dividends				(h)	16,000	
Noncash investing and financing activities:						
Issued stock to purchase equipment		(g2)	5,000	(g1)	5,000	
			366,000		366,000	

15 Stock Investments, Consolidations, and International Operations

Your objectives in studying this chapter should include learning how to:

1. State the criteria for classifying stock investments as current assets or as long-term investments.

2. Describe the circumstances under which the cost method, the equity method, and consolidated financial statements are used to account for long-term stock investments.

3. Prepare entries to account for long-term stock investments according to the cost method and the equity method and to reflect lower of cost or market.

4. Prepare consolidated balance sheets and explain how to report any excess of investment cost over book value or minority interests.

5. Describe the primary problems of accounting for international operations and prepare entries to account for sales to foreign customers.

6. Define or explain the words and phrases listed in the chapter Glossary.

Topical Outline

I. Stocks as investments

    A. Classifying investments

        1. Marketable equity securities—stocks that are marketable and held as investments of cash available for current operations are listed as current assets.

        2. Long-term investments—stocks that are not marketable or are not intended to serve as ready sources of cash are classified as noncurrent assets.

    B. Accounting for investments in stock

        1. Cost method—used when the investor does not have a significant influence over the investee. The investor usually owns less than 20 percent of the investee's voting stock.

            a. Investor records entire cost of stock as a debit to the investment account.
            b. Each portfolio of stock (current or noncurrent) must be reported at the lower of cost or market.
            c. Loss on market decline of long-term portfolio is reported in stockholders' equity section of balance sheet as an unrealized loss.

        2. Equity method—used when the investor has a significant influence (usually owns 20 percent or more of the voting stock of another corporation).

            a. Investor records purchase at cost (as under the cost method).
            b. The investor corporation's share of the investee corporation's earnings is reported as an increase in the Investment account and as Earnings from Investment.

II. Parent and subsidiary corporations

    A. Consolidated financial statements—prepared when one corporation (parent) controls another corporation (subsidiary). The parent must own more than 50 percent of the subsidiary's voting stock.

        1. A work sheet is used to effect the consolidation.

        2. Duplication in items is eliminated so that they are not counted twice (e.g., parent's Investment in Subsidiary and subsidiary's equity accounts).

        3. Minority interest—the portion of the subsidiary that is not owned by the parent.

        4. Excess of investment cost over book value—created when parent pays more than book value for its share of the subsidiary. This excess should be allocated to subsidiary's assets and liabilities so that they are restated at fair values. Any remaining excess is reported as "Goodwill from consolidation."

III. Accounting for international operations

    A. Multinational businesses are those having operations in several different countries.

    B. Foreign exchange rate—the price of one currency stated in terms of another currency.

    C. Sales and purchases denominated in a foreign currency.

        1. Companies making cash sales (or purchases) for which they receive (or pay) foreign currency must translate the transaction amounts into domestic currency.

        2. Receivables or payables stated in terms of foreign currencies result in exchange gains or losses as the foreign exchange rates fluctuate.

    D. Consolidated statements with foreign subsidiaries—prepared using foreign exchange rates to translate the financial statements of the foreign subsidiaries into domestic currency.

Problem I

The following statements are either true or false. Place a (T) in the parentheses before each true statement and an (F) before each false statement.

1. ( ) All corporate stock is listed and traded on an organized stock exchange such as the New York Stock Exchange.

2. ( ) A stock quoted at 14-3/8 means $14.375 per share.

3. ( ) Receipt of a stock dividend affects the per share cost of the old shares.

4. ( ) Under the cost method, when an investment in stock is sold and the proceeds net of any sales commission differ from cost, a gain or loss must be recorded.

5. ( ) At acquisition, the purchase of stock is recorded at cost regardless of which method is used to account for the investment.

6. ( ) When a parent company buys a subsidiary's stock, the subsidiary's (net) assets and the parent company's investment in the subsidiary are both reported on a consolidated balance sheet.

7. ( ) The excess of book value over cost of a purchased subsidiary should be allocated to reduce the balance sheet valuations of any overvalued assets.

8. ( ) A credit sale by a domestic company to a foreign customer required to make payment in U.S. dollars may result in an exchange gain or loss to the domestic company.

Problem II

You are given several words, phrases or numbers to choose from in completing each of the following statements or in answering the following questions. In each case select the one that best completes the statement or answers the question and place its letter in the answer space provided.

_____ 1. On December 31, Inferior Company had the following stockholders' equity:

Common stock, $1 par value, 10,000 shares issued and outstanding $10,000
Retained earnings   7,500
Total stockholders' equity $17,500

Superior Company purchased 7,000 of Inferior Company's outstanding shares on this date (December 31) paying $2 per share. Related to the stock purchase, what is the excess of cost over book value on the date of purchase?

a. $4,000.
b. $7,000.
c. $5,250.
d. $1,750.
e. $2,500.

Problem II (*continued*)

_____ 2. On December 31, Inferior Company had the following stockholders' equity:

Common stock, $1 par value, 10,000 shares issued and outstanding $10,000
Retained earnings   7,500
Total stockholders' equity $17,500

Superior Company purchased 7,000 of Inferior Company's outstanding shares on this date (December 31) paying $2 per share. What amount of minority interest should be reported on the consolidated balance sheet on the date of purchase?

a. $5,250.
b. $4,200.
c. $3,500.
d. $3,000.
e. $6,000.

_____ 3. On January 1, 1990, Allred Company purchased 12,000 shares of Moore Corporation's common stock at 60-1/4 plus a $6,000 commission. On July 1, 1990, Moore Corporation declared and paid dividends of $0.85 per share, and on December 31, 1990, it reported a net income of $156,000. Assuming Moore Corporation has 48,000 outstanding common shares, what should be the balance in the Investment in Moore Corporation account as of December 31, 1990?

a. $729,000.
b. $757,800.
c. $751,800.
d. $723,000.
e. $750,000.

_____ 4. On January 1, 1990, Allred Company purchased 12,000 shares of Moore Corporation's common stock at 60-1/4 plus a $6,000 commission. On July 1, 1990, Moore Corporation declared and paid dividends of $0.85 per share, and on December 31, 1990, it reported a net income of $156,000. Assuming Moore Corporation has 96,000 outstanding common shares, what should be the balance in the Investment in Moore Corporation account as of December 31, 1990?

a. $723,000.
b. $739,200.
c. $738,300.
d. $719,700.
e. $729,000.

Problem III

Many of the important ideas and concepts discussed in Chapter 15 are reflected in the following list of key terms. Test your understanding of these terms by matching the appropriate definitions with the terms. Record the number identifying the most appropriate definition in the blank space next to each term.

Problem III *(continued)*

_____ Consolidated financial statements

_____ Cost method of accounting for stock investments

_____ Equity method of accounting for stock investments

_____ Foreign exchange rate

_____ Long-term investments

_____ Marketable equity securities

_____ Minority interest

_____ Multinational business

_____ Parent company

_____ Reporting currency

_____ Subsidiary

1. Financial statements that show the results of all operations under the parent's control, including those of any subsidiaries. Assets and liabilities of all affiliated companies are combined on a single balance sheet, revenues and expenses are combined on a single income statement, and cash flows are combined on a single statement of cash flows as though the business were in fact a single company.

2. Investments, not intended as a ready source of cash in case of need, such as bond sinking funds, land, bonds, and stocks that are not marketable or, if marketable, are not held as a temporary investment of cash available for current operations.

3. A corporation that owns a controlling interest (more than 50 percent of the voting stock is required) in another corporation.

4. The portion of a subsidiary company's stockholders' equity that is not owned by the parent corporation.

5. An accounting method whereby the investment is recorded at total cost and maintained at that amount; subsequent investee earnings and dividends do not affect the investment account.

6. An accounting method whereby the investment is recorded at total cost, and the investment account balance is subsequently increased to reflect the investor's equity in earnings of the investee, and decreased to reflect the investor's equity in dividends of the investee.

7. The price of one currency stated in terms of another currency.

8. Common and preferred stocks that are actively traded so that sales prices or bid and ask prices are currently available on a national securities exchange or in the over-the-counter market.

9. The currency in which a company presents its financial statements.

10. A corporation that is controlled by another (parent) corporation because the parent owns more than 50 percent of the subsidiary's voting stock.

11. A company that operates in a large number of different countries.

Problem IV

Complete the following by filling in the blanks.

1. If a corporation acquired _____ of another corporation's common stock, the investor is presumed to have a significant influence on the investee corporation's operations, and the investment should be accounted for according to the

_____.

Problem IV *(continued)*

2. When a parent company purchases an interest in a subsidiary, it may pay more than book value for its equity because:

   a) _____

   _____

   _____.

   b) _____

   _____

   _____.

   c) _____

   _____

   _____.

3. Any entries to Exchange Gain or Loss on foreign currency transactions are closed to

   _____ and included on the

   _____.

4. If P Corporation owns 80% of S Corporation's outstanding stock and a consolidated balance sheet

   for P and S is prepared, the consolidated assets will include _____ (80%, 100%) of S Corporation's assets.

5. When a subsidiary pays a cash dividend, the parent company records receipt of its portion with a

   credit to _____

   _____.

6. Common and preferred stocks that are actively traded so that sales prices or bid and ask prices are currently available on a national securities exchange or in the over-the-counter market are known

   as _____.

Problem V

On January 1, 1990, Large Company paid $90,000 for 36,000 of Small Company's 60,000 outstanding common shares. Small Company paid a dividend of $20,000 on November 1, 1990, and at the end of the year reported earnings of $40,000. On January 3, 1991, Large Company sold its interest in Small Company for $120,000.

1. What method should be used in Large Company's books to account for the investment in Small Company?

   _____

2. Complete general journal entries for Large Company to record the facts presented above. Do not give explanations and skip a line between entries.

DATE	ACCOUNT TITLES AND EXPLANATION	P.R.	DEBIT	CREDIT

Problem VI

Complete the working paper below under the assumption that Parent Company paid $95,000 for 90% of the outstanding stock of Subsidiary Company, after which it lent its subsidiary $20,000, taking a promissory note as evidence of the debt.

PARENT COMPANY AND SUBSIDIARY COMPANY
Work Sheet for Consolidated Balance Sheet
As of Date of Consolidation

	PARENT COMPANY	SUBSIDIARY COMPANY	ELIMINATIONS DR.	ELIMINATIONS CR.	CONSOLIDATED AMOUNTS
Assets					
Cash	5 0 0 0 00	2 0 0 0 0 00			
Note receivable	2 0 0 0 0 00				
Investment in Subsidiary Co.	9 5 0 0 0 00				
Plant and equipment	9 0 0 0 0 00	7 3 0 0 0 00			
Excess of cost over book value					
	21 0 0 0 0 00	9 3 0 0 0 00			
Liabilities and Equities					
Accounts payable	8 0 0 0 00	3 0 0 0 00			
Note payable		2 0 0 0 0 00			
Common stock	12 0 0 0 0 00	5 0 0 0 0 00			
Retained earnings	8 2 0 0 0 00	2 0 0 0 0 00			
Minority interest					
	21 0 0 0 0 00	9 3 0 0 0 00			

Solutions for Chapter 15

Problem I

1.	F	5.	T
2.	T	6.	F
3.	T	7.	T
4.	T	8.	F

Problem II

1.	D
2.	A
3.	B
4.	E

Problem III

Consolidated financial statements	1
Cost method of accounting for stock investments	5
Equity method of accounting for stock investments	6
Foreign exchange rate	7
Long-term investments	2
Marketable equity securities	8
Minority interest	4
Multinational business	11
Parent company	3
Reporting currency	9
Subsidiary	10

Problem IV

1. 20% or more, equity method

2. a) certain of the subsidiary's assets are carried on the subsidiary's books at less than fair value
    b) certain of the subsidiary's liabilities are carried on the subsidiary's books at amounts that are greater than fair values
    c) the subsidiary's earnings prospects are good enough to justify paying more than the fair (market) value of its assets less liabilities

3. Income Summary, income statement

4. 100%

5. Investment in Subsidiary

6. marketable equity securities

Problem V

1. The equity method

2. 1990

Jan. 1	Investment in Small Company	....	90,000.00	
	Cash	....		90,000.00
Nov. 1	Cash	....	12,000.00	
	Investment in Small Company	....		12,000.00
Dec. 31	Investment in Small Company	....	24,000.00	
	Earnings from Investment in Small Company	.....		24,000.00

1991

Jan. 3	Cash	....	120,000.00	
	Investment in Small Company	....		102,000.00
	Gain on Sale of Investments	....		18,000.00

Problem VI

PARENT COMPANY AND SUBSIDIARY COMPANY
Work Sheet for Consolidated Balance Sheet
As of Date of Consolidation

	Parent Company	Subsidiary Company	Eliminations Dr.	Eliminations Cr.	Consolidated Amounts
Assets					
Cash	5,000	20,000	....	....	25,000
Note receivable	20,000	.....	....	(a) 20,000	.....
Investment in Subsidiary Co. ...	95,000	.....	....	(b) 95,000	.....
Plant and equipment	90,000	73,000	....	....	163,000
Excess of cost over book value	......	......	(b) 32,000	....	32,000
	210,000	93,000			220,000
Liabilities and Equities					
Accounts payable	8,000	3,000	....	....	11,000
Note payable	......	20,000	(a) 20,000	....	......
Common stock	120,000	50,000	(b) 50,000	....	120,000
Retained earnings	82,000	20,000	(b) 20,000	....	82,000
Minority interest	......	......	....	(b) 7,000	7,000
	210,000	93,000	122,000	122,000	220,000

16 Analyzing Financial Statements

Your objectives in studying this chapter should include learning how to:

1. List the three broad objectives of financial reporting by business enterprises.

2. Describe, prepare and interpret comparative financial statements and common-size comparative statements.

3. Calculate and explain the interpretation of the ratios, turnovers, and rates of return used to evaluate (a) short-term liquidity, (b) long-term risk and capital structure, and (c) operating efficiency and profitability.

4. State the limitations associated with using financial statement ratios and the sources from which standards for comparison may be obtained.

5. Define or explain the words and phrases listed in the chapter Glossary.

Topical Outline

I. Financial reporting

  A. Includes general purpose financial statements and additional financial information such as is presented in news announcements.

  B. Objectives of financial reporting—financial reporting should provide information:

  1. That is useful to present and potential investors and creditors and other users in making rational investment, credit and similar decisions.

  2. To help present and potential investors and creditors and other users in assessing the amounts, timing, and uncertainty of prospective cash flows.

  3. About the economic resources of an enterprise, the claims to those resources, and the effects of transactions, events, and circumstances that change its resources and claims to those resources.

  C. Conceptual framework—the statement of the objectives of financial reporting is part of the FASB conceptual framework project.

II. Comparative statements

  A. Statements with data for two or more successive accounting periods placed in columns side by side in order to better illustrate changes in the data.

  B. Trend percentages emphasize changes that have occurred from period to period and are useful in comparing data covering a number of years.

  C. Common-size comparative statements—statements in which each amount is expressed as a percentage of a base amount.

III. Analysis of short-term liquidity—the amount of working capital is not a measure of a company's ability to meet current debts or take advantage of discounts. Statistics used in the analysis include:

  A. Current ratio—current assets divided by current liabilities.

  B. Acid-test ratio—quick assets (cash, temporary investments, accounts receivable, and notes receivable) divided by current liabilities.

  C. Accounts receivable turnover—net sales or credit sales divided by average accounts receivable.

  D. Days' sales uncollected—an indication of the speed with which a company collects its accounts; calculated by dividing accounts receivable by net credit sales and then multiplying by 365 days.

  E. Merchandise turnover—the number of times a company's average inventory is sold during an accounting period; calculated by dividing cost of goods sold by average merchandise inventory.

IV. Standards of comparison used by financial analysts

  A. Standards acquired from the analyst's own experience.

  B. Information from other competitive companies in the same industry.

  C. Published data such as that put out by Dun & Bradstreet.

  D. Information published by local and national trade associations.

  E. Rule-of-thumb standards.

V. Analysis of long-term risk and capital structure

    A. Debt and equity ratios—show the percentages of total liabilities and owners' equity supplied by creditors and by owners.

    B. Pledged plant assets to secured liabilities—measures the protection provided the secured creditors by the pledged assets.

    C. Times fixed interest charges earned—measures the security of the return to creditors; calculated by dividing income before fixed interest charges and income taxes by fixed interest charges.

VI. Analysis of operating efficiency and profitability

    A. Profit margin—measured by expressing net income as a percentage of net sales. Shows the ability to generate a net income from sales dollars.

    B. Total asset turnover—measured by dividing average total assets employed into net sales. Shows the efficiency of using assets to generate sales.

    C. Rate of return on total assets employed—measures management's performance; calculated as income before interest and income taxes divided by average total assets employed. Also measured as the product of profit margin and total asset turnover.

    D. Rate of return on common stockholders' equity—calculated as net income (minus preferred dividend requirements, if any) divided by average common stockholders' equity.

    E. Price-earnings ratio

        1. Commonly used in comparing investment opportunities.

        2. Calculated by dividing market price per share by earnings per share.

    F. Dividend yield—measured as annual cash dividends per share divided by market price per share.

Problem I

The following statements are either true or false. Place a (T) in the parentheses before each true statement and an (F) before each false statement.

1. ( ) A current ratio of 2 to 1 always indicates that a company can easily meet its current debts.

2. ( ) Accounts receivable turnover of 6.4 times in 1991 and 8.2 times in 1990 indicates that a company is collecting its accounts receivable more rapidly in 1991 than in 1990.

3. ( ) If accounts receivable is $150,000, and net credit sales is $1,000,000, days' sales uncollected is 15.

4. ( ) On a common-size income statement, the amount of net sales is assigned a value of 100%.

5. ( ) To calculate merchandise turnover, cost of goods sold is divided by gross sales.

6. ( ) The ratios and turnovers of a selected group of competitive companies normally are the best bases of comparison for analyzing financial statements.

7. ( ) Return on total assets employed summarizes the two components of operating efficiency— profit margin and return on total asset turnover.

8. ( ) Current ratio, acid-test ratio, accounts receivable turnover, and merchandise turnover are tools for evaluating short-term liquidity.

Problem II

You are given several words, phrases or numbers to choose from in completing each of the following statements or in answering the following questions. In each case select the one that best completes the statement or answers the question and place its letter in the answer space provided.

_____ 1. To analyze long-term risk and capital structure, the following ratios and statistics for analysis would be used:

    a. debt ratio.
    b. equity ratio.
    c. times fixed interest charges earned.
    d. a and b only.
    e. all of the above.

_____ 2. During 1988, a company's sales were $360,000. In 1989 they were $334,800 and in 1990 they were $374,400. Express the sales in trend percentages, using 1988 as the base year.

    a. 1988– 96%; 1989– 89%; 1990–100%.
    b. 1988–100%; 1989–108%; 1990– 96%.
    c. 1988–100%; 1989–100%; 1990–100%.
    d. 1988–104%; 1989–112%; 1990–100%.
    e. 1988–100%; 1989– 93%; 1990–104%.

Problem II *(continued)*

_____ 3. Information from the 1990 income statement of Becker Company follows:

Sales	$320,000
Gross profit on sales	138,000
Operating income	32,000
Income before taxes	22,000
Net income	16,800

If the company's January 1, 1990, accounts receivable were $23,200 and its December 31, 1990, accounts receivable were $28,000, what was the company's accounts receivable turnover?

a.   7.1 times.
b.   5.4 times.
c.   12.5 times.
d.   3.9 times.
e.   10.1 times.

_____ 4. Information from the 1990 income statement of Sumner Company follows:

Sales	$300,000
Cost of goods sold:	
Merchandise inventory, January 1, 1990	$ 28,480
Purchases, net	171,040
Goods available for sale	$199,520
Merchandise inventory, December 31, 1990	19,520
Cost of goods sold	$180,000
Gross profit on sales	$120,000
Operating income	$ 34,000
Income before taxes	$ 22,400
Net income	$ 16,800

Calculate the company's merchandise turnover.
a.   7.5 times.
b.   9.2 times.
c.   12.5 times.
d.   8.3 times.
e.   17.9 times.

_____ 5. The Keyes Company had the following comparative income statements for 1990 and 1989:

	1990	1989
Net sales	$630,000	$552,000
Cost of goods sold	428,400	389,160
Gross profit from sales	$201,600	$162,840
Operating expenses	97,500	78,600
Net income	$104,100	$ 84,240

What are the cost of goods sold in common-size percentages for 1990 and 1989?

a.   110.1% in 1990; 100.0% in 1989.
b.   24.3% in 1990;   21.6% in 1989.
c.   41.2% in 1990;   46.2% in 1989.
d.   68.0% in 1990;   70.5% in 1989.
e.   147.0% in 1990; 141.8% in 1989.

Problem III

Many of the important ideas and concepts discussed in Chapter 16 are reflected in the following list of key terms. Test your understanding of these terms by matching the appropriate definitions with the terms. Record the number identifying the most appropriate definition in the blank space next to each term.

_____ Accounts receivable turnover

_____ Acid-test ratio

_____ Common-size comparative statements

_____ Comparative statement

_____ Current ratio

_____ Days' sales uncollected

_____ Dividend yield

_____ Financial leverage

_____ Financial reporting

_____ General purpose financial statements

_____ Merchandise turnover

_____ Net working capital

_____ Price-earnings ratio

_____ Profit margin

_____ Quick ratio

_____ Return on common stockholders' equity

_____ Return on total assets employed

_____ Times fixed interest charges earned

_____ Total asset turnover

_____ Working capital

1. The use of debt as a source of assets in the hope of earning a return on those assets that is higher than the rate of interest paid to creditors, thereby increasing the return to stockholders.

2. A component of operating efficiency and profitability, calculated by expressing net income as a percentage of net sales.

3. A component of operating efficiency and profitability, calculated by dividing net sales by average total assets.

4. The relation of a company's current assets to its current liabilities, that is, current assets divided by current liabilities.

5. A synonym for working capital.

6. The annual amount of cash dividends paid to a share of stock divided by the market price per share; used to compare the dividend paying performance of different investment alternatives.

7. A financial statement with data for two or more successive accounting periods placed in columns side by side, sometimes with changes shown in dollar amounts and percentages.

8. Current assets minus current liabilities.

9. A synonym for acid-test ratio.

10. Comparative financial statements in which each amount is expressed as a percentage of a base amount. In the balance sheet, the amount of total assets is usually selected as the base amount and is expressed as 100%. In the income statement, net sales is usually selected as the base amount.

11. An indication of how long it takes a company to collect its accounts, calculated by dividing credit sales (or net sales) by the average accounts receivable balance.

12. The number of days of average credit sales volume that would add to the accounts receivable balance, calculated as the product of 365 times the accounts receivable balance divided by charge sales.

Problem III *(continued)*

13. Statements published periodically, which include the income statement, balance sheet, statement of retained earnings or statement of changes in stockholders' equity, and statement of cash flows.

14. A summary measure of operating efficiency and management performance, calculated by expressing net income as a percentage of average total assets.

15. A measure of profitability in the use of assets provided by common stockholders, measured by expressing net income less preferred dividends as a percentage of average common stockholders' equity.

16. A measure of a company's ability to satisfy fixed interest charges, calculated as net income before interest and income taxes divided by fixed interest charges.

17. The number of times a company's average inventory is sold during an accounting period, calculated by dividing cost of goods sold by the average merchandise inventory balance.

18. A measure used to evaluate the profitability of alternative common stock investments, calculated as market price per share of common stock divided by earnings per share.

19. The relation of quick assets, such as cash, short-term investments, accounts receivable, and notes receivable, to current liabilities, calculated as quick assets divided by current liabilities.

20. The process of preparing and issuing financial information about a company.

Problem IV

The sales, cost of goods sold, and gross profits from sales of the Laker Company for a five-year period are shown below:

	1990	1991	1992	1993	1994
Sales	$350,000	$385,000	$413,000	$455,000	$497,000
Cost of goods sold	250,000	280,000	305,000	345,000	375,000
Gross profit	$100,000	$105,000	$108,000	$110,000	$122,000

Laker Company's sales are expressed in trend percentages below. Express its cost of goods sold and gross profit in trend percentages in the spaces provided.

	1990	1991	1992	1993	1994
Sales	100	110	118	130	142
Cost of good sold					
Gross profit					

Comment on the situation shown by the data:

_____

_____

_____

_____

_____

Problem V

Complete the following by filling in the blanks.

1. When calculating accounts receivable turnover, the preferable sales number to use is _____ (cash, credit, total) sales.

2. The acid-test ratio is calculated by dividing _____ by _____. This ratio is a check on _____.

3. Merchandise turnover is calculated by dividing _____ by _____. It is an indication of _____ _____.

4. A slower turnover of merchandise inventory _____ (will, will not) tend to increase working capital requirements.

5. The current ratio is calculated by dividing _____ _____ by _____. It is an indication of _____ with which a company can meet its current obligations.

6. The rate of return on total assets employed is calculated by dividing _____ _____ by _____ amount of assets employed during the year.

7. Times fixed interest charges earned is calculated by dividing income before deducting _____ and _____ _____ by the amount of the _____ _____.

Problem V *(continued)*

8. Days' sales uncollected are calculated by dividing _____

_____ by _____

and multiplying the resulting quotient by _____

_____. Days' sales uncollected are an indication of

_____

_____.

9. The price-earnings ratio for a company's common stock is calculated by dividing the

_____ per share of the common stock by

_____.

10. The rate of return on common stockholders' equity is calculated by dividing _____

_____ by

_____ stockholders' equity.

11. Compared to companies with an average growth rate, companies in a growth industry would be

expected to have a _____ (higher, lower) price-earnings ratio.

Problem VI

1. Following are the condensed income statements of two companies of unequal size.

    Examine the statement amounts and write in this space (_____) the name of the company that operated more efficiently. If you cannot tell from examining the statement amounts, write "cannot tell" in the blank.

COMPANIES A AND Z
Income Statements
For Year Ended December 31, 19—

	Company A	Company Z
Sales	$325,000	$265,000
Cost of goods sold	204,750	164,300
Gross profit on sales	$120,250	$100,700
Selling expenses	$ 61,750	$ 49,025
Administrative expenses	42,250	34,450
Total operating expenses	$104,000	$ 83,475
Net income	$ 16,250	$ 17,225

Problem VI *(continued)*

2. Common-size percentages are often used in comparing the statements of companies of unequal size. Below are the condensed income statements of Companies A and Z with the income statement amounts of Company A already expressed in common-size percentages. Express the income statement amounts of Company Z in common-size percentages in the spaces provided.

COMPANIES A AND Z
Income Statements
For Year Ended December 31, 19—

	Dollar Amounts		Common-Size Percentages	
	Company A	Company Z	Company A	Company Z
Sales	$325,000	$265,000	100.0	_____
Cost of goods sold	204,750	164,300	63.0	_____
Gross profit on sales	$120,250	$100,700	37.0	_____
Selling expenses	$ 61,750	$ 49,025	19.0	_____
Administrative expenses	42,250	34,450	13.0	_____
Total operating expenses	$104,000	$ 83,475	32.0	_____
Net income	$ 16,250	$ 17,225	5.0	_____

3. After expressing the Company Z income statement amounts in common-size percentages, examine the common-size percentages of the two companies and write in this space

(_____) the name of the company that operated more efficiently.

Solutions for Chapter 16

Problem I

1.	F	5.	F
2.	F	6.	T
3.	F	7.	T
4.	T	8.	T

Problem II

1.	E
2.	E
3.	C
4.	A
5.	D

Problem III

Accounts receivable turnover	11	Merchandise turnover	17
Acid-test ratio	19	Net working capital	5 or 8
Common-size comparative statements	10	Price-earnings ratio	18
		Profit margin	2
Comparative statement	7	Quick ratio	9 or 19
Current ratio	4	Return on common stockholders' equity	15
Days' sales uncollected	12		
Dividend yield	6	Return on total assets employed	14
Financial leverage	1	Times fixed interest charges earned	16
Financial reporting	20	Total asset turnover	3
General purpose financial statements	13	Working capital	8

Problem IV

	1990	1991	1992	1993	1994
Sales	100	110	118	130	142
Cost of goods sold	100	112	122	138	150
Gross profit	100	105	108	110	122

Laker Company's sales increased each year throughout the five-year period, but its cost of goods sold increased more rapidly. This slowed the rate of increase in its gross profit.

Problem V

1. credit

2. quick assets, current liabilities, the ability to pay debts that mature in the very near future

3. cost of goods sold, average inventory, merchandising efficiency

4. will

5. current assets, current liabilities, the ease

6. net income, the average

7. income taxes, fixed interest charges, fixed interest charges

Problem V *(continued)*

8. accounts receivable, charge sales, the number of days in a year, collection efficiency (the speed with which a company collects its accounts)

9. market price, earnings per share

10. net income less any preferred dividends, average common

11. higher

Problem VI

1. The average person cannot tell from an examination of the figures which company operated more efficiently.

2.

COMPANIES A AND Z
Income Statements
For Year Ended December 31, 19—

	Dollar Amounts		Common-Size Percentages	
	Company A	Company Z	Company A	Company Z
Sales	$325,000	$265,000	100.0	100.0
Cost of goods sold	204,750	164,300	63.0	62.0
Gross profit on sales	$120,250	$100,700	37.0	38.0
Selling expenses	$ 61,750	$ 49,025	19.0	18.5
Administrative expenses	42,250	34,450	13.0	13.0
Total operating expenses	$104,000	$ 83,475	32.0	31.5
Net income	$ 16,250	$ 17,225	5.0	6.5

3.   Company Z

Appendix E
Special Journals

Your objectives in studying this appendix should include learning how to:

1. Explain how columnar journals save posting labor, and state the type of transaction that is recorded in each journal when special journals are used.

2. Record and post transactions when special journals are used.

3. Define or explain the words and phrases listed in the appendix Glossary.

Topical Outline

I. Special Journals

  A. Reduce writing and posting labor, by grouping similar transactions together and recording them in one place and periodically posting totals accumulated.

II. Sales Journal—typically a single column journal in which all credit sales but no other transactions are recorded.

  A. Individual entries in the Sales Journal are posted to the accounts in the subsidiary Accounts Receivable Ledger.

  B. The column total of the Sales Journal is posted as a debit to Accounts Receivable and as a credit to Sales in the General Ledger.

III. Cash Receipts Journal—a multicolumn journal in which all cash receipts but no other transactions are recorded.

  A. A column titled "Other Accounts—Credit" is used to record all types of receipts that are not frequent enough to justify having separate columns. Each credit in the Other Accounts column must be posted individually.

  B. Separate credit columns, for which only the totals are posted, are usually established for Accounts Receivable and Sales. A separate debit column may be used for sales discounts.

IV. Purchases Journal—all credit purchases but no cash purchases of merchandise are recorded in this journal. Also, separate columns may be established for frequent credit purchases such as store supplies and office supplies.

  A. If the journal does not have columns in which to enter certain types of credit purchases, those purchases must be entered in the General Journal.

  B. Credits to the accounts of particular creditors are individually posted to the subsidiary Accounts Payable Ledger.

V. Cash Disbursements Journal—all cash payments except those made from petty cash are recorded in this journal. (A reimbursement of petty cash is, however, recorded in the Cash Disbursements Journal.)

  A. A Check Register is a cash disbursements journal that includes a column for entering the number of each check.

  B. An "Other Accounts—Debit" column is necessary so that the journal can accommodate all types of cash payments.

VI. General Journal—must be provided even when special journals are used.

  A. Allows the recording of entries which do not fit under any of the special journals.

  B. Examples are:

   1. Adjusting entries.

   2. Closing entries.

   3. Other entries such as credit purchases of items other than merchandise.

VII. Other issues

    A.   If a company collects sales taxes from its customers, the Sales Journal usually has a separate column in which the taxes are recorded.

    B.   In some companies, a collection of all sales invoices serves as a Sales Journal.

    C.   Sales returns may be recorded in the General Journal, or a separate Sales Returns and Allowances Journal is sometimes used.

Problem I

The following statements are either true or false. Place a (T) in the parentheses before each true statement and an (F) before each false statement.

1. (   )   A Purchases Journal is used to record all purchases.

2. (   )   At month-end, the total sales recorded in the Sales Journal is debited to Accounts Receivable and credited to Sales.

3. (   )   Sales is a General Ledger account.

4. (   )   Transactions recorded in a journal do not necessarily result in equal debits and credits to General Ledger accounts.

5. (   )   If a general journal entry is used to record a charge sale, the credit of the entry must be posted twice.

Problem II

You are given several words, phrases or numbers to choose from in completing each of the following statements or in answering the following questions. In each case select the one that best completes the statement or answers the question and place its letter in the answer space provided.

_____   1.   A company that uses a Sales Journal, a Purchases Journal, a Cash Receipts Journal, a Cash Disbursements Journal, and a General Journal borrowed $1,500 from the bank in exchange for a note payable to the bank. In which journal would the transaction be recorded?

    a.   Sales Journal.
    b.   Purchases Journal.
    c.   Cash Receipts Journal.
    d.   Cash Disbursements Journal.
    e.   General Journal.

_____   2.   A company that uses a Sales Journal, a Purchases Journal, a Cash Receipts Journal, a Cash Disbursements Journal, and a General Journal paid a creditor for office supplies purchased on account. In which journal would the transaction be recorded?

    a.   Sales Journal.
    b.   Purchases Journal.
    c.   Cash Receipts Journal.
    d.   Cash Disbursements Journal.
    e.   General Journal.

Problem III

Many of the important ideas and concepts discussed in Appendix E are reflected in the following list of key terms. Test your understanding of these terms by matching the appropriate definitions with the terms. Record the number identifying the most appropriate definition in the blank space next to each term.

_____   Check Register   _____   General Ledger

_____   Columnar journal   _____   Special journal

Problem III (continued)

1. The ledger containing the financial statement accounts of a business.

2. A book of original entry having columns, each of which is designated as the place for entering specific data about each transaction of a group of similar transactions.

3. A book of original entry that is designed and used for recording only a specified type of transaction.

4. A book of original entry for recording cash payments by check.

Problem IV

Complete the following by filling in the blanks.

1. When a company records sales returns with general journal entries, the credit of an entry recording such a return is posted to two different accounts. This does not cause the trial balance to be out of

    balance because _____

    _____.

2. Cash sales _____ (are, are not) normally recorded in the Sales Journal.

3. When special journals are used, credit purchases of store supplies or office supplies should be

    recorded in the _____.

Problem V

Below are eight transactions completed by McGuff Company on September 30 of this year. Following the transactions are the company's journals with prior September transactions recorded therein.

Requirement One: Record the eight transactions in the company's journals.

Sept. 30 Received an $808.50 check from Ted Clark in full payment of the September 20, $825 sale, less the $16.50 discount.

   30 Received a $550 check from a tenant in payment of his October rent.

   30 Sold merchandise to Inez Smythe on credit, Invoice No. 655, $1,675.

   30 Received merchandise and an invoice dated September 28, terms 2/10, n/60 from Johnson Company, $4,000.

   30 Purchased store equipment on account from Olson Company, terms n/10, EOM, $950.

   30 Issued Check No. 525 to Kerry Meadows in payment of her $650 salary.

   30 Issued Check No. 526 for $1,715 to Olson Company in full payment of its September 20 invoice, less a $35 discount.

   30 Cash sales for the last half of the month totaled $9,450.50.

Special Journals   **273**

Problem V *(continued)*

GENERAL JOURNAL   Page 17

DATE	ACCOUNT TITLES AND EXPLANATION	P.R.	DEBIT	CREDIT

SALES JOURNAL   Page 8

DATE		ACCOUNT DEBITED	INVOICE NUMBER	P.R.	AMOUNT
19—					
Sept.	3	N. R. Boswell	651	√	1 875 00
	15	Inez Smythe	652	√	1 500 00
	20	Ted Clark	653	√	825 00
	24	N. R. Boswell	654	√	2 250 00

PURCHASES JOURNAL   Page 8

DATE		ACCOUNT CREDITED	DATE OF INVOICE	TERMS	P.R.	AMOUNT
19—						
Sept.	8	Johnson Company	9/6	2/10, n/60	√	3 750 00
	22	Olson Company	9/20	2/10, n/60	√	1 750 00
	24	Olson Company	9/22	2/10, n/60	√	5 625 00

Problem V (continued)

Page 9

CASH RECEIPTS JOURNAL

DATE	ACCOUNT CREDITED	EXPLANATION	P.R.	OTHER ACCOUNTS CREDIT	ACCOUNTS RECEIVABLE CREDIT	SALES CREDIT	SALES DISCOUNTS DEBIT	CASH DEBIT
19—								
Sept. 1	Rent Earned	Tenant's September rent	711	550 00				550 00
13	N. R. Boswell	Full payment of account	√		1875 00		37 50	1837 50
15	Sales	Cash sales	√			9000 00		9000 00

Page 7

CASH DISBURSEMENTS JOURNAL

DATE	CH. NO.	PAYEE	ACCOUNT DEBITED	P.R.	OTHER ACCOUNTS DEBIT	ACCOUNTS PAYABLE DEBIT	PURCHASES DISCOUNTS CREDIT	CASH CREDIT
19—								
Sept. 15	523	Kerry Meadows	Salaries Expense	611	650 00			650 00
16	524	Johnson Company	Johnson Company	√		3750 00	75 00	3675 00

Requirement Two: The individual postings from the journals of McGuff Company through September 29 have been made. Complete the individual postings from the journals.

Requirement Three: Foot and crossfoot the journals and make the month-end postings.

Requirement Four: Complete the trial balance and test the subsidiary ledgers by preparing schedules of accounts receivable and accounts payable.

Problem V *(continued)*

ACCOUNTS RECEIVABLE LEDGER

N. R. Boswell

2200 Falstaff Street

DATE		EXPLANATION	P.R.	DEBIT	CREDIT	BALANCE
19—Sept.	3		S–8	1 875 00		1 875 00
	13		R–9		1 875 00	–0–
	24		S–8	2 250 00		2 250 00

Ted Clark

10765 Catonsville Avenue

DATE		EXPLANATION	P.R.	DEBIT	CREDIT	BALANCE
19—Sept.	20		S–8	825 00		825 00

Inez Smythe

785 Violette Circle

DATE		EXPLANATION	P.R.	DEBIT	CREDIT	BALANCE
19—Sept.	15		S–8	1 500 00		1 500 00

ACCOUNTS PAYABLE LEDGER

Johnson Company

118 E. Seventh Street

DATE		EXPLANATION	P.R.	DEBIT	CREDIT	BALANCE
19—Sept.	8		P–8		3 750 00	3 750 00
	16		D–7	3 750 00		–0–

Olson Company

788 Hazelwood Avenue

DATE		EXPLANATION	P.R.	DEBIT	CREDIT	BALANCE
19—Sept.	22		P–8		1 750 00	1 750 00
	24		P–8		5 625 00	7 375 00

Problem V (continued)

GENERAL LEDGER

Cash   Account No. 111

DATE	EXPLANATION	P.R.	DEBIT	CREDIT	BALANCE

Accounts Receivable   Account No. 112

DATE	EXPLANATION	P.R.	DEBIT	CREDIT	BALANCE

Store Equipment   Account No. 133

DATE	EXPLANATION	P.R.	DEBIT	CREDIT	BALANCE

Accounts Payable   Account No. 212

DATE	EXPLANATION	P.R.	DEBIT	CREDIT	BALANCE

Sales   Account No. 411

DATE	EXPLANATION	P.R.	DEBIT	CREDIT	BALANCE

Sales Discounts   Account No. 412

DATE	EXPLANATION	P.R.	DEBIT	CREDIT	BALANCE

Problem V *(continued)*

	Purchases			Account No. 511

DATE		EXPLANATION	P.R.	DEBIT	CREDIT	BALANCE

	Purchases Discounts			Account No. 512

DATE		EXPLANATION	P.R.	DEBIT	CREDIT	BALANCE

	Salaries Expense			Account No. 611

DATE		EXPLANATION	P.R.	DEBIT	CREDIT	BALANCE
19— Sept.	15		D–7	650 00		650 00

	Rent Earned			Account No. 711

DATE		EXPLANATION	P.R.	DEBIT	CREDIT	BALANCE
19— Sept.	1		R–9		550 00	550 00

MCGUFF COMPANY
Trial Balance
September 30, 19—

Cash		
Accounts receivable		
Store equipment		
Accounts payable		
Sales		
Sales discounts		
Purchases		
Purchases discounts		
Salaries expense		
Rent earned		

Problem V *(continued)*

MCGUFF COMPANY

Schedule of Accounts Receivable

September 30, 19—

MCGUFF COMPANY

Schedule of Accounts Payable

September 30, 19—

Solutions for Appendix E

Problem I   Problem II

1. F   1. C
2. T   2. D
3. T
4. F
5. F

Problem III

Check Register 4   General Ledger 1
Columnar journal 2   Special journal 3

Problem IV

1. only the balance of one of the accounts, the Accounts Receivable account, appears on the trial balance.

2. are not

3. Purchases Journal

Problem V

Sept. 30 Store Equipment 133   950.00
         Accounts Payable—Olson Company .... 212/√   950.00

SALES JOURNAL   Page 8

DATE		ACCOUNT DEBITED	INVOICE NUMBER	P.R.	AMOUNT
19— Sept.	3	N. R. Boswell	651	√	1875 00
	15	Inez Smythe	652	√	1500 00
	20	Ted Clark	653	√	825 00
	24	N. R. Boswell	654	√	2250 00
	30	Inez Smythe	655	√	1675 00
	30	Accounts Receivable, Dr., Sales, Cr.			8125 00

(112/411)

Problem V *(continued)*

PURCHASES JOURNAL
Page 8

DATE		ACCOUNT CREDITED	DATE OF INVOICE	TERMS	P.R.	AMOUNT
19—						
Sept.	8	Johnson Company	9/6	2/10, n/60	√	3 7 5 0 00
	22	Olson Company	9/20	2/10, n/60	√	1 7 5 0 00
	24	Olson Company	9/22	2/10, n/60	√	5 6 2 5 00
	30	Johnson Company	9/28	2/10, n/60	√	4 0 0 0 00
	30	Purchases, Dr., Accounts Payable, Cr.				1 5 1 2 5 00

(511/212)

CASH RECEIPTS JOURNAL
Page 9

DATE		ACCOUNT CREDITED	P.R.	OTHER ACCOUNTS CREDIT	ACCOUNTS RECEIVABLE CREDIT	SALES CREDIT	SALES DISCOUNTS DEBIT	CASH DEBIT
19—								
Sept.	1	Rent Earned	711	5 5 0 00				5 5 0 00
	13	N. R. Boswell	√		1 8 7 5 00		3 7 50	1 8 3 7 50
	15	Sales	√			9 0 0 0 00		9 0 0 0 00
	30	Ted Clark	√		8 2 5 00		1 6 50	8 0 8 50
	30	Rent Earned	711	5 5 0 00				5 5 0 00
	30	Sales	√			9 4 5 0 50		9 4 5 0 50
	30	Totals		1 1 0 0 00	2 7 0 0 00	18 4 5 0 50	5 4 00	22 1 9 6 50

(√)   (112)   (411)   (412)   (111)

CASH DISBURSEMENTS JOURNAL
Page 7

DATE		CH. NO.	PAYEE	ACCOUNT DEBITED	P.R.	OTHER ACCOUNTS DEBIT	ACCOUNTS PAYABLE DEBIT	PURCHASES DISCOUNTS CREDIT	CASH CREDIT
19—									
Sept.	15	523	Kerry Meadows	Salaries Expense	611	6 5 0 00			6 5 0 00
	16	524	Johnson Company	Johnson Company	√		3 7 5 0 00	7 5 00	3 6 7 5 00
	30	525	Kerry Meadows	Salaries Expense	611	6 5 0 00			6 5 0 00
	30	526	Olson Company	Olson Company	√		1 7 5 0 00	3 5 00	1 7 1 5 00
	30		Totals			1 3 0 0 00	5 5 0 0 00	1 1 0 00	6 6 9 0 00

(√)   (212)   (512)   (111)

Problem V *(continued)*

GENERAL LEDGER

Cash

Date	Debit	Credit	Balance
Sept. 30	22,196.50		22,196.50
30		6,690.00	15,506.50

Sales Discounts

Date	Debit	Credit	Balance
Sept. 30	54.00		54.00

Accounts Receivable

Date	Debit	Credit	Balance
Sept. 30	8,125.00		8,125.00
30		2,700.00	5,425.00

Purchases

Date	Debit	Credit	Balance
Sept. 30	15,125.00		15,125.00

Store Equipment

Date	Debit	Credit	Balance
Sept. 30	950.00		950.00

Purchases Discounts

Date	Debit	Credit	Balance
Sept. 30		110.00	110.00

Accounts Payable

Date	Debit	Credit	Balance
Sept. 30		950.00	950.00
30		15,125.00	16,075.00
30	5,500.00		10,575.00

Salaries Expense

Date	Debit	Credit	Balance
Sept. 15	650.00		650.00
30	650.00		1,300.00

Sales

Date	Debit	Credit	Balance
Sept. 30		8,125.00	8,125.00
30		18,450.50	26,575.50

Rent Earned

Date	Debit	Credit	Balance
Sept. 1		550.00	550.00
30		550.00	1,100.00

ACCOUNTS PAYABLE LEDGER

Johnson Company

Date	Debit	Credit	Balance
Sept. 8		3,750.00	3,750.00
16	3,750.00		–0–
30		4,000.00	4,000.00

Olson Company

Date	Debit	Credit	Balance
Sept. 22		1,750.00	1,750.00
24		5,625.00	7,375.00
30		950.00	8,325.00
30	1,750.00		6,575.00

Problem V (*continued*)

ACCOUNTS RECEIVABLE LEDGER

N. R. Boswell

Date	Debit	Credit	Balance
Sept. 3	1,875.00		1,875.00
13		1,875.00	–0–
24	2,250.00		2,250.00

Inez Smythe

Date	Debit	Credit	Balance
Sept. 15	1,500.00		1,500.00
30	1,675.00		3,175.00

Ted Clark

Date	Debit	Credit	Balance
Sept. 20	825.00		825.00
30		825.00	–0–

MCGUFF COMPANY
Trial Balance
September 30, 19—

Cash	$15,506.50	
Accounts receivable	5,425.00	
Store equipment	950.00	
Accounts payable		$10,575.00
Sales		26,575.50
Sales discounts	54.00	
Purchases	15,125.00	
Purchases discounts		110.00
Salaries expense	1,300.00	
Rent earned		1,100.00
Totals	$38,360.50	$38,360.50

MCGUFF COMPANY
Schedule of Accounts Receivable
September 30, 19—

N. R. Boswell	$ 2,250.00
Inez Smythe	3,175.00
Total accounts receivable	$ 5,425.00

MCGUFF COMPANY
Schedule of Accounts Payable
September 30, 19—

Johnson Company	$ 4,000.00
Olson Company	6,575.00
Total accounts payable	$10,575.00

Appendix F
Present and Future Values: An Expansion

Your objectives in studying this appendix should include learning how to:

1. Explain what is meant by the present value of a single amount and the present value of an annuity, and be able to use tables to solve problems that involve present values.

2. Explain what is meant by the future value of a single amount and the future value of an annuity, and be able to use tables to solve problems that involve future values.

Topical Outline

I. Present value of a single amount

   A. The amount that could be invested at a specific interest rate to generate a fund equal to a given amount at a definite future date.

   B. A table of present values for a single amount shows all of the present values of $1, given a variety of different interest rates and a variety of different numbers of time periods that will lapse before the $1 is received.

II. Present value of an annuity

   A. An annuity is a series of payments that are equal in amount and that are to be received or paid on a regular periodic basis.

   B. Present value of an annuity is the amount that could be invested at a specific interest rate to generate a fund that would be exhausted by a series of payments of a given amount for a given number of periods.

   C. A table of present values for an annuity shows all of the present values of different annuities where the amount of each payment is $1 but where the payments occur over different numbers of periods and a variety of different interest rates are assumed.

III. Future value of a single amount

   A. The amount that would be generated at a definite future date if a given present value were invested at a specific interest rate for a given number of periods.

   B. A table of future values of a single amount shows all of the future values of $1 invested now at a variety of different interest rates for a variety of different time periods.

IV. Future value of an annuity

   A. Future value of an annuity is the amount that would be generated at a given future time if a given series of payments were invested periodically at a given interest rate.

   B. A table of future values for an annuity shows all of the future values of different annuities where the amount of each payment is $1 but where the payments occur over different numbers of periods and a variety of different interest rates are assumed.

Problem I

The following statements are either true or false. Place a (T) in the parentheses before each true statement and an (F) before each false statement.

1. ( ) In discounting, if interest is compounded semiannually, the number of periods must be expressed in terms of 6-month periods.

2. ( ) One way to calculate the present value of an annuity is to calculate the present value of each payment and add them together.

3. ( ) A table for the future values of 1 can be used to solve all of the problems that can be solved using a table for the present values of 1.

4. ( ) Erlich Enterprises should be willing to invest $100,000 in an investment that will return $20,000 annually for 10 years if the company requires a 16% return on its investments. (Use the tables in your text to get your answer.)

Problem II

You are given several words, phrases or numbers to choose from in completing each of the following statements or in answering the following questions. In each case select the one that best completes the statement or answers the question and place its letter in the answer space provided. Use the tables in your text as necessary to answer the questions.

_____ 1. Ralph Norton belongs to a retirement plan whereby $300 is deducted from his monthly paycheck and deposited in a retirement fund which earns an annual interest rate of 12%. If Ralph continues with this plan until his retirement in 4 years, how much will be accumulated in the account on the date of the last deposit? (Round to the nearest whole dollar.)

   a. $ 14,400.
   b. $ 17,205.
   c. $ 18,367.
   d. $220,401.
   e. $573,477.

_____ 2. Maxwell Hammer is going to establish a fund for a future business venture. He makes an initial investment of $15,000 and plans to make semiannual contributions of $2,500 to the fund beginning in six months. The fund is expected to earn an annual interest rate of 8%, compounded semiannually. What will be the value of the fund five years hence, when Mr. Hammer plans to use the funds?

   a. $ 52,218.25
   b. $ 36,706.00
   c. $210,106.75
   d. $ 45,015.25
   e. $102,665.50

Problem II *(continued)*

_____ 3. Tricorp Investment Company is considering an investment which is expected to return $320,000, four years after the initial investment. If Tricorp demands a 14% return, what is the most Tricorp will be willing to pay for this investment?

     a. $320,000.
     b. $109,826.
     c. $189,472.
     d. $ 65,026.
     e. $275,200.

_____ 4. Tom Snap has been offered the possibility of investing $0.3756 for fourteen years, after which he will be paid $3. What annual rate of interest will Mr. Snap earn?

     a.   8.0%
     b.   10.0%
     c.   12.0%
     d.   14.0%
     e.   16.0%

Problem III

Sarah Blue has the option of receiving $1,000 per year for the next ten years, or receiving $6,000 in cash immediately, or receiving $10,000 in cash five years hence. Assuming that Ms. Blue's only goal is to maximize her wealth, and that the current interest rate is 10%, which option should she choose?

Problem IV

Complete the following by filling in the blanks. Refer to the tables in Appendix F in the text to find the answers.

1. Leila Turner expects to invest $2 at an 18% annual rate of interest and, at the end of the investment, receive $39.3466. Ms. Turner must wait _____ years before she receives payment.

2. Jim Ables expects to invest $1 for 37 years, after which he will receive $66.2318. Mr. Ables will earn interest at a rate of _____% on his investment.

3. Mr. Biter expects an immediate investment of $10.6748 to return $1 annually for 25 years, the first payment to be received in one year. Mr. Biter will earn interest at a rate of _____% on his investment.

Solutions for Appendix F

Problem I   **Problem II**

1. T   1. C
2. T   2. A
3. T   3. C
4. F   4. E

Problem III

The present value of $1,000 received annually for ten years discounted at 10% equals $6,144.60. The present value of $6,000 received now is $6,000. The present value of $10,000 to be received five years from now is $6,209. Therefore, Ms. Blue should choose to receive $10,000 five years from now.

Problem IV

1. 18. In Table F-2, where the interest rate per period = 18% and present value = 19.6733 ($39.3466/2), number of periods = 18.

2. 12. In Table F-2, where the number of periods = 37 and the future value = 66.2318, the interest rate = 12%.

3. 8. In Table F-3, where the number of periods = 25 and present value = 10.6748, interest rate = 8%.

Appendix G
The Accounting Problem
of Changing Prices

Your objectives in studying this appendix should include learning how to:

1. Explain why conventional financial statements fail to adequately account for price changes.

2. Explain how price changes should be measured and how to construct a price index.

3. Restate historical cost/nominal dollar costs into constant purchasing power amounts and calculate purchasing power gains and losses.

4. Explain the difference between current costs and historical costs stated in constant purchasing power amounts.

5. Define or explain the words and phrases listed in the appendix Glossary.

Topical Outline

I. Conventional financial statements and price changes

   A. Balance sheet amounts are stated in nominal dollars and fail to show the effects of price changes.

   B. Expenses that are allocations of costs recorded in earlier periods are not stated in terms of current dollars.

II. Measuring the change in prices with price indexes

   A. A price index measures the weighted-average changes in the prices of a particular market basket of goods and/or services.

   B. Specific price indexes measure price changes of a narrow group of products; general price indexes measure price changes of a very broad group of products, or general purchasing power.

   C. General indexes are used to restate dollar amounts of cost paid in one period into dollars with the purchasing power of another period.

III. Historical cost/constant purchasing power accounting

   A. Uses a general price index to restate historical cost/nominal dollar statements into historical cost dollar amounts that represent current, general purchasing power.

   B. Procedures involve:

      1. Calculating general purchasing power gain or loss from owning monetary assets or owing monetary liabilities.

      2. Adjusting nonmonetary items for price changes since the items were first purchased.

   C. Does not reflect current values.

IV. Current cost accounting

   A. Uses specific price indexes and other estimates to report current costs in financial statements.

   B. Only nonmonetary items must be adjusted for specific price changes.

V. Disclosing the effects of price changes

   A. Disclosures are not required, but the FASB recommends that several items of information be disclosed.

   B. Recommended disclosures on a current cost basis include: income from continuing operations; the increase or decrease in the current cost of inventory and property, plant, and equipment, net of inflation; net assets at year-end; and income per common share from continuing operations.

Problem I

The following statements are either true or false. Place a (T) in the parentheses before each true statement and an (F) before each false statement.

1. ( ) In conventional accounting, transactions are recorded in terms of the historical number of dollars received or paid.

2. ( ) If in 1985, the base year of a price index, a market basket of goods has a cost of $8, and in 1990, the same market basket of goods costs $9.50, the price index for 1985 is 84.2.

3. ( ) In 1987, $400 was paid to purchase items A and B when the price index was 105. It would take $476 to purchase items A and B in 1990 if the price index was 125.

4. ( ) Historical cost/constant purchasing power accounting uses a general price index to restate the conventional nominal dollar financial statements.

5. ( ) An investment in bonds is an example of a nonmonetary asset.

6. ( ) Monetary assets are adjusted for general price-level changes on an historical cost/constant purchasing power financial statement to reflect changes in the price level that occurred since the assets were acquired.

Problem II

You are given several words, phrases or numbers to choose from in completing each of the following statements or in answering the following questions. In each case select the one that best completes the statement or answers the question and place its letter in the answer space provided.

_____ 1. Current cost accounting:

    a. is based on the conclusion that current liquidation price is the appropriate valuation basis for financial statements.

    b. matches with current revenues the current costs to replace the resources consumed to earn the revenues.

    c. for inventories, productive capacity, cost of sales, and depreciation is required of all U.S. companies.

    d. has become the primary valuation basis for published financial statements of U.S. companies.

    e. None of the above.

_____ 2. A nonmonetary asset was purchased for $25,000 when the general price index was 125. Five years later, when the general price index was 175, the amount that should be shown for the asset on a historical cost/constant purchasing power balance sheet is:

    a. $17,857.
    b. $25,000.
    c. $31,250.
    d. $35,000.
    e. $43,750.

Problem II *(continued)*

_____ 3. The cost of purchasing a given market basket is as follows:

Year	Price
1990	$25.50
1991	30.00
1992	33.60
1993	36.00

Using 1991 as the base year, the price index for 1992 is:

a. 85.0
b. 89.3
c. 100.0
d. 112.0
e. 120.0

_____ 4. The price index for 1990 was 112. Prices increased 25% by 1993. The price index for 1993 is:

a. 80.
b. 100.
c. 125.
d. 137.
e. 140.

_____ 5. In preparing a historical cost/constant purchasing power balance sheet, which of the following categories must be adjusted from nominal dollar amounts to historical cost/constant purchasing power amounts?

a. Monetary assets.
b. Nonmonetary assets.
c. Monetary liabilities.
d. All assets.
e. All liabilities and equities.

Problem III

Many of the important ideas and concepts discussed in Appendix G are reflected in the following list of key terms. Test your understanding of these terms by matching the appropriate definitions with the terms. Record the number identifying the most appropriate definition in the blank space next to each term.

_____ Current cost

_____ Current cost accounting

_____ Deflation

_____ General price-level index

_____ Historical cost/constant purchasing power accounting

_____ Historical cost/nominal dollar financial statements

_____ Inflation

_____ Monetary assets

_____ Monetary liabilities

_____ Nonmonetary assets

_____ Nonmonetary liabilities

_____ Price index

_____ Purchasing power gain or loss

_____ Specific price-level index

Problem III *(continued)*

1. An accounting system that adjusts historical cost/nominal dollar financial statements for changes in the general purchasing power of the dollar.

2. Assets that are not claims to a fixed number of monetary units, the prices of which therefore tend to fluctuate with changes in the general price level.

3. A general increase in the prices paid for goods and services.

4. In general, the cost that would be required to acquire (or replace) an asset or service at the present time; on the income statement, the numbers of dollars that would be required, at the time the expense is incurred, to acquire the resources consumed; on the balance sheet, the amounts that would have to be paid to replace the assets or satisfy the liabilities as of the balance sheet date.

5. A measure of the changes in prices of a particular market basket of goods and/or services.

6. Conventional financial statements that disclose revenues, expenses, assets, liabilities, and owners' equity in terms of the historical monetary units exchanged at the time the transactions occurred.

7. Fixed amounts that are owed, where the number of dollars to be paid does not change regardless of changes in the general price level.

8. Obligations that are not fixed in terms of the number of monetary units needed to satisfy them, and that therefore tend to fluctuate in amount with changes in the general price level.

9. An accounting system that uses specific price-level indexes (and other means) to develop financial statements that report items such as assets and expenses in terms of the costs to acquire or replace those assets or services at the present time.

10. The gain or loss that results from holding monetary assets and/or owing monetary liabilities during a period in which the general price level changes.

11. A measure of the changing purchasing power of a dollar, spent for a very broad range of items; for example, the Consumer Price Index for All Urban Consumers.

12. Money or claims to receive a fixed amount of money, where the number of dollars to be received does not change regardless of changes in the purchasing power of the dollar.

13. An indicator of the changing purchasing power of a dollar spent for items in a category of items that includes a much narrower range of goods and services than does a general price index.

14. A general decrease in the prices paid for goods and services.

Problem IV

Complete the following by filling in the blanks.

1. If a simple average of the unit prices of several items is calculated for each of two years, a comparison of the averages will indicate the impact of the price changes on most purchasers of

    those items only if _____

    _____.

Problem IV *(continued)*

2. Historical cost/constant dollar accounting is sometimes criticized as being an inadequate response

    to the problem of changing prices because it does not present _____

    _____ in financial statements.

3. The two primary alternatives to conventional accounting that make comprehensive adjustments for

    the effects of price changes are _____

    _____ and _____

    _____.

4. _____ represent money or claims to receive a
    fixed amount of money with the number of dollars to be received not changing regardless of
    changes in the purchasing power of the dollar.

5. If the general price index was 115 in 1990 and was 138 in 1994, it would be appropriate to say that

    the _____

    had fallen by _____% from 1990 to 1994.

6. The basic reason why conventional financial statements fail to adequately account for inflation is

    _____

    _____

    _____

    _____

    _____.

7. _____ is the method of
    accounting that makes adjustments for specific price changes in nonmonetary assets and liabilities.

8. A _____ measures the relative costs of purchasing
    a given market basket of items in each of several years or time periods.

Problem V

A product that originally cost $20,000 was later sold for $30,000. At the time of sale, the cost to replace
the product was $25,500. Also, the general price index rose from 92 at the time of purchase to 115 at the
time of sale. Determine the gross profit from sales assuming (1) historical cost/nominal dollar financial
statements; (2) historical cost/constant purchasing power accounting; and (3) current cost accounting.

Problem V *(continued)*

	Historical Cost/ Nominal Dollar Statements	Historical Cost/ Constant Purchasing Power Accounting	Current Cost Accounting
Sales			
Cost of sales:			
Gross profit			

Problem VI

A company's Cash account showed the following activity and balances during the year:

Balance, January 1	$ 52,000
Receipts from sales	475,000
Payments of expenses	(400,000)
Payment of dividend, December 28	(50,000)
Balance, December 31	$ 77,000

Cash receipts from sales and disbursements for expenses occurred uniformly throughout the year. The general price index during the year was:

January	120
Average during the year	125
December	138

Calculate the purchasing power gain or loss from holding cash during the year.

	Historical Cost/ Nominal Dollar Amounts	Restatement Factor from Price Index	Restated to December 31	Gain or Loss
Balance, January I	$ 52,000			
Receipts from sales	475,000			
Payments of expenses	(400,000)			
Payment of dividend	(50,000)			
Ending balance, adjusted				
Ending balance, actual	$ 77,000			
Purchasing power gain (loss)				

Solutions for Appendix G

Problem I   Problem II

1.	T	1.	B
2.	F	2.	D
3.	T	3.	D
4.	T	4.	E
5.	F	5.	B
6.	F		

Problem III

Current cost 4

Current cost accounting 9

Deflation 14

General price-level index 11

Historical cost/constant purchasing
power accounting 1

Historical cost/nominal dollar
financial statements 6

Inflation 3

Monetary assets 12

Monetary liabilities 7

Nonmonetary assets 2

Nonmonetary liabilities 8

Price index 5

Purchasing power gain or loss 10

Specific price-level index 13

Problem IV

1. those purchasers typically buy an equal number of units of each item

2. current values

3. historical cost/constant purchasing power accounting, current cost accounting

4. Monetary assets

5. purchasing power of the dollar, 16.7

6. that transactions are recorded in terms of the historical number of dollars paid, and these amounts are not adjusted even though subsequent changes in prices may dramatically change the value of the items purchased

7. Current cost accounting

8. price index

Problem V

	Historical Cost/ Nominal Dollar Statements	Historical Cost/ Constant Purchasing Power Accounting	Current Cost Accounting
Sales	$30,000	$30,000	$30,000
Cost of sales:	20,000		
$20,000 × (115/92)		25,000	
....			$25,500
Gross profit	$10,000	$ 5,000	$ 4,500

Problem VI

	Historical Cost/ Nominal Dollar Amounts	Restatement Factor from Price Index	Restated to December 31	Gain or Loss
Balance, January I	$ 52,000	138/120	$ 59,800	
Receipts from sales	475,000	138/125	524,400	
Payments of expenses	(400,000)	138/125	(441,600)	
Payment of dividend	(50,000)	138/138	(50,000)	
Ending balance, adjusted			$ 92,600	
Ending balance, actual	$ 77,000		(77,000)	
Purchasing power gain (loss)				$15,600